FUN WITH THE FAMILY™

in MASSACHUSETTS

HUNDREDS OF IDEAS
FOR DAY TRIPS WITH THE KIDS
SECOND EDITION

by MARCIA GLASSMAN-JAFFE

The
Globe
Pequot
Press

Guilford, Connecticut

Fun with the Family is a trademark of The Globe Pequot Press.

Cover and text design by Nancy Freeborn
Cover photo by Julie Bidwell
Maps by M.A. Dubé

Library of Congress Cataloging-in-Publication Data is available.

ISBN 0-7627-0465-9

Manufactured in the United States of America
Second Edition/First Printing

To Mark, Marisa, Mallory, and Morgan. Thank you for helping me
see the wonders around us as we travel life's many paths.
I am truly blessed with a wonderful and loving family.
Thank you for your understanding and support; I always sensed
your pride in me for my determined perseverance.

THE NORTH SHORE, CAPE ANN, AND THE MERRIMACK VALLEY

GREATER BOSTON

PLYMOUTH AND THE SOUTH SHORE

CAPE COD, MARTHA'S VINEYARD AND NANTUCKET

CENTRAL MASSACHUSETTS

THE PIONEER VALLEY

THE BERKSHIRES

MASSACHUSETTS

Contents

Acknowledgments

The author thanks the members of the Massachusetts Office of Travel and Tourism, the regional travel offices throughout the state, the National Park Service visitor centers, and the sites and attractions contained in this book for their time and cooperation in making this book as accurate and informative as possible. The author would further like to thank Mallory and Marisa Jaffe for their technological assistance, Mark Jaffe and Cyril Glassman for their navigation skills, and Morgan Jaffe for her enthusiasm for exploration.

A personal thanks goes to my mother, Natalie Glassman, who covered for me to allow me free time to do my research. My gratitude, too, to my many friends who put friendship on hold so I could follow my writing dream.

To my dear friend Diane Bair, this project wouldn't have happened without you—many thanks.

Lastly I would like to thank Laurie Kenney, my editor, for her encouragement and guidance.

Introduction

Massachusetts was settled in 1620 by a brave band of 101 men, women, and children. From that initial Plimouth outpost in the "wilds of Massachusetts" grew the state that has garnered a worldwide reputation for its educational institutions, medical facilities, unique sites and culture, rich history, and physical beauty. Boston, the state capital, is considered the gateway to New England and is popular with both domestic and international tourists because of the breadth of its attractions—performing and visual arts, sport facilities, and cultural institutions.

USING THIS BOOK

The book is arranged from the western part of the state toward the eastern end, then proceeds down the Massachusetts coast. Each entry includes address, telephone number, Web site (if available), and description. Where possible, hours, prices, and directions have been added to the entry. The suggested age ranges for a particular site are just that, suggested guidelines. Parents or caregivers must use their own judgment and experience based on the maturity of the child to determine whether a particular site is appropriate.

The maps in the beginning of each chapter are designed to orient you to a particular area, but they are in no way intended to be a substitute for a detailed state road system map.

RATES

The following key indicates pricing by dollar sign instead of a numerical rate for lodging, restaurants, and attractions. Lodging prices fluctuate depending upon location and time of year. Please be aware that lunch is usually a better value at an establishment than dinner. Be sure to inquire about family rates or discounts where indicated in this text.

Rates for Lodging

$	up to $50
$$	$51 to $75
$$$	$76 to $99
$$$$	$100 and up

Rates for Restaurants

$	most entries under $10
$$	most $10 to $15
$$$	most $15 to $20
$$$$	most over $20

Rates for Attractions

$	up to $5 per person
$$	$6 to $10 per person
$$$	$10 to $20 per person
$$$$	more than $21 per person

SPECIAL NOTES OF INTEREST

The Massachusetts Office of Travel and Tourism is eager to send information packages to prospective tourists. The Office of Travel and Tourism can be contacted at the State Transportation Building, 10 Park Plaza, Suite 4510, Boston, Massachusetts 02115; (800) 227–MASS; www.mass-vacation.com. To reserve a stay at any one of the Massachusetts state campgrounds, there is now a central number to call. Contact Reserve America toll-free at (877) 422-6762. The entire state park system is covered by that one number; individual state parks will no longer make reservations.

> The prices and rates listed in this guidebook were confirmed at press time. We recommend, however, that you call establishments to obtain current information before traveling.

The following is a key to the icons found throughout the text.

 Swimming

 Animal Viewing

 Boating / Boat Tour

 Food

 Historic Site

 Lodging

 Hiking / Walking

 Camping

 Fishing

 Museums

 Biking

 Performing Arts

 Amusement Park

 Sports/Athletic

 Horseback Riding

 Picnicking

 Skiing/Winter Sports

 Playground

 Park

Shopping

Help Us Keep This Guide Up to Date

Every effort has been made by the author and editors to make this guide as accurate and useful as possible. However, many changes can occur after a guide is published—establishments close, phone numbers change, hiking trails are rerouted, facilities come under new management, etc.

We would love to hear from you concerning your experiences with this guide and how you feel it could be improved and be kept up to date. While we may not be able to respond to all comments and suggestions, we'll take them to heart and we'll make certain to share them with the author. Please send your comments and suggestions to the following address:

The Globe Pequot Press
Reader Response/Editorial Department
P.O. Box 480
Guilford, CT 06437

Or you may e-mail us at: editorial@globe-pequot.com

Thanks for your input, and happy travels!

The Berkshires

Covering the western end of Massachusetts, Berkshire County changes dramatically, from the high mountains and isolated valleys in the north to the hilly forests and farmland of the area along the Connecticut border. Tell the kids to keep an eye out for the carved wooden Indians that "guard" the tourist shops along the Mohawk Trail. Williamstown, known for Williams College and its world-class art museums, is a classic New England village of white churches and clapboard houses along the edges of the town green. To the southeast is Mt. Greylock, the state's highest mountain, part of a huge park full of hiking trails of varying difficulties, as well as waterfalls, fishing areas, and campgrounds.

The southern Berkshire area is gentler in topography and more cultural in nature. The region abounds with museums, theaters, and outdoor classical music venues, the most famous of which is Tanglewood, summer home of the Boston Symphony Orchestra. Kids will marvel at the round stone barn at Hancock Shaker Village outside Pittsfield. Farther south, in Stockbridge, take the time to walk along the long porch and through the enormous lobby area of the rambling old Red Lion Inn. During the winter Berkshire County is a mecca for skiing families.

MOHAWK TRAIL

The Mohawk Trail, Route 2, is the highway version of the path that Native Americans used to travel from the Connecticut River Valley to the Hudson River Valley. Sixty-seven miles long, the road is only partially in the Berkshires, since it begins in the Connecticut River Valley. Near the town of Florida the trail passes by the entrance to the Hoosuc Tunnel, which was the longest railway tunnel in the country when it was completed in 1875. An engineering marvel in its time, the Hoosuc Tunnel was the first construction to use

THE BERKSHIRES

Williamstown

North Adams

Charlemont

Mt. Greylock

2

New Ashford

7

Adams

8

Hancock

Lanesboro

Dalton

9

Hancock Shaker Village

Pittsfield

Hinsdale

20

8

90

Lenox

Lee

Stockbridge

South Lee

Great Barrington

23

Monterey

Otis

7

8

Mt. Washington

Ashley Falls

nitroglycerin. Stop at the Eastern Summit Gift Shop—not for the shop, but for the telescope (25 cents for about three minutes) on the edge of the steep hill that overlooks the northern Berkshires. The highest point on the trail is the Whitcomb Summit, at 2,240 feet (if the kids are into ascending an observation tower, it's 50 cents per person). The trail makes several hairpin turns on its way into North Adams.

Marcia's Top Family Adventures in the Berkshires

1. Hancock Shaker Village, Pittsfield
2. Mt. Greylock State Reservation, Lanesborough
3. Mohawk Trail
4. Sterling and Francine Clark Art Institute, Williamstown
5. Tanglewood Music Festival, Lenox

North Adams

The City of Spires, as residents like to call it, is a bit run-down nowadays; the beautiful old brick factories and warehouses that produced paper, textiles, and leather goods are mostly empty now. Several of these buildings are the home of the Massachusetts Museum of Contemporary Art, which everyone already calls Mass MoCA.

MASSACHUSETTS MUSEUM OF CONTEMPORARY ART (all ages)

87 Marshall Street, North Adams; (413) 664–4481. Open Memorial Day to Halloween, Sunday through Thursday 9:00 A.M. to 5:00 P.M., Friday and Saturday 9:00 A.M. to 7:00 P.M.; November 1 to Memorial Day, Tuesday through Sunday 9:00 A.M. to 4:00 P.M. Admission: $8.00 for adults, $3.00 for children 6 to 16; Free *for children under 6.*

Opened in May 1999, Mass MoCA is a contemporary international cultural center focusing on visual, media, and performing arts. Call for a family activity schedule. Try the rooftop cafe for a snack. A hotel onsite is in the planning stages.

WESTERN GATEWAY HERITAGE STATE PARK (all ages)

Route 8, North Adams; (413) 663–6312. Open daily year-round 10:00 A.M. to 5:00 P.M., closed Thanksgiving and Christmas. 𝐅𝐫𝐞𝐞*; donations accepted.*

If your family includes a railroad buff or two, visit the Western Gateway Heritage State Park. An introductory twenty-five-minute video sets the tone; along with interesting tidbits about North Adams's history as a bustling railroad town, you'll learn about the construction of the Hoosuc Tunnel. There are family programs throughout the summer and a Kids Korner year-round with arts-and-crafts activities.

Where to Eat

Miss Adams Diner, *53 Park Street, North Adams; (413) 743–5300.* Breakfast (best: waffles) and lunch (bests: fish and chips and meat loaf) in an authentic 1949 lunch car. $

Freight Yard Restaurant, *1 Furnace Park, Western Gateway Heritage State Park, North Adams; (413) 663–6547.* Serving burgers, pasta, steak, and seafood. Open year-round. $–$$

Where to Stay

Twin Sisters Inn, *1111 South State Street/Route 8, North Adams; (413) 663–6933.* Old country house on ten acres that features four large guest rooms, two sharing a bath. Open year-round. Rates are $60 to $85, including breakfast. $$$

Williamstown

Williamstown hasn't changed much since the late nineteenth century. It's home to one of New England's best small liberal arts colleges, Williams College, and to two exceptional art museums: the Sterling and Francine Clark Art Institute and the Williams College Museum of Art.

STERLING AND FRANCINE CLARK ART INSTITUTE (all ages)

25 South Street, Williamstown; (413) 458–9545. Open year-round, Tuesday through Sunday 10:00 A.M. to 5:00 P.M. In July and August a gallery talk takes place every day at 3:00 P.M.

The Clark Art Institute has a world-class collection of late-nineteenth-century paintings by Renoir, Monet, Corot, Pissaro, and Degas, among others. Also interesting is a room with paintings by the American artists Sargent, Remington, and Homer. They were contemporaries, and all were celebrated in their time for very different styles and subject matter: Sargent for his exquisite portraits of high-society figures; Remington for his depiction of cowboys and western life; and Homer for his haunting New England sea and mountain scenes. The beautiful grounds are a great spot for a picnic.

 WILLIAMS COLLEGE MUSEUM OF ART (all ages)
Main Street, Williamstown; (413) 597–2429. Open Tuesday through Saturday 10:00 A.M. to 5:00 P.M., Sunday 1:00 to 5:00 P.M., and major holidays that fall on Monday. In addditon, the museum is open Mondays in July and August.
Free.

The Williams College Museum of Art is one of the best college art museums in the country, in terms of the breadth of its collection of contemporary and modern American and non-Western art. The museum's ARTWORKS program, a series of one-person exhibitions of contemporary art, has been particularly well received. Good traveling exhibitions stop here, too. Special family days and activities; call ahead.

Play time From late June through August, the **Williamstown Theatre Festival** (Box 517, Williamstown 01267; 413-597-3399 or 413-597-3400), one of the country's preeminent theater groups, presents musicals, dramas, children's theater, and special events. Most performances are at Williams College's Adams Memorial Theater.

Other Things to See and Do

Sand Springs Pool and Spa, *158 Sand Springs Road, Williamstown; (413) 458–5205.* Olympic pool, tiny tot pool, hot tubs, snack bar, seasonal.

Water Street Books, *26 Water Street, Williamstown; (413) 458–8071.* Children's section and Saturday morning children's programs.

Natural Bridge State Park, *off Route 8, North Adams; (413) 663–6392.* White marble natural bridge that was formed 500 million years ago.

Where to Eat

Hobson's, *159 Water Street, Williamstown; (413) 458–9101.* Homemade soups and abundant salad bar. Kids can order a half-plate. $$–$$$

Store at Five Corners, *corner of Routes 7 and 43, Williamstown; (413) 458–3176.* Great sandwiches and dessert goodies, all packed to go. Open year-round. $

Where to Stay

Berkshire Bed and Breakfast, *Main Street, Williamstown; (413) 268–7244* reservation service.

The House on Main Street B&B, *1120 Main Street, Williamstown; (413) 458–3031.* Three rooms with private baths; three others share one full and one half bath. The big screened-in porch is a nice spot to relax. $$$–$$$$.

The Orchards, *222 Adams Road, Williamstown; (413) 458–9611 or (800) 225–1517.* Antiques, four-poster beds, fireplaces, pond. $$$–$$$$

Adams and Lanesborough

Adams, birthplace of Susan B. Anthony, the suffragist who led the struggle to gain the vote for women, is still remembered with an annual summer festival in July called Susan B. Anthony Days. Adams is set peacefully along the banks of the Hoosac River and shadowed by Mt. Greylock. The southern entrance to Mt. Greylock is in Lanesborough.

Take Me Out to the Fair! The only major agricultural fair in the Berkshires, the **Adams Fair** takes place the last days of July/first days of August at Bowe Field off Route 8 (Old Columbia Street). Call (413) 663-3977 for more information.

MT. GREYLOCK STATE RESERVATION (all ages)

Visitor center, Rockwell Road, Lanesborough; (413) 499–4263. Park is open from sunrise until a half hour before sunset. Visitor center open daily year-round, 9:00 A.M. to 5:00 P.M. There are several ways to approach the mountain; one is from North Adams (1 mile west of North Adams on Route 2, take Notch Road through a residential area that turns into woody hills; signs will direct you from there); the other is via Route 7 in Lanesborough (follow the signs).

Mt. Greylock State Reservation is an enormous park (10,327 acres), with 45 miles of hiking trails of varying difficulties, as well as camping, fishing, canoeing, cross-country skiing, and snowmobiling. The visitor center in Lanesborough is an excellent first stop. A large tabletop relief map shows the park's layout and topography. Even if your family hasn't done a lot of hiking, don't be discouraged. Many of the park's trails leave from the parking area on top of the mountain (this is one of the reasons it's such a terrific family place; you can drive right to the best part). One of the best routes is a 4-mile hike from the summit down Overlook Trail to Hopper Trail, then on to March Cataract Falls. Coming back up, you can walk part of the Appalachian Trail rather than retracing your steps along the Hopper Trail. *Note:* The weather can change quickly and unexpectedly on Mt. Greylock. Every year a few experienced hikers find themselves stranded. Get a map and talk to rangers in the visitor center before you begin your hike.

Whether or not you hike, don't end your visit to Mt. Greylock without climbing the War Memorial Tower. On a clear day you'll be able to see Mt. Monadnock in New Hampshire, 115 miles away, as well as the full Berkshire range, the Taconics in New York, and the southern part of the Appalachians. The tower is open 9:00 A.M. to 5:00 P.M. daily, mid-May through mid-October.

Each Columbus Day, the town of Adams sponsors the Mt. Greylock Ramble, an annual trek to the mountain summit.

Amazing Massachusetts Fact Mt. Greylock, at 3,491 feet, is the highest point in the state.

Where to Eat

Greylock's Bascom Lodge, *(413) 743–1591 or 443–0011.* The lodge, built in the 1930s, sits atop Mt. Greylock. Breakfast, lunch, and dinner; reservations suggested. The Appalachian Mountain Club manages the lodge. $–$$$

Where to Stay

Greylock's Bascom Lodge, *(413) 743–1591 or 443–0011.* The eight rooms are rustic but comfortable, and vary in size from dormitory-style rooms that sleep eight people to private doubles. All rooms share baths and are provided with linens. The Appalachian Mountain Club offers guided nature walks and hikes from here. Call ahead. Open mid-May through mid-October. $–$$$

Florida, Dalton, and Hinsdale

It's rumored that the small village of Florida is the most frigid spot in the state because of its location, not quite the tropical picture its name would suggest. Savoy State Park in Florida is a hidden gem. Dalton is home to the Crane Paper Company, with bragging rights to fine quality paper (Crane is the only supplier of paper for U.S. paper currency). Hinsdale takes great pride in native son Israel Bissell, who gave Paul Revere a run for his money.

SAVOY MOUNTAIN STATE FOREST (all ages)

260 Central Shaft Road, Florida; (413) 663–8469. From Route 2 in Florida, turn onto Central Shaft Road. Open year-round dawn to dusk.

Savoy Mountain State Forest on 11,000 acres is a less crowded version of Mt. Greylock State Reservation. The park is especially appealing to children because of the good swimming in North Pond (there isn't much legal swimming on Greylock). Hiking is less challenging, too, and the pleasant hike to Tannery Falls brings you to one of the nicest falls in the Berkshires. There are four cabins on the banks of South Pond and forty-five campsites available Memorial Day to Columbus Day.

*B*erkshire Skiing Meccas During the winter Berkshire County is a mecca for skiing families. Some of New England's best small-scale, family-oriented downhill and cross-country ski areas are here. All can boast of excellent ski schools, family packages, and reasonably priced accommodations either at the base of the mountain or within a few miles:

- **Brodie Mountain,** *Route 7, New Ashford; (413) 443–4752 or (413) 443–4751 (ski conditions).* Known for its lively Irish approach to everything. On St. Patrick's Day the snow magically turns green, and people named Kelly ski for Free. There's a ski school and day care program. The vertical drop is 1,250 feet. There are six lifts, twenty-eight trails (nearly all beginner and intermediate; the black diamonds aren't tough), cross-country and night skiing, and a hotel.

- **Bucksteep Manor,** *885 Washington Mountain Road, Washington; (413) 623–5535.* Offers 15 miles of groomed trails. The Cross-country Center is open December through March, and rentals are available. A twenty-two-room inn is on site, as well as one-hundred campsites, a pool, tennis courts, and an outdoor hot tub.

- **Butternut Basin,** *Route 23, Great Barrington; (413) 528–2000 or (800) 438–SNOW.* Cross-country and downhill skiing (1,000-foot vertical drop), lodge, camping, and rentals. Children ski **Free** weekdays with an accompanying adult skier ticket purchase.

- **Catamount,** *Route 23, South Egremont; (413) 528–1262; www.cata-mountski.com.* One thousand-foot vertical drop; longest run is 2 miles. Ski school, nursery, rentals, night skiing, and special **Free** days (call for a schedule).

- **Cranwell Resort,** *Route 20, Lenox; (413) 637–1364 or (800) CRANWELL.* Cross-country skiing, rentals and lessons, ninety-five deluxe rooms in a rambling Tudor mansion, with gourmet dining in a historic setting.

- **Jiminy Peak,** *Corey Road, Hancock; (413) 738–5500, (800) 882–8859 (lodging) or (413) 738–PEAK (ski conditions).* Self-contained resort with nice condominiums and a slopeside inn. The state's first quad chair is here, along with five other lifts. Challenging steep intermediate runs and black-diamond slopes deserve their rating. There's a kids-only area for SKIwee lessons, and the day care center takes kids from 6 months. A snowboard park, an ice-skating rink, and night skiing are other fun options. During the summer the Alpine Slide is a popular attraction.

- **Notchview Reservation,** *Route 9 Windsor, (413) 298–3239.* Trustees of Reservations property with over 3,000 acres for cross-country skiing and hiking.

- **Otis Ridge,** *Route 23W, Otis; (413) 269–4444.* A small downhill ski area oriented to families. The vertical drop is only 400 feet, and there are just ten runs. Come here if you want your kids to learn to ski in an intimate setting; experienced skiers will be bored.

CRANE PAPER COMPANY (all ages)

Housatonic Street, off Route 8, Dalton; (413) 684–2600. Open June through mid-October, Monday through Friday 2:00 to 5:00 P.M. **Free**.

Crane Paper Company makes the paper on which all U.S. currency is printed. Tour the museum to learn how paper is made and see a display about the history of paper money.

The Midnight Ride of Israel Bissell?

A few miles southeast of Dalton is the small town of Hinsdale, whose claim to fame is Israel Bissell. Bissell is the man who outdid Paul Revere: In five days he rode from Hinsdale through Connecticut to New York and on to Philadelphia to carry the news of the colonists' confrontation with the British in 1775. Bissell is buried in the Maple Street Cemetery (take Route 143 East; the cemetery is at the top of the first small hill after Route 8).

Where to Stay

Dalton House, *955 Main Street, Dalton; (413) 684–3854.* Eleven rooms (all with private bath, some with fireplace) in two buildings. The rooms in the carriage house are larger and quieter, with period furniture and exposed beams. During the winter, ski packages can include ski tickets and dinner. $$–$$$$

Pittsfield

The residents of Pittsfield are extremely dedicated to preserving the contributions of the Shakers to the American lifestyle at Hancock Shaker Village. Pittsfield offers many recreational and cultural opportunities, with its many lakes, museums, and parks.

BERKSHIRE MUSEUM (all ages)

Route 7, 39 South Street, downtown Pittsfield; (413) 443–7171; www.berkshireweb.com/berkshiremuseum. Open Tuesday through Saturday 10:00 A.M. to 5:00 P.M., Sunday 1:00 to 5:00 P.M. and Mondays in July and August. Admission: $6.00 for adults, $4.00 for ages three to eighteen, Free *for under three.*

An eclectic museum that is a little bit of everything. Somehow the museum combines a hands-on aquarium with science and history exhibits, paintings, sculpture, and decorative arts. There is a cinema that runs a montage of first-rate films (call for a schedule). Children's programs crowd the museum during vacation week; the museum specializes in blockbuster interactive family exhibitions February through May. A popular Refrigerator Art Gallery features guest artists (local children who create artwork), which are hung on a series of thirteen refurbished refrigerator doors.

Pittsfield's Summerfest

Pittsfield's Summerfest A summer-long celebration, this festival features music, art, and recreation geared to appeal to all age groups. Call (413) 442-6769 for information.

HANCOCK SHAKER VILLAGE (all ages)

Junction of Routes 20 and 41, Pittsfield; (413) 443–0188; www.hancockshakervilage.org. Guided tour April 1 to mid-May and late October through November, 10:00 A.M. to 3:00 P.M. Admission $10.00 for adults, $5.00 for children 6 to 17. Self-guided tour mid-May through October 9:30 A.M. to 5:00 P.M. Admission: $13.50 adults, $5.50 for kids age 6 to 17. There is a family ticket for $25 (guided season) or $33 (self-guided season), which includes two adults and an unlimited number of children under 17.

Our culture reveres the Shakers for their simple, beautiful furniture and building designs. What most people don't know is that their crafting skill was a direct expression of their religious devotion to express their reverence to God by making their environment a "heaven on earth." Hancock Shaker Village was the third of eighteen Shaker communities established in the United States. Its heyday was in 1830, just after the round stone barn was completed, when 300 Shakers lived, worked, and worshiped here. They farmed, sold seeds and herbs, manufactured medicines, and made and sold all types of goods, from boxes to textiles. Eventually their population dwindled, and in 1960 the Shaker ministry in Canterbury, New Hampshire, sold the Hancock property to a group of Pittsfield residents. The following year they opened Hancock Shaker Village as a museum. It's best to come at self-guided season, since the entire property consisting of twenty restored buildings is open to the public. Kids learn how the Shakers spun wool, made furniture, cooked, and did such crafts as basketmaking. The staff is knowledgeable, dedicated, and enthusiastic; tour guides welcome and encourage questions. A cafe is open during the season.

WAHCONAH PARK (all ages)

105 Wahconah Street, Pittsfield; (413) 499–6387; www.pittsfield.com. Games are usually at 7:00 P.M. For a schedule, write to Box 328, Pittsfield 01202.

From June through early September, the Pittsfield Mets, a Class A farm team of the New York Mets, play at Wahconah Park three or four times a week. This is old-time baseball in a park that's so small, every seat is a good seat, and the players are happy to sign autographs.

Other Things to See and Do

Arrowhead, *78 Holmes Road, Pittsfield;* *(413) 442–1793.* Home of Herman Melville, author of *Moby-Dick.*

Bousquet Ski Area, *Dan Fox Drive, Pittsfield; (413) 442–8316.* Downhill skiing and snowboarding.

Pittsfield State Park, *Cascade Street, Pittsfield; (413) 442–8992.* Hiking, cross-country skiing, swimming, canoeing, and fishing on over 10,000 acres.

Where to Eat

Bagels Too, *166 North Street, Pittsfield; (413) 499–0119.* Specializing in bagels and sandwiches, eat in or take-out. $

Dakota, *Route 7, 1035 South Street, Pittsfield; (413) 499–7900.* Steaks, seafood, salad bar, fabulous Sunday brunch; children's menu. $–$$$

Where to Stay

Crowne Plaza, *Berkshire Common, Pittsfield; (413) 499–2000 or (800) 2–CROWNE.* A 175-room hotel in central location. $$$–$$$$

Southern Berkshires

The southern Berkshires have been a haven for the wealthy for well over a century, and the cultural life in the towns of Lenox and Stockbridge reflects their passions: music and theater. During the high season of July and August, kids can see more live performances here than they could in many large cities—and much of it goes on outdoors. There are several excellent museums; gracious historic inns for families with well-behaved children; and parks, wildlife sanctuaries, and good skiing.

Lenox

The summer home of the Boston Symphony Orchestra, Lenox has become a tourism mecca for lovers of fine music, theater, and dance. Earlier settled by wealthy New York aristocrats at the turn of the century, many Lenox mansions are experiencing a rebirth as some of the finest hostelries in the area.

TANGLEWOOD MUSIC FESTIVAL (all ages)

West Street, Lenox; (413) 637–5165 (box office) or (617) 266–1492 (off-season). Shed and Hall tickets range from $12 to $70. Lawn tickets (purchased on site only) are $12 to $16, depending on the event; lawn tickets for children under 12 are Free *(four per family). Children under 5 are not allowed in the Shed or the Hall during concerts. Write ahead for a full summer schedule: Symphony Hall, 301 Massachusetts Avenue, Boston, 02115.*

Tanglewood is the summer home of the Boston Symphony Orchestra, whose members, on summer weekends, perform concerts from the afternoon into the evening, often with the assistance of internationally known musicians and conductors. Most people who come to hear them sit outside on the lawn, arriving early with elaborate picnics and making a day of it. Some devotees choose to sit "inside," which means under the roof of one of the two buildings: the Shed (which is anything but), with seating for more than 5,000, and Seiji Ozawa Hall, with seating for 1,180. If your kids are lucky enough to have

Tanglewood on Parade is a daylong outdoor celebration in early August, finishing with a gala evening performance topped off with fireworks.

music lovers for parents, your entire family will enjoy an outing to Tanglewood, especially on a warm summer evening when the BSO plays the *1812 Overture,* complete with fireworks under the stars.

Other Things to See and Do

The Berkshire Scenic Railway and the Railway Museum, *Willow Creek Road, Lenox; (413) 637–2210.* A restored 1902 Lenox railway station and the Railway Museum.

Pleasant Valley Wildlife Sanctuary, *472 West Mountain Road, Lenox;* *(413) 637–0320.* Seven miles of walking trails.

Edith Wharton Restoration, The Mount, *Plunkett Street, Routes 7 and 7A, Lenox; (413) 637–1899. House and gardens open daily June through October.* Look closely, things aren't what they seem.

Where to Eat

Church Street Cafe, *65 Church Street, Lenox; (413) 637–2745.* Pasta and grilled fish specialties. Dine under the stars in season. $$–$$$

The Village Snack Shop,
27 Housatonic Street, Lenox; (413)
637–2564. Low-key breakfast and

lunch place with homemade soup and
good lunch specials. $

Where to Stay

Apple Tree Inn and Restaurant,
10 Richmond Mt. Rd., Lenox; (413)
637–1477. Thirty-five rooms on lovely

22-acre estate. Family friendly, heated
pool, tennis. Near Tanglewood.
$$–$$$$

Stockbridge and Lee

Authentic New England charm permeates this town that was home to Norman
Rockwell and where he drew his inspiration for his scenes of Americana. The
Red Lion Inn's long wraparound porch is a town fixture for a welcoming cool
summer drink. Lee has turn-of-the-century charm, and its downtown is listed
in the National Registry of Historic Areas.

BERKSHIRE BOTANICAL GARDEN (all ages)
*Junction of Routes 102 and 183, Stockbridge; (413) 298–3926. Open daily May
through October 10:00 A.M. to 5:00 P.M. Admission: $5.00 for adults, $3.00 for
students;* **Free** *for children under 12.*

Berkshire Botanical Garden offers fifteen acres of gardens that vary
from herbs to lilies to vegetables of all kinds. This is a different kind of
green space that young children will enjoy: It's accessible to them
because the plants are just their size. Picnicking is encouraged here.

NORMAN ROCKWELL MUSEUM (all ages)
*Route 183, Stockbridge; (413) 298–4100; www.nrm.org. Open May through
October, daily, 10:00 A.M. to 5:00 P.M.; November through April, weekdays
10:00 A.M. to 4:00 P.M., weekends 10:00 A.M. to 5:00 P.M. The studio building is
open from May through October. Admission: $9.00 for adults, $2.00 for children
6 to 18,* **Free** *for children under 6.*

Rockwell, chronicler of life in America for seven decades, lived in
Stockbridge for the last twenty-five years of his life. The Norman Rock-
well Museum holds the largest collection of original Rockwells. Chang-
ing exhibits feature works of other illustrators. The museum has special
family days, programs, and art activities. The grounds are a pleasant
spot for a walk or a picnic. Outdoor sculptures are by Rockwell's son
Peter.

"Sedgewick Pie" Route 102 in Stockbridge is the village cemetery, where, among other local notables, the Sedgewick family is buried. In 1781 Thomas Sedgewick, a lawyer, successfully defended Elizabeth "Mumbet" Freeman, who became the first slave freed by law in the United States. The trial also rendered slavery illegal in Massachusetts. Mumbet is buried with the Sedgewick family in the **"Sedgewick Pie,"** the family grave plot, so called because family members are buried in a circle with their feet in the center. Why? They hoped that when they sit up on Judgment Day, they will see each other before they see anything else.

 OCTOBER MOUNTAIN STATE FOREST

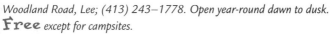 *Woodland Road, Lee; (413) 243–1778. Open year-round dawn to dusk.*

 Free *except for campsites.*

Covering over 16,127 acres, October Mountain is the largest of the state forests. Most people come here to hike, fish, or boat, but in the winter cross-country skiing and snowshoeing trails have a following as well. There are forty-five campsites, flush toilets, and showers. No swimming.

Other Things to See and Do

Berkshire Mountain Llama Treks, *322 Landers Road, Lee; (413) 243–6074.*

Berkshire Outlet Village, *50 Water Street, Lee.* Savings on designer brands.

Chesterwood, *off Route 183, Stockbridge; (413) 298–3579.* Estate of sculptor Daniel Chester French.

Naumkeag, *Prospect Hill Road, Stockbridge; (413) 298–3239.* Joseph Hodges Choate's summer home designed by Stanford White in the Shingle style. Gardens by Fletcher Steele, famous landscape architect.

Santarella, *Main Road (3 miles from Lee), Tyringham; (413) 243–3260.* Gingerbread house, museum, and gardens of sculptor Sir Henry Hudson Kitson.

Where to Eat

Joe's Diner, *63 Center Street, Lee; (413) 243–9756.* Serving classic diner food—open-faced sandwiches, fries and gravy, and the like. Open from noon to midnight daily, year-round. $

Red Lion Inn, *Main Street, Stockbridge; (413) 298–5545.* Meals served in the main dining room, a small tavern, and downstairs in a pub called the Lion's Den (live music at night). $$–$$$

Shanahan's Market, *Elm Street (off Main Street), Stockbridge; (413) 298–3634.* An old-fashioned general store with a lunch counter serving plain food—eggs, bacon, pancakes, sub sandwiches—and lots of local gossip. Breakfast and lunch only. $

Theresa's Stockbridge Cafe (aka the infamous "Alice's Restaurant"), *40 Main Street; (413) 298–5465.* Vegetarian food, pizza, and Middle Eastern dishes. Kid's menu. $

Where to Stay

Historic Merrell Inn, *1565 Pleasant Street, South Lee; (413) 243–1794 or (800) 243–1794.* Original wide-plank floors, fireplaces, and antiques. Breakfasts are delicious and filling. Not appropriate for young children. $$–$$$$

Red Lion Inn, *Main Street, Stockbridge; (413) 298–5545; www.redlioninn.com.*

Treat yourselves to a stay at this quintessential rambling New England inn that many others try to emulate. Rooms vary in size, from quite small to almost palatial. Families will be happiest in the suites with connecting bathroom. The annex buildings tend to be quieter than the main inn building. Open year-round (very crowded in July and August). $$$–$$$$

Hidden Berkshires

Picturesque towns and villages near the corner of the state bordering Connecticut and New York are a bit off the beaten path but not to be overlooked. Butternut Basin and Catamount are nice beginner downhill ski areas for families (see sidebar on Ski Meccas in this chapter). Many properties managed by the Trustees of Reservations are found here, as well as many wilderness areas.

  ### MT. WASHINGTON STATE FOREST AND BASH BISH FALLS (all ages)

Route 344, Mt. Washington; (413) 528–0330. Directions: From Route 23 South, turn right at the signs for Mt. Everett–Bash Bish Falls. Follow the road west to the foot of the mountain, then follow the signs for Bash Bish Falls. Turn into the second parking area. Open daily, dawn to dusk. **Free.**

Bash Bish Falls is a great name for a great place. From the second parking area you can hike 1 mile, then clamber, climb, or walk down a stone stairway to see the 60-foot waterfall that plunges into a churning pool. Unfortunately, you can't swim here—too dangerous—but the boulders that border the falls are still a cool spot to relax on a hot day.

Great Barrington and Monterey

BEARTOWN STATE FOREST (all ages)
Blue Hill Road, Monterey; (413) 528–0904. Open year-round. Parking is $2.00

Crossed by the Appalachian Trail, the park has good hiking and cross-country skiing, but its highlight is Benedict Pond, one of the region's best swimming holes.

MONUMENT MOUNTAIN RESERVATION (all ages)
Route 7, Great Barrington. Open dawn to dusk. **Free**.

Noted for its easy hiking trails and outcrops of quartzite rock, Monument Mountain has a colorful history. Squaw Peak at the summit got its name from an Indian maiden, who wasn't allowed to marry her lover, plunging to her death from this spot. A cluster of rocks mark where she landed, put there as a tribute to her by members of her tribe. It is also the meeting place of famous writers Herman Melville and Nathaniel Hawthorne, arranged, by a group of friends. They enjoyed a picnic, drank champagne, and became lifelong friends. Owned by the Trustees of Reservations.

Other Things to See and Do

Moon Mountain Llama, *Great Barrington; (413) 528–5056.* Picnic and tours by guides, transportation by llama.

Where to Eat

Martin's, *49 Railroad Street, Great Barrington; (413) 528–5455.* Serves breakfast all day, along with lunch specials. Try the omelet made with Monterey chèvre, the strawberry-banana pancakes, or the lentil stew. $

Four Brothers, *Route 7, Great Barrington; (413) 528–9684.* Part of a chain of Greek pizza places that covers upstate New York and the Berkshires, serving delicious pizza and eggplant dishes. $–$$

Where to Stay

Windflower, *684 South Egremont Road, Great Barrington; (413) 528–2720 or (800) 992–1993; www.windflowerinn.com.*

Thirteen rooms, fireplaces, gardens, pool. Children welcome. $$$$

Marcia's Top Annual Events

in the Berkshires

- **Butternut Basin Kids' Festival,** January, Great Barrington; (413) 528-2000

- **Winter Week at Hancock Shaker Village,** February, Pittsfield; (413) 443-0188

- **Brodie Mountain Pro Cup Race, March,** New Ashford; (413) 443-4752

- **Shearing Days at Hancock Shaker Village,** May, Pittsfield; (413) 443-0188

- **Chesterwood Antique Car Show,** May, Stockbridge; (413) 298-3579

- **Summerfest,** June, Great Barrington; (413) 442-1793

- **Berkshire Theatre Festival,** June through August, Stockbridge; (413) 298-5576

- **La Festa,** June, North Adams; (413) 66-FESTA

- **Big Apple Circus,** June/July, Great Barrington; (413) 528-4200

- **Jacob's Pillow Dance Festival,** June through August, George Carter Road, Becket; (413) 243-0745

- **Tanglewood Music Festival,** June through August, Lenox; (413) 637-5165 or (617) 266-1492

- **Williamstown Theatre Festival,** June through August, Williamstown; (413) 597-3400

- **Annual Monument Mountain Climb,** August 2, Great Barrington; (413) 442-1793

- **Autumn Farm Weekend,** August, Pittsfield; (413) 443-0188

- **Great Josh Billings Runaground,** triathalon, mid-September, Great Barrington to Lenox; (413) 442-1090

- **Fall Foliage Festival,** October, North Adams; (413) 663-3735

- **Tub Parade,** September, Lenox; (413) 637–3646

- **Berkshire Music Festival of Trees,** November through December, 39 South Street, Pittsfield; (413) 443-7171

- **Main Street at Christmas,** Main Street, first weekend in December, Stockbridge; (413) 298-5200

Ashley Falls

This tiny town near the Connecticut border is the site of two interesting attractions owned by the Trustees of Reservations: the oldest dwelling in Berkshire County, the Colonel John Ashley House; and Bartholomew's Cobble, a national natural landmark.

BARTHOLOMEW'S COBBLE (all ages)

Off Route 7A, Ashley Falls; (413) 229–8600. Museum and information center open from mid-April through mid-October daily; other times of the year Wednesday through Sunday and holidays, 9:00 A.M. to 5:00 P.M. Admission: $3.00 for adults, $1.00 for children 6 to 12.

Bartholomew's Cobble is an unusual natural hilly rock garden, studded with limestone outcroppings (the cobbles) and featuring distinctive flora, such as forty species of ferns and many wildflowers. Bird-watching is excellent here, due to the abundant plant life. There are 6 miles of hiking trails (the easygoing Ledges Trail is particularly pleasant for families with younger kids), picnic facilities, and a small natural history museum.

COLONEL JOHN ASHLEY HOUSE (all ages)

Cooper Hill Road, Ashley Falls; (413) 229–8600. Open Memorial Day weekend through mid-October, Wednesday through Sunday and Monday holidays, 1:00 to 5:00 P.M. Admission: $5.00 for adults, $2.50 for children.

Colonel John Ashley House is named for one of the first citizens of what was then the town of Sheffield, which was purchased in 1722 from Native Americans for 460 pounds sterling, three barrels of cider, and thirty quarts of rum. Ashley, a surveyor and lawyer, built his house in 1735. In 1773 the Ashley house was the site of the signing of the Sheffield Declaration, now considered the first "declaration of independence" from Britain. The house features a collection of Colonial-era tools and tableware. The colonial-style herb gardens are particularly interesting. Learn how seventeenth-century Americans used herbs for cooking meals, healing the sick, and freshening their homes.

The Pioneer Valley

The Pioneer Valley borders the Connecticut River, which stretches north to south through the state. The river valley is broad and fertile, making it excellent farming country. Many crops are raised here, including corn, tobacco, and sod for golf courses. The area was one of the first regions of inland New England to be secured by English settlers during the turbulent late seventeenth and early eighteenth centuries, when they battled Native American tribes and French militia. The town of Deerfield is one of the best sources of information about this early period of colonial history. At Turners Falls there's an interesting underwater view of a fish ladder, where salmon and shad swim during the spring. In Agawam, Riverside Park is New England's largest amusement park. It features all the essentials—roller coasters, bumper cars, water rides, stock car races, and lots of sticky fried food. Finally, for twelve days every September, the Big E (the Eastern States Exposition), in Springfield, is the biggest annual fair on the East Coast. It's family fare all the way—livestock shows, crafts contests, musical entertainment, rides, and midways. For information on where to stay, call New England Bed and Breakfast (413-773-7557). The Greater Springfield Convention and Visitors Bureau, 1500 Main Street, Box 15589, Springfield 01115 (413-787-1548 or 800-723-1548; www.valleyvisitor.com), has information on the entire Pioneer Valley.

Mohawk Trail Region

The Mohawk Trail (Route 2) was the first road designated a Scenic Byway. The route is much more dramatic when you drive it from east to west. The trail starts in central Massachusetts and ends on the New York/Massachusetts border. As the road begins climbing into the foothills, look back over the Connecticut River Valley.

THE PIONEER VALLEY

Northfield

Bernardston •

91

Greenfield •

Deerfield •

Cummington •

9

Amherst •

Northampton

South
Hadley
•

20

10

202

23

Holyoke •

90

90

20

Westfield •

West Springfield

Southwick •

202

Agawam

Springfield

91

Marcia's Top Family Adventures in the Pioneer Valley

1. Historic Deerfield and Yankee Candle Company, Deerfield

2. Riverside Park, Agawam

3. Basketball Hall of Fame, Springfield

Northfield and Bernardston

The historic village of Bernardston boasts several buildings on the National Register of Historic Places, including the library, the Unitarian Church, the town halls, and the old high school, all of which are on Main Street. The quaint New England town of Northfield on the banks of the Connecticut River is home to the prestigious private secondary school Northfield/Mt. Hermon.

NORTHFIELD MOUNTAIN RECREATION AND ENVIRONMENTAL CENTER (all ages)

99 Millers Falls Road, off Route 63, Northfield; (413) 659–3714. Cross-country skiing mid-December through March. Call for hours and fees. Hiking in the off-season is **Free***.*

Beneath Northfield Mountain is Northfield Mountain Recreation and Environmental Center, an enormous power-generating facility that's owned by Northeast Utilities. Atop the mountain is a water reservoir that's used to generate power when consumer demand exceeds other power sources. Tours on energy and the environment are offered at the hydroelectric station, but the schedule varies, so call ahead. The property is open to the public for cross-country skiing, hiking, picnicking, and wildlife viewing. The altitude makes for fairly consistent snow on the 25 miles of cross-country skiing trails, which in warm weather are used for hiking. The lodge offers ski and snowshoe rentals and lessons.

QUINNETUKUT II (all ages)

Route 63, Northfield; (413) 659–3714. Operates Wednesday through Sunday, mid-June to mid-October (call for a schedule). Price: $8.00 for adults, $4.00 for children under 14. Sunset Cruises are $17 for adults and children 10 and older.

The *Quinnetukut II* takes passengers on an hour-and-half cruise on the Connecticut River between Northfield and Gill. Knowledgeable guides comment on the flora, fauna, and history of the areas. Boats leave from the River View area, across from the entrance to Northfield Mountain. Reservations required.

Tap into This!

Tap into This! Many of the maple sugaring houses in the Pioneer Valley offer tours and eating facilities. For a copy of the Massachusetts Maple Producers Directory, contact the Massachusetts Maple Producers Association, Watson-Spruce Corner Road, Ashfield 01330 (413-628-3912; www.massmaple.org).

BARTON COVE (all ages)

Route 2, Gill; (413) 863–9300. Open Memorial Day to Columbus Day. Kayak and canoe rentals are $10 per hour, $25 for the day.

You can rent canoes at Barton Cove (operated by the Northfield Mountain Recreation and Environmental Center) on the Connecticut River. There's a campground with showers (call for reservations).

Cross-country Skiing Meccas

- **Hickory Hill Ski Touring Center,** *Buffington Hill Road, Worthington; (413) 623–5535.* A 500-acre farm with 12 miles of carefully groomed trails and a funky old lodge. During snow season it's open Friday through Monday.

- **Northfield Mountain Cross-country Ski Area,** *Route 63, Northfield; (413) 659–3713.* Offers 26 miles of trails. Rentals available.

- **Stump Sprouts Ski Touring Center,** *West Hill Road, West Hawley; (413) 339–4265.* Twelve miles of groomed trails on 450 acres. Instruction, rentals, and guided tours available. Simple rooms accommodating two to six people can be reserved, but bring your own linens.

- **The Worthington Inn,** *Old North Road/Route 143, Worthington; (413) 238–4441.* A three-bedroom B&B ($$$–$$$$) located near an excellent cross-country ski center.

Where to Eat

Four Leaf Clover, *Route 5, Bernardston; (413) 648–9514.* Family-oriented restaurant open for lunch and dinner year-round. $–$$

Falls River Inn, *junction of Routes 5 and 10, Bernardston; (413) 648–9904.* Large main dining room with a working stove, smaller dining areas with working fireplaces. $$

Where to Stay

Falls River Inn, *junction of Routes 5 and 10, Bernardston; (413) 648–9904.* Federal-style building with seven guest rooms, all with private bath, most with claw-foot tubs, some with fireplaces. Breakfast and dinner served in the large main dining room. Near skiing and Northfield Mountain. Rates are $55 to $90 a night, including full breakfast.

Greenfield and Turners Falls

Longview Tower in Greenfield has observation decks that offer views of Massachusetts, Vermont, and New York. From Greenfield, drive through the town of Montague to reach Turners Falls, the site of the first dam on the Connecticut River.

TURNERS FALLS FISH LADDER (all ages)

First Street (off Avenue A), Turners Falls; (413) 659–3714. Open mid-May through mid-June, Wednesday through Sunday. **Free**.

The draw here is the underground/under-river viewing facility that allows kids to watch salmon, shad, and other anadromous fish (those that migrate upriver from the sea to breed in freshwater) pass by a window on their way to their favorite spawning grounds upstream. The facility is on the south side of the dam, just before the bridge; look for the sign. Just below the dam, Unity Park is a nice spot for a picnic; there's a playground here, too.

Amazing Massachusetts Facts Longview Tower is the highest steel observation tower in Massachusetts.

Cruising Down the River

The Connecticut River Greenway State Park extends from the border with Connecticut (Chicopee) to the New Hampshire/Vermont border. The park encompasses six public boat accesses to the Connecticut River, the Mount Sugarloaf Observation Area, the Norwottuck Rail Trail, and public lands acquired to create a public greenway along the Connecticut River. The gentlest portion of the river for kayaking and canoeing is from Turners Falls in Montague south for 15 miles to Hatfield. The Connecticut River was designated one of fourteen American Heritage Rivers in 1998. For further information, call (413) 586-8706.

Other Things to See and Do

Lunt Design Center, *298 Federal Street (off I–91 exit 27), Greenfield; (413) 772–8643.* Tour of factories; gardens and cafe.

Poets Seat Tower, *Mountain Road and Maple Street, Greenfield; (413) 773–5453.* Hiking, birding, and views.

Where to Eat

Famous Bill's, *30 Federal Street/Route 5, Greenfield; (413) 773–9230.* Serves down-home food—meat loaf, burgers, and such—in a friendly atmosphere. Children's menu. $-$$

Taylor's Tavern Restaurant, *238 Main Street, Greenfield; (413) 773–8313.* Voted best restaurant in Greenfield by the local paper; children's menu. $-$$

Where to Stay

Berkshire Bed and Breakfast; *(413) 773–7557.* Reservation service that inspects all host homes regularly to be sure that they meet stringent standards of cleanliness and hospitality. Accommodations range from working farms to modest suburban dwellings to gracious Victorian homes.

Brandt House Country Inn, *29 Highland Avenue, Greenfield; (800) 235–3329; www.brandt-house.com.* Estate with eight guest rooms (some with fireplaces), clay tennis courts, billiards, and a wraparound porch. Well-behaved dogs are allowed with prior notice. Rates are $100 to $195, including breakfast.

Shelburne and Charlemont

At Shelburne's Bridge of Flowers, over 500 varieties of flowers are planted and cultivated. The Mohawk Trail State Forest (Route 2, Charlemont; 413–339–5504) has camping, hiking, cabin rentals, fishing, nature programs, swimming, and a good picnic area.

THE BRIDGE OF FLOWERS (all ages)

16–22 Water Street (in the center of town), Shelburne Falls; (213) 625–2143; www.shelburnefalls.com. The bridge is in full bloom from May to October. **Free** *parking on the Shelburne side.*

In the riverside village of Shelburne Falls, a quick detour off Route 2, see the Bridge of Flowers. It's a 400-foot retired trolley bridge that has been planted with flowerbeds. The best time for viewing the bridge is in the months of July and August. Don't miss the nearby Salmon Falls, with the country's most numerous glacial potholes formed by retreating ice from the glaciation period.

Hail to the Sunrise Just beyond Charlemont on Route 2 is a 900-pound bronze statue of an Indian chief figure with his arms and face lifted to the east. The piece is called **Hail to the Sunrise.** It's one of many statues that you'll see along the Mohawk Trail.

Where to Eat

Gould's SugarHouse, *587 Mohawk Trail, Route 2, Shelburne; (413) 625–6170.* Good breakfast- or lunch-break stop along the Mohawk Trail, especially if you're into pancakes and syrup. Open daily March and April and September and October, 8:00 A.M. to 2:00 P.M. $

The Warfield House, *200 Warfield Road, off Rte.2, Charlemont; (413) 339–6600 or (888) 339–VIEW; www.warfieldhouse.com.* Located on 530 mountaintop acres of farmland, featuring llama treks, emus, a sugar house, snowshoeing, and hayrides and a gourmet restaurant. $$–$$$

Where to Stay

The Charlemont Inn, *Route 2, Mohawk Trail, Charlemont; (413) 339–5796.* Interesting guest list including Benedict Arnold, Mark Twain, Calvin Coolidge and the sighting of a ghost named Elizabeth. Great location and pricing. $

U̶p the Creek without a Paddle

Contact these tour companies for whitewater adventures and calmer river trips on the Deerfield, West, and Millers Rivers. All tours provide lunch, offer instruction and equipment, and have a variety of trips suited for the neophyte and the old hand.

- **Crab Apple Whitewater,** Mohawk Trail, Route 2, Charlemont; (800) 553-7238

- **North American Whitewater Expeditions,** Mohawk Trail, Route 2, Charlemont; (800) RAPIDS-9

- **Wilderness Plus Rafting Company,** Mohawk Trail, Route 2, Charlemont; (800) 866-6943

- **Zoar Outdoor,** Mohawk Trail, Route 2, Charlemont; (800) 532-7483

Deerfield

Deerfield has survived more than just 300 years of farming in New England's unpredictable climate. In 1675 the Bloody Brook Massacre battle of King Philip's War resulted in the deaths of sixty-seven Deerfield residents. In 1704 a band of French and Indian soldiers attacked, killing forty-nine of the inhabitants and carrying off 111 more to Quebec. Miraculously, a few of these people survived and were able to make their way back to Deerfield. Historic Deerfield has an interesting story to reveal of the history and lifestyles of a struggling inland settlement.

HISTORIC DEERFIELD (ages 6 and up)

Route 5/The Street, Deerfield; (413) 774–5581. Open daily 9:30 A.M. to 4:30 P.M.; closed Thanksgiving and Christmas. Admission (good for two consecutive days): $12.00 for adults, $5.00 for children 6 to 17.

Twelve of the restored houses along The Street form an association called Historic Deerfield. These spectacular examples of eighteenth- and nineteenth-century architecture, design, furnishings, and lifestyles will probably be most interesting to older kids, who can appreciate the work that has gone into these houses, as well as the rich history of the town and its inhabitants. Don't try to see more than three houses in one day; they're all worth visiting, but more than three would be too much for any but the most ardent historic preservationist, let alone a family with children. A popular outdoor family education program offered by Historic Deerfield is a child pack that is rented for use along the Channing Blake Trail (a child-friendly ½-mile meadow walk). The pack comes equipped with a mini-microscope, a workbook, pencils, pens, and various measurement devices to explore nature and the outdoors.

THE YANKEE CANDLE COMPANY (all ages)

Route 5, South Deerfield; (413) 665–2929. Open daily 9:30 A.M. to 6:00 P.M.; closed Thanksgiving and Christmas. Admission to all is **Free** *except for the car museum, which costs $5.00 for adults, $2.00 for children 4 to 11;* **Free** *for children under 4.*

The Yankee Candle Company began in 1969 in a kitchen here, and the rest is history—at least, the company thinks so. At this complex that seems to sprout new buildings every season, you can dip your own candles, and visit a car museum, a Bavarian Christmas village, a toy factory with Santa and Mrs. Claus, and a candle-making museum that demonstrates candle making through history. Of course, selling candles is the main focus of the Yankee Candle Company, and there's a huge variety. Chandler's Restaurant is on site if you get hungry. Call for a schedule of special events.

Other Things to See and Do

Carriage Rides and sleigh rides can be booked at the Deerfield Inn. (see description below.)

Where to Eat

Wolfie's, *205 South Main Street, South Deerfield; (413) 665–7068.* Great sandwiches and a calm atmosphere. Open for lunch and dinner year-round, Monday through Saturday, 11:00 A.M. to 10:00 P.M. $

Deerfield Inn, *81 Old Main Street, Deerfield; (413) 774–5587; www.deerfieldinn.com.* Historic setting for delicious regional dishes. $$–$$$

Where to Stay

Deerfield Inn, *81 Old Main Street, Deerfield; (413) 774–5587 or (800) 926–3865.* With only twenty-three rooms in this historic setting, make your reservation early (Deerfield Academy parent weekends tend to sell out the inn). Room rates range from $127 to $241, including breakfast.

The Five College Area of Amherst, Hadley, Northampton, and South Hadley

Families with near-college-age children will find lots to do here, especially if the kids are interested in visiting any of the "five colleges"—the University of Massachusetts (which everyone calls U. Mass), Amherst College, Hampshire College, Smith College, and Mount Holyoke College. Campus tours are given several times a week at most colleges, and each has a lovely campus with a different flavor.

Museums of the Five Colleges of the Pioneer Valley

- **University Gallery,** University of Massachusetts, Amherst; (413) 545-3670

- **Mead Art Museum and Pratt Museum of Natural History,** Amherst College, Amherst; (413) 542-2335

- **Hampshire College Art Gallery,** Amherst; (413) 549-4600

- **Smith College Museum of Art,** Northampton; (413) 585-2760

- **Mount Holyoke College Art Museum and the Arboretum,** South Hadley; (413) 538-2245

AMHERST

This quintessential college town is home to Amherst College, Hampshire College, and the University of Massachusetts. Two well-known Amherst poets are the beloved Robert Frost, who taught poetry at Amherst College, and Emily Dickinson.

EMILY DICKINSON HOMESTEAD (all ages)

280 Main Street, Amherst; (413) 542–8161. Open March to mid-December, Wednesday through Saturday 1:00 to 4:00 P.M. (last tour at 4:00 P.M.); reserve your spot ahead of time. Admission: $4.00 for adults, $2.00 for children 6 to 11; Free *for children under 6.*

If you have a poetry fan in the family, be sure to walk by the Emily Dickinson Homestead near the campus of Amherst College. Dickinson was born and spent most of her life in this house. Her gravesite is not far from the house. Ask for directions, and recite one of her poems over her grave, as do the U. Mass American poetry students.

JONES LIBRARY (all ages)
43 Amity Street, Amherst; (413) 256–4090. **Free**, *call for a schedule.*
The library's special collections rooms hold a precious store of handwritten works by Dickinson, as well as a comprehensive collection of papers and other articles owned by Robert Frost, another native of Amherst.

The Belle of Amherst A beautifully illustrated and riveting children's bedtime storybook on Emily Dickinson is *Emily* (Bantam/Doubleday) by Michael Bedarn, illustrated by Barbara Cooney. This sweet tale would be a great read prior to a tour of the Emily Dickinson Homestead.

Other Things to See and Do

Mullins Center, *University of Massachusetts, Amherst; (413) 545–0505.* Athletic and entertainment complex.

Red Wing Meadow Trout Farm, *Route 116, Amherst; (413) 549–3558.* Rods and bait for a fee; no license required, safe for young children.

Stone House Museum, *20 Maple Street, Belchertown; (413) 323–6573.* Sculpture, antique carriages and sleighs, and late 1700s furnishings

Where to Eat

La Veracruzana, *63 South Pleasant Street, Amherst; (413) 253–6900.* Mouth-watering Mexican food; great art collection. $–$$

Where to Stay

The Lord Jeffrey Inn, *30 Boltwood Avenue, Amherst; (413) 253–2576 or (800) 742–0358.* Forty-eight-room inn loaded with charm, facing Amherst Common. Highly regarded pub fare and dining room. $$$$

HADLEY

Don't be surprised if you drive by tobacco drying in the tobacco barns at harvesttime. This is a sleepy agricultural community bordered by its sophisticated sister communities of Amherst and Northampton.

SKINNER STATE PARK (all ages)

Route 47, Hadley; (413) 586–0350 or (413) 253–2883 (visitor center). Open May through October; seasonal hours. **Free**.

    A road and several hiking trails lead to the summit of Mt. Holyoke and extends to the Holyoke Range State Park. The summit is a great picnic spot, with tables, a few grills, and a superb view of the Connecticut River Valley. The Summit House at Skinner State Park (413–586–0350; open weekends May through October) is a recently restored old mountain inn that's now the site of summer concerts.

Norwottuck Rail Trail Bike Path

The Norwottuck is a 10-mile bike path on the former Boston and Maine Railroad railway bed. The path is a paved 8-foot-wide trail connecting Northampton, Hadley, Amherst, and Belchertown. Run by the Department of Environmental Management (DEM) and part of the Connecticut River Greenway State Park, the path meanders through forest, pastureland, and residential areas. A highlight of the route is Beaver Pond in South Amherst. Bikes can be rented at the Valley Bicycle Trailside Store, 8 Railroad Street, Hadley (413–584–4466). For an off-trail bite, try the Ice Cream Pedaler, 8 Railroad Street, Hadley, for sandwiches and desserts. For a trail map, write DEM, 136 Damon Street, Northampton 01060, Attention: Conn. River Greenway State Park (413–586–8706).

Other Things to See and Do

Hadley Farm Museum, *147 Russell Street (Route 9) Hadley; (413) 584–8279.* Colonial farm tools in a restored barn.

Where to Stay

Howard Johnson, *401 Russell Street, Hadley; (413) 586–0114 or (800) 654– 2000.* One hundred rooms in central location on Route 9; outdoor pool. $$$–$$$$

NORTHAMPTON

Northampton, an artsy town, is a cultural mecca for this region, influenced by Smith College.

SMITH COLLEGE MUSEUM OF ART, THE LYMAN PLANT HOUSE, AND THE BOTANIC GARDENS (all ages)

Elm Street; (413) 585–2760. Open mid-September through May, Tuesday through Sunday 10:00 A.M. to 5:00 P.M.; June, by appointment only; July and August, Tuesday through Saturday 10:00 A.M. to 5:00 P.M. **Free***.*

Art lovers will enjoy a visit to the Smith College Museum of Art, whose fine collection of more than 18,000 works of art are displayed in an outstanding building. The greenhouses have annual flower spectaculars in March and November.

WORDS AND PICTURES MUSEUM (all ages)

140 Main Street, Northampton; (413) 586–8545. Open year-round, Tuesday through Sunday noon to 5:00 P.M. Admission $3.00 for adults, $1.00 for children under 18; on Tuesday and Wednesday it's $1.00 for adults, **Free** *for kids.*

Located in an old brownstone on Main Street, the Words and Pictures Museum displays outstanding examples of "sequential art," which most of us would call comic strips. Aspiring artists and writers will be inspired by the highly creative works.

LOOK MEMORIAL PARK (all ages)

300 North Main Street, Route 9, Florence (northwest of Northampton); (413) 584–5457. Open dawn to dusk. Parking is $1.00 on weekdays, $2.00 on weekends. Seasonal hours and activities; call for a schedule. Separate fees for paddleboats, train rides, mini-golf, and bumper boats.

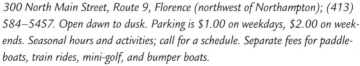

Look Memorial Park is a 150-acre conservation area with many water activities available—swimming, bumper boats, and paddleboats— as well as a miniature railroad, an outdoor theater, where summer concerts are held on most weekends, a small zoo, mini-golf, and lots of picnic tables and grills. Other activities include cross-country skiing, snowshoeing, biking, and hiking.

Other Things to See and Do

Beyond Words Bookstore, *189 Main Street, Northampton; (413) 586–6304.* Excellent children's section.

Pioneer Valley Balloons, *Old Ferry Road, Northampton Airport; (413) 584–7980.* Sunrise or sunset rides, with complimentary champagne for adults.

Where to Eat

Ben and Bill's Chocolate Emporium, *141 Main Street, Northampton; (413) 584–5695.* Indulge in handmade chocolate treats made right on the premises. $

Spoleto, *50 Main Street, Northampton; (413) 586–6313.* Voted Best in the Valley, specializing in Italian cuisine. $$–$$$

The Tailgate, *159 Main Street, Northampton; (413) 584–4458.* Homemade soups, sandwiches, salads, and some hot entrees, too. $

Where to Stay

Hotel Northampton and Historic Wiggins Tavern, *36 King Street, Northampton; (413) 584–3100 or (800)* 547–3529. Lovely seventy-seven-room hotel, great cafe and dining room, centrally located. $$$$

SOUTH HADLEY

A charming, quieter college town very proud of the Mount Holyoke campus, South Hadley is between Northampton and Springfield.

Other Things to See and Do

Joseph Skinner Museum, *35 Woodbridge Street, South Hadley; (413) 538–2085.* Musical instruments, minerals, glassware, and regional furnishings.

Dino Land, *off Route 116, South Hadley; (413) 467–9566.* Dinosaur tracks.

Holyoke

Like Lowell, Holyoke is a mill city, planned around the canals built in the mid-nineteenth century as the power source for the Holyoke Water Power Company. The 150-year-old system still generates hydroelectric power and supplies process water to manufacturing companies that occupy the old mill buildings.

 HOLYOKE HERITAGE STATE PARK (all ages)
21 Appleton Street, Holyoke; (413) 534–1723. The visitor center can be contacted at (413) 534–1723. Open Tuesday through Sunday noon to 4:30 P.M.
Holyoke Heritage State Park is an eight-acre complex of enormous mill buildings and outdoor spaces, with exhibits about the city's growth. There are two main attractions for families here: the **Holyoke Merry-Go-Round** and the **Children's Museum.**

- **Holyoke Merry-Go-Round;** *(413) 538–9838. Open year-round, weekends noon to 4:00 P.M. and during Holyoke School vacations. Price: $1.00 per ride.* The antique merry-go-round was built in 1929 in Philadelphia. Housed in a colorful new building near the entrance to the park, the large carousel has forty-eight horses and two chariots, all carved by hand, plus a loud, cheerful band organ.

- **The Children's Museum (age 8 and under);** *444 Dwight Street, Holyoke; (413) 536–KIDS. Open Tuesday through Saturday 9:30 A.M. to 4:30 P.M., Sunday noon to 5:00 P.M. Admission: $4.00 per person.* The Children's Museum emphasizes family participation in educational games and interactive exhibits. Make your own paper, or try your hand at one of the mock-ups of local businesses set up here, including a "working" TV station.

The Holyoke Dam Located on Route 116, left at the fishway sign just before the South Hadley Falls Bridge, the Holyoke Dam has a viewing window and observation platform for watching over a million migrating shad and salmon in early May and June. Call (413) 659-3714 for more information.

Other Things to See and Do

Wistariahurst Museum, *238 Cabot Street, Holyoke; (413) 534–2216.* Mansion of silk manufacturer William Skinner. *Tip:* Abuts questionable section of town.

Mt. Tom State Reservation, *off Route 5, Holyoke; (413) 527–4805.* Hiking,

natural history museum, wildlife watchtower, snowshoeing and cross-country skiing trails.

Volleyball Hall of Fame, *444 Dwight Street (at Heritage State Park), Holyoke; (413) 536–0926; www.volleyball.org.* A look at this sport's history.

Where to Eat and Stay

Yankee Pedlar Inn, *1866 Northampton Street (Route 5), Holyoke; (413) 532–9494.* Twenty-eight-room Victorian-

style inn known for its fine food and decor. $$$

Springfield

Dr. James Naismith invented basketball here when he made a game of throwing a soccer ball into a peach basket at Springfield College in 1891. Homeboy Theodor Seuss Geisel (alias Dr. Seuss) has a national memorial in tribute to his work at the Quadrangle. The Naismith Basketball Hall of Fame is a family favorite, as well as the museums of the Quadrangle. Springfield is the largest city in the Greater Springfield region, as well as in the entire Pioneer Valley. It is also considered the gateway to western Massachusetts and Connecticut.

NAISMITH BASKETBALL HALL OF FAME (all ages)

1150 West Columbus Avenue, Springfield; (413) 781–6500. Open daily, September through June, 9:30 A.M. to 5:30 P.M., July through Labor Day, 9:00 A.M. to 7:00 P.M.; closed major holidays. Admission: $8.00 for adults, $5.00 for children 7 to 15; **Free** *for children under 7. Directions: Exit 4 off the Mass. Turnpike to Route 91S. Take exit 7, then follow the signs.*

The Naismith Basketball Hall of Fame is an entertainment center/museum that will be interesting to any visitor who's ever had even a remote connection to the game. Walk through the Shoe Tunnel, which is hung with the enormous footwear of inductees. Challenge your basketball knowledge. Shoot hoops of various shapes, sizes, and heights. Play Bill Walton in the Virtual Reality game. Or compare your height and arm span to those of the game's biggest players. Enshrinement into the Basketball Hall of Fame in October.

QUADRANGLE

Corner of State and Chestnut Streets, Springfield; (413) 263–6800. Open year-round, Wednesday through Sunday noon to 4:00 P.M. Admission (includes entry to all four museums): $4.00 for adults, $1.00 for children 6 to 18; **Free** *for children under 6.*

Springfield's Quadrangle, a complex that incorporates four museums and the main branch of the Springfield City Library, is a nice place to spend time. Parking is **Free** at the museums' and library's lots on State Street and Edwards Street. The plaza includes six bronze sculptures, which are a tribute to Theodor Geisel, author of the *Dr. Seuss* series. Museums of the Quadrangle include:

- **Connecticut Valley Historical Museum**—350 years of Pioneer Valley history.

- **George Walter Vincent Smith Art Museum**—Islamic rugs, largest collection of Chinese cloisonné in the West, Shinto shrine, and nineteenth-century American paintings

- **Springfield Museum of Fine Art**—European and American paintings

- **Springfield Science Museum**—The African Hall focuses on the diverse wildlife of the African continent, and Dinosaur Hall (the kids' favorite) includes a full-size replica of a towering tyrannosaur. Other attractions include a hands-on Exploration Center, several interactive life science exhibits, an antique airplane, and a planetarium

FOREST PARK (all ages)

Route 83, off Route 21/Sumner Street; (413) 733–2251; www.the-spa.com/zoo/. Open daily April 14 to November 15. Open weekends November 15 to December 31 and mid-February to April 15. Closed Thanksgiving, Christmas, and New Year's Day through mid-February. Price: in-state cars $2.00 midweek, $3.00 weekends; out-of-state vehicles $3.00 midweek, $4.00 weekends.

Forest Park is a large city park with a small zoo, nature trails, picnic spots, swimming pools, and other recreational activities. During the December holidays the park has several drive-through lighting displays with various themes, such as the North Pole and Barney's Victorian Village (admission is $8.00 per car).

Major Agricultural Fairs in the Pioneer Valley

- **Blandford Fair,** early September, North Street, Blandford; (413) 848–2888

- **Cummington Fair,** late August, Fairgrounds Road, Cummington; (413) 238–7724

- **Eastern States Exposition,** mid-September, 1305 Memorial Avenue, West Springfield; (413) 737–2443

- **Franklin County Fair,** early September, Wisdom Way, Greenfield; (413) 774–4282; www.fcas.com

- **Heath Fair,** mid-August, Heath; (413) 337–4733

- **Littleville Fair,** early August, Kine Brook Road, Chester; (413) 296–4354

- **Middlefield Fair,** mid-August, Bell Road, Middlefield; (413) 623–6423

- **Northampton Fair,** late August, Bridge Street, Northampton; (413) 584–2237

- **Westfield Fair,** mid-August, Russellville Road; (413) 562–4640

Other Things to See and Do

Indian Motorcycle Museum and Hall of Fame, *33 Hender Street, Springfield; (413) 737–2624.* Collection of toy, motorcycles, and related memorabilia.

Riverfront Park and Tinkerbell Cruises, *foot of State Street, Springfield; (413) 787–6440 (park) and (413) 781–3320 (cruise line).* Seven-acre park with playground. Cruises May through October.

Springfield Armory National Historic Site, *One Armory Square, Springfield; (413) 734–8551 or www.nps.gov/index.html.* First National Armory, site chosen by General Washington. Museum features huge firearm collection, interactive exhibits, introductory film, and bookstore.

Springfield Civic Center, *1277 Main Street, Springfield; (413) 787–6600 or (800) 639–8602.* Sports and entertainment venue.

Springfield Falcons, *Springfield Civic Center, 1277 Main Street, Springfield; (413) 739–3344; www.falcons ahl.com.* American Hockey League teams. Price: $12.00 for adults, $7.00 for children 18 and under.

Storrowton Village Museum, *Eastern States Exposition, 1305 Memorial Avenue, West Springfield; (413) 787–0136 or* *www.thebige.com.* Re-created New England village.

Where to Eat

Gus and Paul's, Tower Square, *1500 Main Street, Springfield; (413) 781–2253.* Deli and bakery in a family setting. $

Spaghetti Warehouse, *60 Congress Street, Springfield; (413) 737–5454.* Fun spot with great homemade sauces and pastas. $–$$

Where to Stay

Springfield Marriott Hotel, *Boland and Columbus Avenues; (413) 781–7111 or (800) 228–9290.* Indoor pool and health club, 265 rooms, downtown location. $$$–$$$$

Agawam

Riverside Park in Agawam is an enormous amusement park, New England's largest.

RIVERSIDE PARK (all ages)

Route 159/Main Street, Agawam; (413) 786–9300 or (800) 370–7488. Open April through late October; call for prices and hours.

With a hundred rides, shows, and attractions spread over 170 acres, Riverside can be terribly crowded on summer weekends, but the tumult can add to the experience. There are four water rides, four roller coasters (one is inverted) a monorail, a Ferris wheel, two Kiddieland areas, a nice old merry-go-round, and a speedway (auto racing) on the grounds. Favorite rides for those with nerve and verve is the *Helivation* (a twenty-story free fall drop) and *Shipwreck Falls* (a twenty-passenger boat climbing a gradual 100-foot grade, with a steep plunge from the top). There are daily performances. The Island Kingdom Waterpark has eight waterslides, a lazy river, and a wavepool. No pets, no picnicking.

Marcia's Top Annual Events

in the Pioneer Valley

- **1704 Weekend at the Indian House,** February, Deerfield; (413) 774-7476

- **Spring Bulb Show,** March, Northampton; (413) 585-2740

- **Dr. Seuss Birthday,** early March, the Quadrangle, Springfield; (413) 263-6800

- **Massachusetts International Festival of the Arts,** late April, Amherst, Northampton, Holyoke, and Springfield; (800) 224-MIFA

- **Spawning migrations,** May/June, Holyoke Dam and Turners Falls; (413) 659-3714

- **Springfield Arts Festival,** June, Springfield; (413) 736-ARTS

- **Shelburne Falls Riverfest,** early June, Shelburne Falls; (413) 625-2544

- **Green River Music and Up-Country Hot-Air Balloon Fair,** July, Greenfield; (413) 773-5463

- **Turn-of-the-Century Ice Cream Social,** July, Deerfield; (413) 774-7476

- **Teddy Bear Rally,** August, Amherst Town Common; (413) 256-8983

- **The Big E (Eastern States Exposition),** September, West Springfield; (413) 737-2443

- **Greenfield Fall Festival and Street Fair,** October, Greenfield; (413) 774-2791

- **Volleyball Hall of Fame Enshrinement,** October, Springfield; (413) 536-0926

- **Book and Plow Festival,** October, Amherst; (413) 253-0700

- **Basketball Hall of Fame Enshrinement,** October, Springfield; (413) 781-6500

- **Chrysanthemum Show,** mid-November, Smith College, Northampton: (413) 585-2740

- **Bright Nights,** December, Forest Park, Springfield; (413) 733-2251

Central Massachusetts

Rolling hills run through most of this peaceful area, a region that Boston families treasure as a nearby source of seasonal rural activities. In spring, pastures are full of young animals kicking up their heels. Clear lakes and large parks welcome picnickers on summer afternoons. The city of Worcester has several good family-oriented museums. Orchards provide hours of fun for enthusiastic apple-pickers from late August through late October. Quiet country roads lead to the hiking and cross-country skiing trails that crisscross the region. The Central Massachusetts Tourism Council, 33 Waldo Street, Worcester (800-231-7557), is a helpful resource. South of Worcester, Old Sturbridge Village is an early-nineteenth-century "village" that was constructed in 1946. Unpaved roads, costumed interpreters, and working artisans give kids a flavor of what it might have been like to visit a typical New England village during the first fifty years of the Republic.

The Nashoba Valley and the Johnny Appleseed Trail

A hilly region that's served Bostonians as an easy escape for well over a century, the Nashoba Valley hasn't changed much since the Alcott family set up a commune in Harvard with other transcendentalists in 1843. The **Johnny Appleseed Visitor Center,** Route 2 West, Lancaster (978-534-2302), and the **North Central Massachusetts Chamber of Commerce,** 110 Erdman Way, Leominister (978-840-4300), offers maps and brochures on the area sights and attractions.

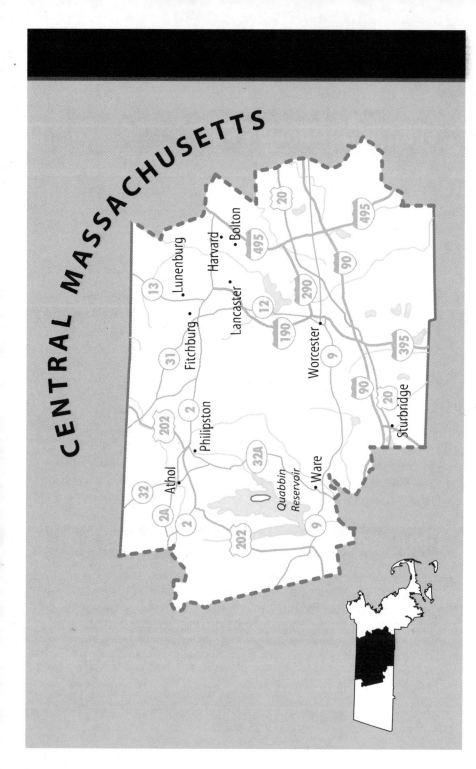

CENTRAL MASSACHUSETTS

Marcia's Top Family Adventures

in Central Massachusetts

1. Old Sturbridge Village, Sturbridge

2. Quabbin Reservoir and Park, Ware

3. Museum of the New England Landscape, Harvard

4. Worcester museums (Worcester Art Museum, Ecotarium, and Higgins Armory)

5. Farm fun on the Johnny Appleseed Trail

MUSEUM OF THE NEW ENGLAND LANDSCAPE (all ages)

102 Prospect Hill Road, Harvard; (978) 456–3924; www.fruitlands.org. Open daily from mid-May to mid-October, 10:00 A.M. to 5:00 P.M. Admission: $6.00 for adults, $3.00 for children.

Formerly the Fruitlands Museum and Farmhouse, the 200-acre property surrounding the four museums provides stunning views of the Nashua River Valley and, in the far distance, of mountains in southern New Hampshire. The Fruitlands Farmhouse Museum is dedicated to the memory of the transcendentalists, many of whom spent seven months of 1843 in the farmhouse at the bottom of the hill. The transcendentalists believed that God exists in humans and nature alike. Their beliefs led them to a distinct "back-to-nature" lifestyle, very unusual during their time. They tried living in a communal building on a farm where they could be as self-sufficient as possible. Among them were the Alcott family (Louisa, her three sisters, and her parents). The group gave its communal home the hopeful name of Fruitlands in the expectation that its orchards would produce an abundance of fruit. Unfortunately, the site wasn't optimal, and the trees didn't provide as much sustenance as the group had hoped. For this reason and others, its members left Harvard and went back to Concord.

In 1910 Clara Endicott Sears purchased the property, which had become run-down. She restored the farmhouse and opened it as a museum in honor of the Alcotts and their friends Emerson, Thoreau, and Margaret Fuller. The building houses mementos of the group.

Also on the property are the Shaker Museum, the Picture Gallery, and the Indian Museum. The Shaker Museum is dedicated to the Shaker towns of Harvard (which donated journals and an original Shaker office building) and Shirley. Exhibits depict the many industries of the Shaker communities' (look for the Sister's Work Room full of looms and spinning wheels) and illustrate how business was conducted between the Shakers and the outside world. The Picture Gallery houses portraits by primitive folk artists, and landscape paintings, with a sizable collection of paintings from the Hudson River School of painters. The Indian Museum holds Thoreau's rock and mineral collection and other interesting artifacts of the Native Americans who once lived in the area.

Nature trails (used for cross-country skiing in the winter), two archaeological sites depicting different periods of New England history, the Museum Store, and the Tea Room round out your day at the museum. Watch for the summer concert series and the Harvest Festival in September.

NASHOBA VALLEY WINERY AND ORCHARDS (all ages)

100 Wattaquadoc Hill Road, Bolton; (978) 779–5521; www.NashobaWinery.com. Open year-round; twenty-minute tours are given Saturday and Sunday, 11:00 A.M. to 5:00 P.M. (last tour at 4:00 P.M.). Tours are $3.00 for adults, **Free** *for children.*

Pick berries during the summer and early fall, apples throughout the fall, and be sure to bring a picnic. In the winter it's a nice place to cross-country ski. Regardless of the season, you can take a tour of the winery. Horseback riding is allowed, but bring your own horse. A restaurant on the premises is open Tuesday through Saturday for lunch, Wednesday through Saturday evening for dinner, and Sunday for brunch. An annual Harvest Festival is held the first Saturday in September.

WHALOM PARK (all ages)

Route 13, Lunenburg; (978) 342–3707; www.whalompark.com. Call for prices and hours.

An old-fashioned amusement park, Whalom Park isn't huge, and there are nearly as many kiddie rides as adults-only rides. Clowns wander the premises, and there's a parade every day. Attractions include roller coasters, a water slide, mini-golf, and paddleboats. There's swimming in the lake on weekends. The shady, grassy picnic area is very pleasant.

Tour de Fitchburg

Tour de Fitchburg Fitchburg's **Longsjo Classic Bicycle Race**—a tribute to former Olympian cyclist Arthur Longsjo—is a four-day race held in early July. It's one of the premier amateur bicycle races, attracting competitors from around the world. For more information, call (978) 582-0226, or check out the Web site at users.cyberzone.net/longsjo.

 DRAWBRIDGE MARIONETTE THEATER (ages 10 and under)
181 Main Street, Fitchburg; (978) 342–2552 or (800) 401–3694. Admission: $3.00. Performances are every weekend on Saturday at 11:00 A.M., Sunday at 2:00 P.M.

Each marionette show has original songs, skits, and special effects and ends with a demonstration of the art of "mastering the strings."

 FITCHBURG ART MUSEUM (ages 8 and up)
185 Elm Street, Fitchburg; (978) 345–4207. Open Tuesday through Saturday 11:00 A.M. to 4:00 P.M., Sunday 1:00 to 4:00 P.M. Admission: $3.00 for adults, $2.00 for seniors; Free *for children.*

The focus is on American and European art and local contemporary New England artists. There's also a minor collection of classical art and antiquities from Greece, Rome, Asia, and South America. A big hit is the permanent Egyptian exhibit.

The Rat Pack

The Rat Pack The **River Rat Race (mid-April)** from Athol to Orange started as a bet in 1963 among friends as to whether or not the Millers River was navigable for canoeists (dams and rapids were problems). The bet escalated into a 6-mile race, and today the best canoeists in North America take the challenge to be crowned the King River Rat. The affair starts with a pancake breakfast, River Rat Parade, and Duck Race, leading to the River Rat Race, with a field of over 320 canoeists. For more information, contact the North Quabbin/Athol/Orange Chamber of Commerce, 521 Main Street, Athol (978-249-3849).

WACHUSETT MOUNTAIN SKI AREA AND STATE RESERVATION (all ages)

499 Mountain Road, Princeton; (978) 464–2300, www.wachusett.com. Open seasonally from dawn to dusk from late November to late March. Skiing from late November to late March.

Full snowmaking coverage makes this a fun family ski mountain. Features day and night skiing, five lifts (including the only high-speed detachable quad in the state), and eighteen trails. During the off-season you can hike and picnic here, or take the auto road to reach the summit.

Farm Fun

- **Alta Vista Farm,** 80 Hillside Road, Rutland; (508) 886–4365. Bison herd, tours, picnicking.

- **Arrowhead Acres,** 92 Aldrich Street, Uxbridge; (508) 278–5017. Petting farm, pumpkins, hayrides.

- **Berlin Orchards,** 200 Central Street, Berlin; (978) 838–2400. Apples, hayrides, farm animals, ice cream, picnicking, cider press, and Family Festivals.

- **Bolton Spring Farm,** 159 Main Street, Bolton; (978) 779–2898. Apples and pumpkins, hayrides, helicopter rides.

- **Brookfield Orchards,** 12 Lincoln Road, North Brookfield; (508) 867–6858. Apples, cross-country skiing, farm tours, harvest festivals, country store, playground.

- **Clover Hill,** 1839 Lower Road, Hardwick; (413) 477–0316. Petting farm, hayrides, sleigh rides, llamas, emus.

- **Davis Farmland/Family Farm Adventure,** 145 Redstone Hill, Sterling; (978) 422–6666. Children's farm and museum, petting farm, play park, largest collection of endangered livestock in United States.

- **Fay Mountain Farm,** 12 Cemetery Road, Charleston; (508) 248–7237. Apples, peaches, pears, blueberries, raspberries, cider mill tours, hayrides, picnic area, and pond.

- **George Hill Orchard,** George Hill Road, Lancaster; (800) 699–4331. Pick-your-own farm, home of Apple Tree Theatre.

- **Great Brook Trout Farm,** 120 Meadow Road, Bolton; (978) 779–0077 or (978) 779–6899. Fee fishing for trout, bass, perch, and sunfish.

- **Nourse Farm,** 70 Norse Street, Westboro; (508) 366–2644. Tours, pony rides, hayrides, farm animals.

- **Overlook Farm,** 216 Wachusett Street, Rutland; (508) 886–2221. Heifer Project International, hay and sleigh rides, hiking, picnicking.

- **Red Apple Farm,** 455 Highland Avenue, Phillipston; (800) 628–4851. Scenic views and trails, apples, blueberries, raspberries, pumpkins, picnicking, farm animals, hayrides, mazes, bonfires, groomed cross-country skiing trails.

- **Tougas Family Farm,** 246 Ball Street, Northborough; (508) 393–6470. Pick-your-own fruits, petting zoo, hay- and wagon rides, cider pressing, farm tours.

- **Zukas Homestead Farm and B&B,** 89 Smithville Road, Spencer; (508) 885–5320. Heifers, miniature horses, small animals, hiking, sledding, cross-country skiing, B&B.

Other Things to See and Do

Johnny Appleseed Visitor Center, *Route 2 West, Lancaster; (978) 534–2302; www.appleseed.org.* Farmers' market held every Sunday from June through mid-October from 9:00 A.M. to 2:00 P.M.

Mountain Lynx Outdoor Adventures, *180 Central Street, Leominster; (978) 840–6464.* Adventures in rock climbing, canoeing, and caving.

National Plastics Center and Museum, *210 Lancaster Street, Leominster; (978) 537–9529.*

Nashoba Paddler Rentals, *Groton; (978) 448–8699.* Open May 1 through November. Daily canoe rentals are $33, hourly rate is $11 ($8.00 for each additional hour).

Where to Eat

Fox Run Restaurant, *185 Ward Hill Road, Phillipston; (800) 695–8267.* Historic setting, specialties include plank steak, rack of lamb, and Chateaubriand. Children's menu. $$

The 1761 Old Mill, *Route 2A East, Westminster; (978) 874–5941.* Former saw mill. Standard New England fare—hearty, filling, and delicious. Children's menu. $-$$$

Where to Stay

Friendly Crossways, *247 Littleton County Road, Harvard; (978) 456–3649; www.ultanet.com.* The first youth hostel in the United States, this stay over offers family rooms, dorm rooms, or private rooms. Rent linens or bring your own; kitchen privileges. $

Sheraton Four Points, *99 Erdman Way (junction of Routes 2 and 12), Leominster;* *(978) 534–9000.* 187 deluxe guest rooms, restaurant, and pub with children's menu; indoor heated pool. $$$$

Wachusett Village Inn, *9 Village Inn Road, Westminster; (978) 874–2000 or (800) 342–1905.* Full recreation center with indoor pool and hot tubs; restaurant with children's menu. $$$–$$$$

Greater Worcester and the Blackstone Valley

The second largest city in Massachusetts as well as New England, Worcester loses a lot of tourists to Boston, but it's managed to build a busy cultural life for itself with several good museums.

The Worcester Tourism Bureau, 33 Waldo Street, Worcester (508-753-2920; www.worcester.org), can provide you with information and maps.

The Blackstone Valley, designated a National Heritage Corridor, has several formerly company-owned mill towns representative of the Industrial Revolution. It's a picturesque area with recreational opportunities.

Worcester

 JOHN WOODMAN HIGGINS ARMORY (12 and under)
100 Barber Avenue, Worcester; (508) 853–6015. Open year-round Tuesday through Saturday, 10:00 A.M. to 4:00 P.M., Sunday noon to 4:00 P.M.; closed most holidays. Admission: $5.75 for adults, $4.75 for children 6 to 16; **Free** *for children under 6.* **Free** *admission on Founder's Day (second weekend in January).*

Try on a helmet—or perhaps a full suit of armor, if you're big enough—at this remarkable collection, the only museum in the Western Hemisphere dedicated to arms and armor. The orientation is fun for everyone; the interpreter selects a visitor to "suit up," encouraging him or her to describe how uncomfortable and restrictive the armor actually is. The Quest Gallery has costumes for everyone: princesses and princes, queens and kings, and helmets for moms and dads. The museum runs interesting workshops for kids in which they learn to make gargoyles, books, masks, pennants, and shields; call for a schedule. Chess games are always going on in the Quest Gallery.

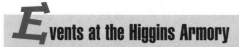

*E*vents at the Higgins Armory

- **Higgins Faire,** second weekend in June; Medieval festival with games, food, face painting, hair wraps, and period entertainment and demonstrations.

- **Falconry Demonstrations at the Higgins Armory Museum,** November.

- **Knight before Christmas,** second weekend in December. Decorate gingerbread ornaments and castles, listen to traditional holiday songs and entertainment.

WORCESTER ART MUSEUM (all ages)
55 Salisbury Street, Worcester; (508) 799–4406. Open year-round, Wednesday through Friday and Sunday 11:00 A.M. to 5:00 P.M., Saturday 10:00 A.M. to 5:00 P.M.; closed major holidays. Admission: $8.00 for adults, $6.00 for seniors and students; Free *for children under 18.* Free *admission on Saturday from 10:00 A.M. to noon. Sunday museum tours at 2:00 P.M.*

Nearly every period of art is featured in this small, excellent city museum. Highlights include a sixth-century floor mosaic in the central court area; a twelfth-century Romanesque house that was moved here, stone by stone, from France; an eleven-headed, ninth-century Japanese sculpture; and an extensive collection of pre-Columbian sculpture in various media, including gold and ceramic. The Museum Cafe serves light snacks and lunches. A garden cafe is open during the summer.

ECOTARIUM (all ages)
222 Harrington Way, Worcester; (508) 791–9211; www.ecotarium.org. Open year-round, Monday through Saturday 10:00 A.M. to 5:00 P.M., Sunday noon to 5:00 P.M. Admission: $7.00 for adults, $5.00 for children 3 to 16.

The focus at the Ecotarium (formerly the New England Science Center) is on the environment. An $18 million expansion and renovation plan created trails, an outdoor observation walkway, and renovations to the existing building's architecture. The Nature Trail traverses the property and rounds the two existing ponds, the Water Pavilion, and the Pier, giving access to over sixty acres of lake and woods. A Tree Canopy Walkway allows you to study and inspect the leafline of the trees. The walkway, suspended approximately 20 feet above the ground, allows you to observe the habitat of birds, insects, and wildlife. There's a zoo with larger animals, such as polar bears and big cats. Inside the three-story building are several good interactive environmental exhibits, three large aquariums, and a planetarium show (the planetarium is open on weekends only; call for a schedule).

BLACKSTONE RIVER VALLEY NATIONAL HERITAGE CORRIDOR (all ages)

The visitor center at River Bend Farm, located in the Blackstone River and Canal Heritage State Park, Oak Street in Uxbridge, has information on the corridor; (508) 278–7604.

The Blackstone River Valley National Heritage Corridor covers communities from Worcester, Massachusetts, to Providence, Rhode Island. The area's mills, villages, and canals help to reveal the history of the Industrial Revolution. Recreational opportunities include hiking, hayrides, canal boat rides, historic sites and natural areas, canoeing, cross-country skiing, and ice-skating. Ask for the auto route tour map.

SOUTHWICK'S WILD ANIMAL FARM (12 and under)
Follow signs off Route 16, Mendon; (508) 883–9182; www.southwickzoo. Open daily mid-April to mid-October (call for off-season hours). Hours: Mother's Day through Labor Day, 10:00 A.M. to 5:00 P.M. Admission: $8.95 for adults, $6.95 for children 3 to 12; Free *for children under 3.* Free *parking.*

If the kids are into animals, they'll love a visit to Southwick's Wild Animal Farm, where they're likely to see giraffes, peacock, alligators, and more than a hundred other species of animals on a 300-acre farm. There's a petting zoo and a deer forest, where they can approach the deer. Kids can take rides on ponies, elephants, and sometimes camels. During the summer there's a circus every day. An education building has informative presentations.

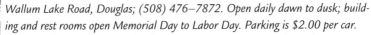

DOUGLAS STATE FOREST AND WALLUM LAKE (all ages)

Wallum Lake Road, Douglas; (508) 476–7872. Open daily dawn to dusk; build-

ing and rest rooms open Memorial Day to Labor Day. Parking is $2.00 per car.

Douglas State Forest and Wallum Lake is an enormous state forest—
nearly 5,200 acres—with a plethora of picnic sites and a big lake for
boating and swimming. The beach has a bathhouse and lifeguards.
Activities include hiking, mountain biking, horseback riding, swimming,
boating, snowmobiling, cross-country skiing, and snowshoeing.

PURGATORY CHASM STATE RESERVATION (all ages)

*Purgatory Road, Sutton; (508) 234–3733. Open daily dawn to dusk. Parking is
$2.00 per car.*

The deep chasm is a dramatic sight and a nice spot to hike any time
of year, but in the summer the cool, damp air is especially pleasant. A
marked path leads down the series of ravines that form the chasm. *Note:*
This path is steep in spots and isn't appropriate for children under 10.
There are numerous picnic spots in the reservation, as well as a good
playground area and a short marked path through the woods that's
more appropriate for younger kids.

Other Things to See and Do

Broad Meadow Brook Wildlife Sanctuary, *414 Massasoit Road, Worcester; (508) 753–6087.* Largest urban wildlife sanctuary in New England. Open daily dawn to dusk.

Willard House and Clock Museum, *11 Willard Street, North Grafton; (508) 839–3500; www.NAWCC.org/museum/williard/willard.htm.* One-hour guided tour offered on the hour Tuesday through Saturday 10:00 A.M. to 4:00 P.M., Sunday 1:00 to 5:00 P.M. Admission: $5.00 for adults, $2.00 for children 12 and under.

Worcester Common Outlets, *100 Front Street, Worcester; (888) GET–IN–ON–IT.* Discount outlet shopping.

Worcester Centrum Centre, *50 Foster Street; (508) 755–6800; www.centrumcentre.com.* Home of the AHL Ice Cats. Buy tickets at the box office, or call Ticketmaster at (617) 931–2000.

Where to Eat

Firehouse Cafe, *1 Exchange Place, Worcester; (508) 753–7899.* Pub-style food, indoor and outdoor dining. $$

Hebert Candies Mansion, *575 Hartford Turnpike (Route 20), Shrewsbury; (508) 845–8051.* Headquarters of Heberts Candies, **Free** factory tour given at this national landmark (America's first roadside candy store). Great chocolates and make-your-own sundae bar. $

Maxwell Siverman's Toolhouse, *25 Union Street, Worcester; (508) 755–1200.* Restored factory building; steak and seafood specialties. $$-$$$

Webster House, *1 Webster Street, Worcester (508) 757–7208.* Family-friendly; homemade pies. $

Where to Stay

Crowne Plaza, *10 Lincoln Square, Worcester; (508) 791–1600.* Offers 243 rooms. $$$-$$$$

Quabbin Reservoir and the Greater Sturbridge Area

Quabbin, which means "place of many waters," lives up to its name. The Quabbin Reservoir covers over 39 square miles, with 120,000 acres of state-owned watershed land surrounding it. Scenic hikes and trails are especially magnificent in the autumn. Another draw is Old Sturbridge Village, one of the best outdoor living history museum/villages in the country. Contact the Sturbridge Chamber of Commerce (800–628–8379; www.sturbridge.com) for more information.

QUABBIN RESERVOIR AND PARK (all ages)

485 Ware Road, entrance on Route 9 between Ware and Belchertown; (413) 323–7221. Open daily dawn to dusk. Visitor center has seasonal hours. **Free,** *except for charge for fishing.*

Quabbin Reservoir and Park is a protected watershed of the Quabbin Reservoir, which supplies water to 2.4 million residents of Massachusetts. The man-made watershed lands also supply wilderness, wildlife, forest, research, historical, and recreational resources. The visitor center, located at Winsor Dam, provides information about the many hiking trails on the 87-square-mile reservation and a few exhibits about the reservoir's construction. The reservoir was begun in 1926; the towns of Dana, Prescott, Greenwich, and Enfield were "discontinued," which means that the state bought the land from the residents and moved them away, then flooded the land. Enfield Lookout, up a winding road after you cross the dam, overlooks a spectacular view of the reservoir and the hills that were once the town of Enfield. A good, though hilly, walk begins across the road from the lookout (pick up maps at the visitor center). Fishing and boating for fishing purposes only are at designated areas. No dogs, swimming, camping or fires, off-road vehicles, sliding on dams, or cross-country skiing.

THE SALEM CROSS INN FARM AND RESTAURANT (all ages)
Route 9, West Brookfield; (508) 867–2345. Restaurant is open year-round, Tuesday through Friday 11:30 A.M. to 9:00 P.M., Saturday 5:00 to 10:00 P.M., Sunday noon to 9:00 P.M.

Listed in the National Register of Historic Places, the Salem Cross Inn is named for the hexmark on the front door latch that was placed there to fend off witchcraft when the building was erected in 1720. It was built by a grandson of Peregrine White, the only baby born on the *Mayflower*. The 600-acre property is a working farm. In winter there is an 11-kilometer snowshoeing and cross-country skiing track, and sleigh rides are offered. Hayrides are offered in the warmer months, and hiking is allowed. The dining room menu changes with the season. During the winter, roasts are cooked on a roasting jack (the only one remaining in the country) and breads are baked in an original beehive oven. A spring or summer evening might feature a roast cooked outdoors over a pit, served with chowder. There is a special children's menu for $6.95.

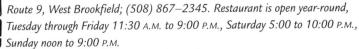

More Than a Mouthful The Native American name for Webster Lake (off Routes 16 and 193, Webster) is Lake Chargoggagog-manchauggagoggchaubunagungamaugg. Not surprisingly, this is the longest geographic name in the United States. Rough translation: I fish on my side of the lake, you fish on yours, and no one fishes in between.

Marcia's Top Annual Events

in Central Massachusetts

- **Washington's Birthday Celebration,** February, Old Sturbridge; (508) 347–3362

- **Athol to Orange River Rat Race,** April, Athol; (978) 249–3849

- **Eastern Sprints Regatta rowing championships,** May, Lake Quinsigamond, Quinsigamond State Park, Worcester; (508) 757–2140

- **The Brimfield Flea Market,** May, July (Fourth of July weekend), and September (Labor Day weekend), Brimfield Common; (413) 283–6149 or (413) 283–2418

- **New England Aerobatics Championships,** mid-May, Orange Municipal Airport; (978) 249–3849

- **Harvest weekend,** September, Old Sturbridge Village; (508) 347–3362

- **Three Apples Storytelling Festival,** late September, Harvard; (617) 499–9529.

- **Spooky World,** October, 100 River Road, Berlin; (978) 838–0200

- **Pumpkin Commission Weigh In and Festival,** October, Phillipston; (978) 249–3849

- **Thanksgiving at Olde Sturbridge Village,** November, Old Sturbridge Village; (508) 347–3362

- **Chain of Lights Holiday Celebration,** December, Worcester County; (508) 753–2920

OLD STURBRIDGE VILLAGE (all ages)

1 Old Sturbridge Village Road, Sturbridge; (508) 347–3362. Open January 1 to Washington's Birthday, weekends only, 10:00 A.M. to 4:00 P.M.; Washington's Birthday to the last weekend in March daily, 10:00 A.M. to 4:00 P.M.; April through the end of October daily, 9:00 A.M. to 5:00 P.M.; November through December daily, 10:00 A.M. to 4:00 P.M. Closed Christmas. Admission (good for two consecutive days): $16.00 for adults, $8.00 for children 6 to 15; Free *for children under 6.*

Worth at least one full day's visit for any family, the village re-creates the daily life of a rural early-nineteenth century community, with its farms, fields, shops, houses, and outlying mill areas. More than forty buildings from all over New England were carefully dismantled and transported here in the mid-1940s, then painstakingly reassembled and furnished in period style. The period portrayed by the village is particularly significant because it was a time when New Englanders' lives were transformed by the rise of commerce and manufacturing, improvements in agriculture and transportation, emigration and growing urbanization, and the political and social changes of a prospering young country. Younger children will enjoy seeing the costumed interpreters who set the scene, as well as the animals, the unpaved streets, and the interesting simple tools and machines that the interpreters use. Older kids will enjoy the interaction with the interpreters, who welcome questions and participation in many activities such as sheep shearing, spinning, weaving, gardening, fireplace cooking, tinsmithing, watercolor painting, and candle making. Special events occur all year, call for a schedule.

Note: Advance registration is required for fee-based activities. Wear comfortable shoes; the property is large. Bring a stroller for younger children, although you'll have to leave it outside many of the buildings. The village is accessible for visitors with disabilities (more than half of the buildings are wheelchair accessible), and sign-language interpreters are available by prior arrangement.

Where to Eat

Publick House Restaurant, *Route 131, 187 Main Street (on the common), Sturbridge; (508) 347-3313.* Six dining rooms in a traditional setting. New England cooking: thick chops, pot roast, lobster pie, and Indian pudding for dessert. $-$$$

Rom's, *Route 131, Sturbridge; (508) 347-3349.* Six dining rooms serving classic meals at reasonable prices. $-$$

Where to Stay

Publick House Properties, *Route 131 (on the Common), Sturbridge; (508) 347-3313.* Large complex of accommodations consisting of the 1771 **Publick**

House Historic Inn, the modern **Country Motor Lodge,** and the **Chamberlain House,** with suite accommodations. A mile away is the gracious

Colonel Ebenezer Crafts Inn, furnished with four-poster beds. All guests have access to the pool, tennis courts, and playground at the Publick House. Packages during the Yankee Winter Weekends (January–March) include admission to Old Sturbridge Village. $$$–$$$$

Sturbridge Host, *Route 20, Sturbridge; (508) 347–7393 or (800) 582–3232.* Great location, indoor pool, sauna, health club, tennis, mini-golf, boating, and fishing on Cedar Lake. $$$–$$$$

The North Shore, Cape Ann, and the Merrimack Valley

The ragged coastline of the North Shore begins in the shipyards on Boston's north edges. As the crow flies, it stretches for 30 miles, up and around the island of Cape Ann, in and out of Ipswich Bay, and so along to the New Hampshire border. Along the way are the historic towns of Saugus, Lynn, Marblehead, Salem, Gloucester, Rockport, Ipswich, and Newburyport. Families flock to the museums of old Salem to hear the dark tales of the country's early history, retold here on-site and in chilling detail. Enchanting Marblehead's narrow streets and dollhouselike buildings stand in stark contrast to the workaday fishing villages of Gloucester and Rockport. Beautiful beaches and state parks bring families to Ipswich, Salisbury, Topsfield, and Newburyport. Mill towns like Lowell, which were on the cutting edge of the Industrial Revolution, are now sites of learning and history.

Marcia's Top Family Adventures for the North Shore, Cape Ann, and the Merrimack Valley

1. Parker River National Wildlife Refuge and Plum Island, Newburyport
2. Crane Beach, Ipswich
3. Salem Maritime National Historic Site and the Peabody and Essex Museums, Salem
4. Marblehead Harbor, especially during Race Week
5. Boott Cotton Mills and the American Textile History Museum, Lowell
6. Bearskin Neck, Rockport

THE NORTH SHORE, CAPE ANN and THE MERRIMACK VALLEY

Newburyport

Lowell

Ipswich

Essex

Rockport

Beverly

Gloucester

Manchester-By-The-Sea

Salem

Marblehead

Saugus

Saugus's main commercial street is Route 1, which divides the town into two parts. On either side of the highway are found two interesting tourism sites, the Saugus Ironworks and the Breakheart Reservation. Saugus was settled in 1630, and the first successful ironworks in the country was established here. The Breakheart Reservation is a 600-acre oasis straddling the communities of Saugus and Wakefield. For more information, contact the **Saugus Chamber of Commerce** (781-233-8407).

SAUGUS IRONWORKS NATIONAL HISTORIC SITE (all ages)

244 Central Street; (781) 941-2372; www.nps.gov/sair. Directions: From Route 1 take the Walnut Street exit and follow the National Historic Site signs. Open daily November 1 to March 31, 9:00 A.M. to 4:00 P.M., April 1 to October 31, 9:00 A.M. to 5:00 P.M.; closed Thanksgiving, Christmas Day, and New Year's Day. Call for times of guided tours. **Free**.

The Saugus Ironworks is the birthplace of the ironmaking industry in the colonies. The Iron Works House, the last seventeenth-century building in Saugus, was saved and restored in 1915 by Wallace Nutting, an authority on colonial American buildings and furniture. Archeological digs unearthed the remains of the ironworks, and in 1954 reconstruction of the site was completed. The ironworks has seven functioning water wheels. There are four sets of bellows, a 500-pound water-powered hammer, and a rolling and slitting mill. Park guides run the machinery, but the water wheels operate only from April through October. Blacksmiths demonstrate their skills year-round. Special programs for kids are offered. Don't forget to visit the interpretive museum.

BREAKHEART RESERVATION (all ages)

177 Forest Street; (781) 233-0834. Open dawn to dusk year-round. **Free**.

Breakheart is busy year-round. The property includes forest land with a variety of hiking trails, two freshwater lakes, playgrounds, and picnicking shelters with stoves. Pearce Lake, framed by Eagle Rock, is a great spot for a cooling splash on a hot summer's day. The beach is lifeguarded in season (July 4 to Labor Day) and handicap-accessible. Activities include hiking, mountain biking, cross-country skiing, rollerblading, swimming, fishing, bicycling, snowshoeing, and wildlife viewing. Annual events include Maple Sugarin', a First-Day Hike, and birding tours. Reservations for special events are required, and a small fee may be charged. For schools and nonprofit groups, there is **Camp Nihan Environmental Education Camp and Center,** with overnight facilities. For more information call (781-662-5230; fax 781-727-8228). Adjacent to Breakheart is the **Kasabuski Ice Skating Arena** (781-231-8107), which can be paired with a visit to the reservation.

Where to Eat

Brew Moon Restaurant and Microbrewery, *Route 1 North; (781) 941–BREW.* Part of a local four-restaurant chain, the restaurant offers tasty fare and prize-winning home-brewed beer. Open for lunch and dinner. $-$$

The Hilltop Steak House and Butcher Shop, *Route 1 South; (781) 233–7700.* Local landmark famous for its large portions. Children's menu. $-$$

Lynn and Nahant

Once part of the same township, Lynn and Nahant evolved into two separate entities. Lynn is an urban center, while Nahant has retained its charm as a small seaside village. A popular seaside haven for the wealthy in the 1800s, Nahant is connected to Lynn by a causeway. Lynn's earliest settlers were shoemakers by trade, giving birth to a city that in its heyday would earn an international reputation for shoe production.

LYNN HERITAGE STATE PARK (all ages)

590 Washington Street; (781) 598–1974. Visitor center open Wednesday to Sunday 9:30 A.M. to 4:30 P.M. **Free**.

The Lynn Heritage State Park includes a visitor center/exhibition area and Waterfront Park. Start your tour of the center with the informative eight-minute video, then wind your way through the interactive displays depicting Lynn's history, its industries, and its citizens. Once you've finished your tour, follow the yellow footsteps to Waterfront Park. The park sponsors outdoor concerts and recreational activities, such as paddleboat rentals and fishing at the marina. There are water shuttles for a fee to the Boston Harbor Islands National Recreational Area. Schedules can be picked up at the visitor center.

Halloween in August Dress up as your favorite sea monster at the **Harbor Monster Day** festival at Waterfront Park. Prizes are given. Look for the arrival of Seamore! Contact the Lynn Heritage State Park Visitors Center for a schedule of events.

LYNN WOODS RESERVATION (all ages)

Main entrance is accessed from Walnut Street. Open dawn to dusk; (781) 477–7123; www.flw.org. **Free**.

Upon entering the park, stop in at the park headquarters for a map. Lynn Woods is the second-largest city-owned park in the country, covering 2,200 acres. A favorite hike for kids is the Jackson Path trail leading to Dungeon Rocks. There's a cave here that you can enter May 1 to October 31 from 11:00 A.M. to 4:00 P.M. For a special treat, a guide, costumed as a pirate, will take the children to the bowels of the cave the Saturday before Halloween. Other fun trails lead to the stone tower on Burrill Hill, the rose garden, and the steel tower on Mount Gilead. Other activities are mountain biking, horseback riding, and cross-country skiing. There's also a playground. Landscape architect Frederick Law Olmsted consulted here and advised that Lynn Woods be left a rugged forest environment; thus, the park is not wheelchair- or stroller-friendly. Call for a schedule of seasonal events.

LYNN SHORE RESERVATION/NAHANT BEACH (all ages)

1 Causeway Street, Nahant; (617) 727–1368. Main parking lot open dawn to dusk, end of June to the end of September. Side parking lots accessible year-round. Parking is $2.00 in-season.

Nahant Beach, also known as Long Beach, is a crescent of pure white sand lifeguarded until 6:00 P.M. in-season. There are swings and a playground near the Lynn end of the beach. The beach promenade goes from King's Beach on the Lynn/Nahant line to Swampscott.

Raiders of the Lost Rock The notorious pirate Thomas Veal is said to be buried with his treasure in Dungeon Rock. As the legend goes, Veal was trapped in the cave while examining his treasure when an earthquake struck, bringing down boulders and burying him with his booty for eternity. Children dream of uncovering the treasure.

Woman of Valor

Woman of Valor Mary Baker Eddy, a resident of Lynn from 1875 to 1882, was honored in the National Women's Hall of Fame as the only American woman to found a world religion. The Christian Science Church, which she founded, advocates healing through prayer.

Where to Eat

Dockside Restaurant and Bar, *28 Wilson Road, Nahant Beach; (781) 593–7500.* This restaurant has great views of Nahant Beach and the Lynn/Boston skyline. Varied kid's menu; standard menu runs from sandwiches to seafood. Open year-round for lunch and dinner 11:30 A.M. to 10:00 P.M. $-$$.

Marblehead

In the picturesque harbor town of Marblehead, the streets are so narrow and many of the buildings so small that the town resembles a scaled-down model, but it's a real place where real people live. Walk the twisting streets, eat seafood while you watch the boats, see a historic painting, and immerse yourselves in one of the best-preserved seaside villages in Massachusetts.

When you arrive in Marblehead, visit the **information booth** (62 Pleasant Street/Route 114, corner of Pleasant and Spring Streets; 781–631–2868; www.marbleheadchamber.org) to pick up a copy of the self-guided walking-tour brochure and to ask questions about the day's activities. The booth is open daily, 10:00 A.M.–5:30 P.M., from Memorial Day through Columbus Day.

ABBOT HALL AND THE WATERFRONT PARKS AND SIGHTS (all ages)

Washington Square; (781) 631–0528. Open Monday, Thursday, and Friday 8:00 A.M. to 5:00 P.M., Tuesday and Wednesday 8:00 A.M. to 9:00 P.M., Saturday 9:00 A.M. to 6:00 P.M., and Sunday 11:00 A.M. to 6:00 P.M. **Free**.

Abbott Hall, which still operates as the town hall, is the prime tourist destination in Marblehead. Walk through the lobby and then into the room on your left. You'll be confronted by an enormous painting, the original *Spirit of '76*, by Archibald Willard, given to the town by General John Devereaux in 1876, whose son was the model for the drummer boy. After you've seen the painting, follow the walking tour through Marblehead's narrow streets, ending up by the water. Watch the boats from **Clark Landing** (at the end of State Street) or from **Crocker Park** (off State Street). If you want to have a picnic lunch, there are two excellent sites to choose from: **Fort Sewall,** at the end of Front Street, and **Chandler Hovey Park,** at the end of Follett Street on the eastern end of Marblehead Neck, overlooking **Marblehead Lighthouse** and the harbor.

Hide and Seek Militia weapons were stored in Marblehead Powder House in 1775, when the British occupied Boston. Today, the Powder House on Green Street stands as one of the few powder houses left in the United States.

JEREMIAH LEE MANSION (ages 6 and up)

170 Washington Street; (781) 631–1768. Open mid-May through October 31, Monday through Saturday 10:00 A.M. to 4:00 P.M., Sunday 1:00 to 4:00 P.M. Admission: 4.00 for adults, $3.50 for students and seniors; **Free** *for children 10 and under.*

Tour this outstanding example of Georgian architecture, with original handpainted wallpaper dating from 1771. There's a collection of nineteenth-century children's furniture and toys scattered throughout the mansion. Across the road from the Lee home is the **J. O. J. Frost Folk Art Museum,** which has a model of life in Marblehead from a seafarer's point of view. Open year-round, call for hours.

Amazing Massachusetts Facts

- Both the town of Marblehead and the city of Beverly lay claim to being the birthplace of the American Navy.

- The Wenham Tea House is the oldest teahouse in America.

- Marco the Magi's "Le Grand David and His Own Spectacular Magic Company" is the longest running family stage attraction.

- The Myopia Polo Field is the oldest polo field in the country (since 1888) and is the oldest polo club in America.

- The American Textile History Museum in Lowell is the world's largest textile museum.

***B*race for the Race** The America's Cup Title was held for three consecutive years in Marblehead in the 1880s. While it may not be the America's Cup, **Race Week in Marblehead** is big doings nowadays, with competitors from around the globe. Race week is held the last week in July. Call the Boston Yacht Club at (781) 631-3100 for details.

Other Things to See and Do

Marblehead Model Yacht Club. Races are held every Sunday at 10:00 A.M. at Redd's Pond on Pond Street from the end of March through mid-November. When the ice freezes, the location shifts to harbor sailing at the Boston Yacht Club, 1 Front Street. There are regattas held four to five times a year. For information, contact Worth Marine at (781) 639-1835.

Crowninshield Island. *Beacon Street to Dolliber Cove.* **Free**.. This island off the coast of Marblehead is owned by the Trustee of Reservations. The idyllic setting is great for nature walks, birding, picnicking, swimming, and fishing. To reach the island, you may walk across during low tide or go by boat. *Warning:* Check the tide schedule, or you'll get caught on the island.

***S*pecial Times** Sandwiched around the Fourth of July holiday, the Marblehead Festival of the Arts is the big kick-off to summer. There is an arts competition for all ages, food, street performances, derbies, and competitions sponsored by area organizations. Parking for some events can be scarce, particularly in Old Town Marblehead.

Where to Eat

The Barnacle, *141 Front Street; (781) 631–4236.* Great chowder and harbor views. Lunch and dinner. $-$$$

Flynnies at the Beach, *Devereux Beach; (781) 639-3035. Open May through November.* Deck and beach dining, with ocean views of Marblehead Neck, the harbor, and the Atlantic. Inside dining on chillier days. Breakfast, lunch, and dinner. Serving sandwiches,

seafood, chicken, and beef. Handicap-accessible. $-$$

Jacob Marley's, *9 Atlantic Avenue; (781) 631-5594.* Fun dining with a diversified menu. $-$$

King's Rook, *12 State Street; (781) 631-9838.* Restored 1747 building; serving lunch and dinner. Long list of unusual nonalcoholic drinks.

Where to Stay

The Bishop's B&B, *10 Harding Lane; (781) 631–4954.* All rooms with water-view; walking distance to historic Old Marblehead. Small beach. Children over 6 are welcome, but pets and smoking are banned. $$$-$$$$

The Marblehead Inn, *264 Pleasant Street; (781) 639–9999 or (800) 399–5843.* Ten suites with private bath; great for nonsmoking families. Rates include continental breakfast. $$$$

Salem

Salem makes the most of its reputation as the location of the infamous Salem witch trials during the seventeenth century. But there's a lot more to it than this sad and rather gruesome period: A top-notch waterfront area, a world-class museum, and a historic house with a secret stairway are among the highlights of Salem that have nothing to do with witches or trials.

When you arrive in Salem, go to the **Chamber of Commerce** (Old Town Hall, Front Street; 978-744-0004) for **Free** self-guided tour maps and information about the day's activities. Another place for information on Salem and Essex County is the **National Park Service Regional Visitor Center** at the corner of New Liberty and Essex Streets (978-740-1650). The Park Service has created three heritage trails through thirty-four communities based on three themes: Early Settlement, the Maritime, and the Industrial Trails. Brochures on area attractions not included in these themes are also available.

SALEM TROLLEY TOURS (all ages)

8 Central Street; (978) 744–5469. Open from March through November 10:00 A.M. to 5:00 P.M. (weekends only in March and November). Price: $8.00 for adults, $4.00 for children 5 to 12; **Free** *for children under 5. Price includes discounts to some attractions.*

If you'd rather let someone else do the driving (and that's not a bad idea in busy Salem), the trolley tours are a good deal. The trolley covers 8 miles with fourteen stops that include the major sights and attractions of Salem. You can get on and off all day long. Tours start hourly at the Salem Visitor Center.

SALEM MARITIME NATIONAL HISTORIC SITE (all ages)

174 Derby Street; (978) 740–1680. Open daily year-round, 9:00 A.M. to 5:00 P.M.; closed Thanksgiving, Christmas, and New Year's Day. Admission: $3.00 for adults; $2.00 for seniors and children 6 to 16.

Located on the waterfront, the site encompasses the Custom House (where Nathaniel Hawthorne worked), the Derby House, and the Narbonne House, among other historic buildings. Start your tour with the seventeen-minute video presentation on the early maritime history of Salem and its role in international trade. Then take the tour of the Custom House, the Elias Derby mansion, and the Narbonne House. The weights and measures at the Custom House are especially fascinating to kids. They'll also enjoy watching demonstrations of the intricate skills required in shipbuilding. When the work is completed (sometime in 2000), you'll be able to tour the replica of the three-masted square rigger *The Friendship*. Special programming and demonstrations are given by park rangers; call for a schedule.

F**riendship Renewed** The Salem Maritime National Historic Site is proud of the newest addition to its collection, *The Friendship*, a replica of a 1797 ship built in Salem and owned by Waitt and Pierce. At press time the ship was under construction, but it may be open for public tours sometime in 2000. Be sure to pick up a copy of *The Friendship* newspaper; it's full of fun and games.

PEABODY ESSEX MUSEUM (all ages)

East India Square; (978) 745–9500 or (800) 745–4054. Open Monday through Saturday 10:00 A.M. to 5:00 P.M., Sunday noon to 5:00 P.M.; closed Monday, Labor Day through Memorial Day. Admission: $8.50 for adults, $5.00 for children 6 to 16; senior, and family discounts.

This collection of items gathered by Salem sea captains on their round-the-world voyages is varied and eclectic, from elephant tusks to intricate navigational instruments to exotic plants to Chinese armor. The Asian art wing holds a superb collection of porcelain, furniture, and decorative arts. Try to take the **Free** one-hour tour of the museum, given each day at 2:00 P.M. Historic homes representing three centuries in Salem are included in the admission price. The original court documents from the Salem witchcraft trials are part of the collection at Phillip's Library.

HOUSE OF THE SEVEN GABLES (all ages)

54 Turner Street; (978) 744–0991.Open daily 10:00 A.M. to 5:00 P.M. (except Sunday December 1 through April 30, noon to 5:00 P.M.). Closed Thanksgiving, Christmas, New Year's Day, and the first two weeks in January. Admission: $7.00 for adults; $6.00 for seniors; $4.00 for children 6 to 17.

A fun place to visit, even for people who aren't familiar with Nathaniel Hawthorne's book. Begin your visit by watching the short multimedia presentation of Hawthorne's story, then walk through the house to see the secret staircase, which winds up through a wall (this may be all that the younger kids will remember about the house), and the low-beamed attic. Hawthorne's birthplace is on the property; it's furnished with period furniture, and the guides know a lot about the family and their times.

SALEM WITCH MUSEUM (ages 7 and up)

19½ Washington Square; (978) 744–1692; www.salemwitchmuseum.com. Open daily, September through June, 10:00 A.M. to 5:00 P.M.; July and August, 10:00 A.M. to 7:00 P.M. Admission $5.50 for adults; $3.50 for children 6 to 14.

Can't keep the kids away from the witch stories? Head for the thirty-minute multimedia presentation about the witchcraft hysteria that gripped seventeenth-century Salem. The show is a bit scary and gruesome, and it is definitely *not* appropriate for kids under seven.

How Salem Got Its Name To smooth over conflict between groups of settlers on the Naumkeag Peninsula (near present-day Pioneer Village), the area was renamed Salem, from the Hebrew word *Shalom*, or peace.

THE SALEM WAX MUSEUM OF WITCHES AND SEAFARERS (ages 6 and up)

282 Derby Street; (978) 740–2929. Open daily, December through April, 10:00 A.M. to 5:00 P.M.; July, August, and October 9:00 A.M. to 7:00 P.M.; May, June, September, and November 9:00 A.M. to 6:00 P.M. Extended hours during Haunted Happenings. Admission: $4.50 for adults, $2.75 for children. Ask about the combination ticket for Salem Witch Village.

Featuring wax figures of life-size witches, the museum puts the witch stories in the context of Salem's seventeenth-century life as a major seaport, and it's not nearly as scary as the Salem Witch Museum.

SALEM WITCH VILLAGE (ages 6 and up)

288 Derby Street; (978) 740–9229. Open November through April 10:00 A.M. to 5:00 P.M., May through October 9:00 A.M. to 6:00 P.M. Extended hours during Haunted Happenings. Admission: adults $4.50; children $2.75. Ask about the combination ticket for the Salem Wax Museum.

Traces the history of witchcraft from medieval Europe to modern-day America. The guides are all practicing witches. Burning incense permeates the museum and can be headache-inducing. Even though the displays can be trite at times, the guides are interesting and informative. The only way to describe the experience is "All you wanted to know about witchcraft but were afraid to ask." Call for a schedule of workshops. If you visit during Halloween (the Celtic New Year), be sure to ask for the Terror ticket. *Caution:* Displays can be scary.

NEW ENGLAND PIRATE MUSEUM (all ages)

274 Derby Street; (978) 741–2800; www.piratemuseum.com. Open May through October, 10:00 A.M. to 5:00 P.M. Extended hours during Haunted Happenings. Admission: $5.00 for adults, $4.00 for seniors, $3.00 for children 4 to 13.

Buried treasure and pirates are actually part of the North Shore's history. This attraction has it all; it's educational, historical, and fun for kids who enjoy learning about the local looters such as Blackbeard and Captain Kidd.

FRIENDSHIP CARRIAGE TOURS (all ages)

(978) 745–3806. Open year-round. Price: $40 to $60 for a half-hour reserved tour.

All aboard for a narrated carriage ride with commentary and gossip of the 1800s. Guides dress in period costume. Toby the horse is very fond of children and likes to eat the unwrapped mint provided by your guide. Specialty rides can be arranged. My family's favorite is the Chocolate Ride, which stops at Harbor Sweets. In the winter, sleigh rides on Salem Common are very popular.

For Your Amusement At the tip of land that juts into Salem Bay is **Salem Willows Park,** a fine destination for an afternoon of picnicking and outdoor activities. The views are good—Beverly's harbor on one side, the south coast of Cape Ann on the other. There's a small amusement park with a nice merry-go-round and a pier for fishing.

mazing Salem

- Ye Olde Pepper Candy Companie of Salem is the oldest candy company in the United States.

- The Salem Maritime National Historic Site was the first place designated as a National Historic Site.

- Pioneer Village was the first outdoor museum in America.

- The first elephant to set foot in this country disembarked in Salem in the late 1700s.

- In 1650 Salem resident Anne Bradstreet became the first woman to publish a book of verse in America.

- Elias Derby became the first millionaire in America (his home is part of the Salem Maritime National Historic Site).

- The telephone was first demonstrated at Lyceum Hall by Alexander Graham Bell.

- Monopoly was produced and sold by Salem toy and game company Parker Brothers.

HAUNTED FOOTSTEPS GHOST TOUR (ages 8 and up)

8 Derby Square; (978) 745–0666. Open May 7 through October 31. Price: $8.00 for adults, $4.00 for children 6 to 12. Reservations suggested.

Under the cover of night, Haunted Footsteps Ghost Tour is a historically based one-hour walking tour geared to older unflappable kids and their families. Some of the topics covered are sites of documented hauntings and the witchcraft hysteria of the 1600s. The guides are costumed, adding to the spooky atmosphere.

MOBY DUCK AMPHIBIOUS SIGHTSEEING (all ages)

Visitor Center at New Liberty Street; (978) 741–4FUN; www.mobyduck.com. Offered seven days a week, weather permitting, Memorial Day through Halloween; also open weekends in May. Price: $13.00 for adults, $8.00 for children. No credit cards.

This land-and-sea tour of Salem and Salem Harbor is offered on a "duck," an amphibious vessel on wheels.

MISERY ISLANDS (all ages)

Salem Bay, ½ mile from West Beach. Price: $3.00 for adults, $1.00 for children 12 and under.

Great Misery and Little Misery are accessible by boat. According to local lore, the islands got their moniker from a man who was shipwrecked and stranded there for three frigid December days in the 1600s.

Nowadays, they're a great spot for fishing, picnicking, swimming, hiking, and bird sightings. If you don't have your own boat, don't worry; Sunline Cruises can get you there (see entry below). Great views, particularly of Manchester-by-the-Sea.

Very Bewitching Laurie Cabot, "Official Witch of Salem," has been invited to the season opener of the Red Sox for many years to bring them good luck. Laurie is very generous with her time and is willing to pose for photographs. You can find her at her store The Cat, the Crow and the Crown, at Pickering Wharf, where she sells her paintings and does readings.

SALEM 1630: PIONEER VILLAGE (all ages)

Located in Forest River Park; (978) 744–0991. Directions: Take Lafayette Street to West Street; enter Forest River Park. Open May through November, Monday through Saturday 10:00 A.M. to 5:00 P.M., Sunday noon to 5:00 P.M. Admission: $5.00 for adults, $3.00 for children 6 to 17, Free *for children under 6. Ask about the combination ticket for House of Seven Gables.*

Want to see how the settlers lived in one of the first enclaves of the Massachusetts Bay Colony? Pioneer Village is the recreated seventeenth-century fishing village bordering Salem Harbor managed by the House of the Seven Gables. This area was originally referred to as Naumkeag, or fishing place, by local tribes. Thatched roof cottages, a wigwam, and live barnyard animals await you. Guides dress in period costume and demonstrate culinary skills of the time using authentic recipes. Hands-on activities allow kids to test their skills at spinning, churning butter, and carding. A special event occurring in late June is **the Muster,** a reenactment of military operations of the 1600s.

SUNLINE CRUISES (all ages)
Salem Willows Waterfront Park; (978) 741–1900. Operates October through May, weekends only; daily from May through the beginning of September. Rates vary ($2.00 to $27.00), depending on cruise. Ask about Salem's Best Pass.

Cruises include tours of Misery Islands, sunset and meal cruises (breakfast, lunch, or dinner), and deep-sea fishing excursions. Four boats allow you to enjoy the coast and islands of the North Shore. A new tour cruises to Gloucester's Rocky Neck art colony.

 EAST INDIA CRUISE/SALEM WHALE WATCH (all ages)
57 Wharf Street and Pickering Wharf; (978) 741–0434 or (800) 745–9594; www.salemwhalewatch.com or www.cestacean.org. Operates May through October; call for schedule. Price: $25 for adults, $16 for children 16 and under.

The ship heads out to both Stellwagen Bank and Jeffrey's Ledge, popular feeding grounds of a variety of whales and dolphins. Experienced naturalists give a background of the area's history and will help you spot marine creatures that are encountered along the way. New this year is a classroom at sea, with an anatomically correct scale model of a whale, a touch tank aquarium with various crustaceans, and a microscope area to examine the plankton and microscopic animals that the whales eat. This interactive experience is not limited to school groups. Full galley and bar onboard.

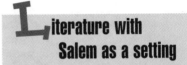

CHILDREN'S

1. *Carry on Mr. Bowditch,* by Jean Lee Latham

2. *Early Thunder,* by Jean Fritz

TEEN AND ADULT

1. *The House of Seven Gables,* by Nathaniel Hawthorne

2. *The Crucible,* by Arthur Miller

 WITCH DUNGEON MUSEUM (ages 6 and up)
16 Lynde Street; (978) 741–3570; www.witchdungeon.com. Open April through December 10:00 A.M. to 5:00 P.M. Admission: $5.00 for adults, $4.00 for seniors, $3.00 for children ages 4 to 13, Free *for children under 4.*

A highly acclaimed reenactment of the witch trial of Sarah Good by professional actors leads to a chilling conclusion. A tour of the dungeon completes this thought-provoking experience.

WINTER ISLAND MARITIME PARK (all ages)

50 Winter Island Road; (978) 745–9430. Open daily May through October, 6:00 A.M. to 10:00 P.M.; 7:00 A.M. to 4:00 P.M. in the winter. Closed Christmas. Admission: $5.00 per car for nonresidents.

Owned by the city of Salem, this hidden gem features the remains of a historic fort and a working lighthouse. Unique to most cities, there is camping with fifty-seven RV and tent sites, with showerhouse. Other facilities include a boat launch area, a picnic area, and a camp store. If you wish to leave your vehicle, the Salem Trolley services the park in the summer. Every summer there is a **Blues Festival** in July and a **Taste of the North Shore.** Call for the schedule.

Other Things to See and Do

Cry Innocent, *St. Peter's Church, 24 St. Peter's Street; (978) 927–2306 ext. 4747; www.gordon.edu/internet/acad/ theatre/historyalive.html. Performances: the three weeks before Halloween. $.* You are the jury at the trial of Bridget Bishop, the first person hanged for witchcraft in 1692.

Harbor Sweets, *85 Leavitt Street; (978) 745–7648.* Take a tour to see how delicious, preservative-free chocolates are made. **Free** samples.

Pickering Wharf, *Wharf Street (off of Derby Street).* Funky shops and restaurants on the harbor near sights and attractions.

Harbor Express Company, (all ages) *Salem Ferry to Marriott Long Wharf Boston. Blaney Street Landing (2 blocks past the House of Seven Gables); (978) 741–3442. Seasonal. $$–$$$, under 12* **Free** *with an adult.* Travel one way or round trip to Boston's Long Wharf and Logan Airport.

Salem Willows Boat Livery, *Salem Willows Pier; (978) 745–6996. Seasonal. Prices are per hour depending upon rental.* Kayak, rowboat, or motorboat rentals. Bait and tackle shop.

The Witch House, (ages 6 and up) *310 Essex Street; (978) 744–0180. Web site: www.salemweb.com.* Original home of Judge Jonathan Corwin, judge at the Salem Witch Trials. Period furniture.

Where to Eat

Bella Verona, *197 Essex Street; (978) 825–9911.* Italian specialties of the Verona region served up with pride and care. Serving lunch and dinner. $–$$

The Crypt, *121 Essex Street; (978) 745–8181.* What an awesome idea—a restaurant with a haunted cafe theme in the heart of enchanting Salem. Standard fare is sandwiches and wraps. Kid's menu; breakfast served on weekends. Closed Mondays. $–$$

Engine House Pizza, *71 Lafayette Street; (978) 745–1744.* Specialties include pizza, subs, salads, and pasta. $

In a Pig's Eye, *148 Derby Street; (978) 741–4436; www.inapigseye.com.* The restaurant's slogan—"Dine up—Dress down"—pretty much sums up its philosophy. Casual fare; not to be missed is Mexican night. $-$$.

Museum Cafe, *Peabody Essex Museum, East India Square; (978) 740–4551.* The Cafe overlooks an Oriental garden, and the tableclothed seating is in an elegant room that exhibits some of the museum's collection. Lunch only; children's menu. $-$$

Rockmore Dry Dock, *94 Wharf Street, Pickering Wharf; (978) 740–1001.* Views of Salem Harbor and Salem Maritime National Historic Site. Seafood specialties in a fun atmosphere. Lunch and dinner; children's menu. $-$$.

Whatever Floats Your Boat The only floating restaurant at sea that isn't ship based is **The Rockmore Floating Restaurant** *(Salem Harbor; 978–740–1001 or 781–639–0600).* Take the water shuttle from Pickering Wharf, Rockmore Dry Dock, or Village Street, Marblehead. Both the water shuttle and parking are free. The menu includes sandwiches, hot dogs, and fried seafood. The kid's get a kick out of the fish that swim up, hoping for leftover crumbs. The food is good, but the views and the ambience are what attract people here year after year. This restaurant has been a real hit with my children and their friends. They love to feed the fish, but I do worry that in their excitement, I'll be fishing them out of the water!

Where to Stay

Amelia Payson Guest House, *16 Winter Street; (978) 744–8304.* A small B&B with three rooms, all with private bath, plus a studio apartment. Closed in winter. $$-$$$$

The Clipper Ship Inn, *40 Bridge Street, Route 1A; (978) 745–8022.* Sixty-room motel with annex. Handicap-accessible. $$-$$$

Hawthorne Hotel, *on the Common; (978) 744–4080.* Designated a Historic Hotel of America, the eighty-three-room Hawthorne has great charm and class. Restaurant serves breakfast, lunch, and dinner. $$$$

Salem Inn, *7 Summer Street; (978) 741–0680 or (800) 446–2995; www.salemweb.com/biz/saleminn.* European-style inn; great location. Some rooms have canopy beds, fireplaces, and Jaccuzzis. Suites available with kitchenettes. Complimentary breakfast. $$$-$$$$

Cut 'Em off at the Pass Contact **Destination Salem**, 10 Liberty Street (978–741–3252), to find out about combo tickets and special savings. These have included Salem's Best Pass and Salem Fun Pass. Ask about combination passes during **Haunted Happenings** in October.

Peabody

BROOKSBY FARM (all ages)
Felton Street; (978) 531–1631. Open year-round.

A municipally owned farm since 1976, Brooksby is a fun place to visit at almost anytime of the year. Pick your own strawberries in June, blueberries and raspberries in July and August, apples in late summer and fall; cut flowers in summer, or choose that special Christmas tree in December. A barn is home to goats, a llama, sheep, pigs, chickens, a rooster, geese, and ducks. Feeding the animals is allowed. Brooksby offers hayrides for $65 that seat twenty-five to thirty people, a great idea for a kids' party. Cross-country skiing is available for **Free**. However, there is a small charge for equipment rental ($6.00) and lessons ($3.00). The trails can also be used for snowshoeing and hiking. Ice skating is allowed on the ponds (check to see if the pond is properly frozen). A farm store sells produce from the farm and related products. The third weekend in October is **Harvest Happenings,** with lots of **Free** events.

Peabody Festivals

- **International Festival,** third Sunday in September. Celebrates the diversity of the city, with ethnic food, dance, and cultural events. (978) 532–3000.

- **Harvest Happenings at Brooksby Farm,** third weekend in October. Old-fashioned fun includes apple pie-baking contests, hay rides, a horseshoe pitch, pony rides, and pumpkin decorating.

Where to Eat

Porcini's, *10 Foster Street; (978) 538–3111.* Great Italian food in a charming family atmosphere. Closed Mondays. $$

Johnny Rocket's, *Northshore Shopping Center; (978) 532–2999.* Fifties retro diner complete with a lunch counter, jukeboxes, and booths. Great burgers and shakes; cash only. $

Where to Stay

Marriott Hotel, *8A Centennial Drive; (978) 977–9700.* Nicely appointed rooms; pool. Great daily brunches with special pricing for children. $$$$

Danvers

ENDICOTT PARK (under 10)

57 Forest Street; (978) 774–6518. Open daily 7:00 A.M. to 9:00 P.M. Admission: $1.00 for residents on weekends and holidays, $3.00 for nonresidents. Groups of twenty or more must have a permit.

This 165-acre park is owned by the town of Danvers. Attractions include a barn with farm animals, trails, a pond with a fishing platform, playing fields, and picnic tables. A state-of-the-art playground is a big attraction for kids. Also on the grounds are Glen Magna and the Derby Tea House, owned by the town historical society.

REBECCA NURSE HOMESTEAD (ages 5 and up)

149 Pine Street; (978) 774–8799. Open mid-June to September, Tuesday through Sunday 1:00 to 4:30 P.M.; September and October, Saturday and Sunday 1:00 to 4:30 P.M. Admission: $4.00 for adults, $3.00 for kids.

If you're fascinated by tales of the Salem witch trials, you'll enjoy this. This is the original saltbox homestead of the Nurse family. The matriarch, Rebecca Nurse, was accused in 1692 of practicing witchcraft. Her accusers were a group of rebellious teenage girls who were having fits of hysteria and blaming Rebecca as one of their tormentors. Executed in July 1692, her remains were brought back to the family plot and buried in an unmarked grave. The property includes the original Nurse homestead, with seventeenth- and eighteenth-century period furnishings; a reproduction of the Olde Salem Village Meeting House (featuring a multimedia presentation); the family cemetery, with a monument to Rebecca bearing a poem by John Greenleaf Whittier; and a gift shop.

WITCH HYSTERIA MONUMENT (all ages)

176 Hobart Street. Open year-round. **Free**.

Erected 300 years after the Witchcraft Hysteria of 1692, this monument stands in solemn testimony to the memory of the twenty-five innocent people who lost their lives. It's located on town land, across from the original site of the Olde Salem Village Meeting House, where many of the accused were questioned.

Top Ice Cream Spots

1. **Treadwell's**, *30 Hobart Street, (978) 777–3858.* Homemade ice cream and yogurt. Awarded first place in 1996 by *Northshore* magazine. Open year-round.

2. **Cherry Hill Farm**, *210 Conant Street; (978) 774–0519.* Homemade ice cream—huge portions and a long list of flavors. For adults, there's the Sun n'Air Driving Range behind the ice cream stand to work off those excess pounds from the ice cream you just consumed. Open March through Thanksgiving; outdoor seating.

3. **Putnam Pantry Ice Cream and Candies**, *Route 1 North, just after the Route 62/Danvers exit; (978) 774–2383.* Opened in 1951, the big attraction is the make-your-own sundae bar (all the toppings and candies are made on the premises). Extremely popular with groups is the Battle of Bunker Hill, with seventeen scoops of ice cream, for $17.76. Indoor seating is reminiscent of ice cream parlor decor of the 1940s and 1950s.

Other Things to See and Do

The Plains Park Skateboard Park

(57 Conant Street) is a great place for children to practice their moves. Structures include a pyramid, a spine, the Bench, the fun box, a half pipe, a flat pyramid, steel rails, and a cement rail edge. Open dawn to dusk in season.

Special Time The Danvers Family Festival (starting the weekend prior to and ending the weekend after the Fourth of July) features road races, dog shows, a bike rodeo, Fireman's Muster, Endicott Park Day, Irish Night, a golf tournament, various band concerts, Oldies Night, and, of course, the requisite Fourth of July fireworks.

Where to Eat

Essex Agricultural Institute/The Ram's Inn, *562 Maple Street; (978) 774–0050.* Students attending the culinary school at Essex Aggie operate a restaurant to showcase their skills. Try the Belgian waffles with fresh fruit and whipped cream. Open Wednesday and Thursday 11:00 A.M. to 12:15 P.M. for lunch, Friday 7:30 A.M. to 11:00 A.M. for breakfast during the school term. $

Two Moon Cafe at the Danvers Courtyard, *275 Independence Way; (978) 739–4478.* Gourmet dining in a welcoming setting. $$–$$$

Danvers Yacht Club Restaurant, *161 Elliott Street; (978) 774–8621.* Save room for Gilda, the swan-shaped cream puff ice cream dessert. Surf-and-turf specialties. $$

Where to Stay

Danvers Courtyard by Marriott, *275 Independence Way; (978) 777–8630.* A 122-room hotel located near the Liberty Tree Mall. Seasonal outdoor pool. $–$$$$

Day's Inn, *152 Endicott Street; (978) 777–1030.* A 130-room motel near the highway and close to mall. **Free** continental breakfast. $$–$$$

King's Grant, *Route 128 North/Exit 21 at Trask Lane; (978) 774–6800.* Offers 124 rooms, twenty-nine of them clustered around an indoor atrium pool. Popcorn machine and **Free** continental breakfast. $$$–$$$$

Topsfield

IPSWICH RIVER WILDLIFE SANCTUARY (all ages)
Perkins Row; (978) 887–9264. Open year-round Tuesday through Sunday, dawn to dusk, and Monday holidays. Admission: $3.00 for adults, $2.00 for seniors and children 3 to 15.

The sanctuary has 10 miles of trails on 2,400 acres of land that are protected by the Massachusetts Audubon Society. Start your visit at the information center, where you can pick up a trail map. For families, the best trail leads to the Rockery, a pile of enormous boulders that kids love to climb up, through, into, and over. Continue around the pond (look for ducks, turtles, and frogs), then around the marsh, from which you can look over the wetlands of Topsfield and Ipswich. *Note:* Don't bring your dog; this is a wildlife sanctuary. Do bring bug repellent, especially during the spring.

BRADLEY PALMER STATE PARK (all ages)

Asbury Street; (978) 887–5931. Park open year-round; **Free**. *Parking for wading pool is $2.00; accessible in summer only.*

Bradley Palmer, a successful attorney and friend of presidents and kings, bequeathed his mansion and grounds to the state of Massachusetts for public use. The mansion has been recently renovated and is now a B&B (see Willowdale Lodge entry in Where to Stay). An extensive trail system is used for hiking, horseback riding, mountain biking, snowmobiling, cross-country skiing, and snowshoeing. The Ipswich River winds through the north end of the property, giving access to canoeing (rentals available at Foote Brothers in Ipswich) and fishing. It's also a great spot to teach a child to ride a bike since there is a large stretch of flat paved road. A real treat for the under 10 set is the wading pool, open from Father's Day to Labor Day. The centerpiece of the lifeguarded pool is a mushroom-shaped structure with water cascading over it.

TOPSFIELD FAIRGROUNDS (all ages)

Route 1 North (exit 50 off Route 95); (978) 887–5000.

The 83-acre fairground is home to the Topsfield Fair, an agricultural fair held every October. In addition to the Topsfield Fair, there are numerous off-season events that take place here. Some of the more popular kid-oriented events held in May and June are dog shows, the 4-H Horse Show, the Alpaca Show, the Native American Festival, the Gem and Mineral Show, and the Horse Training Tour. Prices and schedule vary according to event; call the Topsfield Fairgrounds for more information.

Where to Stay

Willowdale Lodge, *Asbury Street, Bradley Palmer State Park; (978) 887–0707.* This carefully renovated

B&B is set in Bradley Palmer State Park. Full breakfast included in rate. $$$$

It's a Family Affair

Topsfield Fair, *Topsfield Fairgrounds, Route 1 North/exit 50; (978) 887–5000; www.topsfieldfair.org. Admission: $6.00 for adults weekdays/ $7.00 weekend;* Free *for children under 10.* The Topsfield Fair, held on the Topsfield Fairgrounds, is the oldest agricultural fair in the United States. Held every October the ten days preceding the Columbus Day holiday, the fair features exhibit halls, a flower show, livestock shows, a petting zoo, a vegetable show (with the New England Giant Pumpkin contest), pig races, and a horse and ox pull. There's a midway and lots of food concessions. Local and national talent performs at the grandstand or on one of five smaller stages. On the final evening there's a fireworks celebration.

Hamilton

MYOPIA HUNT CLUB AND POLO FIELDS (all ages)

435 Bay Road; (978) 468–7956. Polo season begins the last Sunday in May and continues to the first Sunday in October. Matches begin at 3:00 P.M.; gates open at 1:30 P.M. Admission: $5.00 for adults; Free *for children under 12.*

Need an activity that involves the little ones when they get antsy? During halftime spectators are asked to help prepare the field for the next half by stomping on the divots that have been dislodged by the racing polo ponies. Bring a blanket to spread out under the trees, and watch that the little ones don't run out into the field during play.

APPLETON FARM GRASS RIDES AND APPLETON FARMS (all ages)

Intersection of Cutler Road and Highland Street, Ipswich; (978) 356–4755. Open year-round 8:00 A.M. to sunset. Free.

The Appleton Grass Rides are a series of trails used for hiking, nature study, cross-country skiing, and snowshoeing. Due to the fragile nature of the trail, horseback riding is no longer allowed. One of the oldest continuously running farms in America, Appleton Farms has been newly acquired by the Trustees of Reservations and will be used to educate children on the workings of a farm.

Wenham

WENHAM MUSEUM (all ages)

132 Main Street; (978) 468–2377. Open year-round Tuesday through Sunday, 10:00 A.M. to 4:00 P.M. Closed Monday (except for certain holidays), Thanksgiving, Christmas, and New Year's. Admission: $4.00 for adults, $3.50 for seniors, and $3.00 for children 3 to 16.

The Wenham Museum is often called "the doll museum" because of its enormous collection of dolls and dollhouses from around the world. Local children love to have their birthday parties here (by prior arrangement only), coupled with a visit to the Wenham Tea House for dessert.

WENHAM TEA HOUSE (all ages)

4 Monument Street; (978) 468–1398. Open from 9:30 A.M. to 5:00 P.M. Restaurant open from 10:30 to 11:30 A.M. for continental breakfast, 11:30 A.M. to 2:30 P.M. for lunch, 3:15 to 4:30 P.M. for tea. Reservations suggested.

Operated by the Village Improvement Society, the Tea House has a restaurant, a gourmet shop, a gift shop, a baby shop, and an adult clothing store. It's best known for its luncheon menu and afternoon tea. There is a side room for birthday parties. The Tea House profits support local scholarships and playgrounds.

Beverly

LYNCH PARK (all ages)

55 Ober Street; (978) 921–6067. Open year-round from 7:00 A.M. to 8:00 P.M. in the winter, until 10:00 P.M. in the summer. Parking for nonresidents is $5.00 weekdays, $10.00 weekends.

On a windy spring day, Lynch Park is a great spot for kite flying. Once part of the Evan's estate, it is now the number one choice of settings for many bridal pictures and weddings that take place in the park's beautiful rose garden. Children will delight in the extensive play structure, swings, and band shell (with summer concerts). The two small lifeguarded beaches tend to be rocky, but there's a small snack bar and kayak rentals. The annual **Beverly Homecoming** weeklong festival (first week in August) is centered in Lynch Park.

MARCO THE MAGI'S "LE GRAND DAVID AND HIS OWN SPECTACULAR MAGIC COMPANY" (all ages)

Cabot Street Cinema, 286 Cabot Street, Beverly; (978) 927–3677. Performances are from mid-September through July, Sunday at 3:00 and 5:30 P.M.

An afternoon of family vaudeville is in the don't-miss category. Even while you're waiting for the show to start, there's plenty to watch—jugglers and puppeteers keep the kids fascinated while attendees take you to your seats. The shows are long (about two and a half hours), but don't let their length dissuade you from bringing younger kids to see the magic shows, dancing, singing, and spectacular sets, all created by the dedicated resident stage troupe. Marco the Magnificent and Le Grand David have been named Magicians of the Year twice by the Academy of Magical Arts in Hollywood and by the Society of American Magicians in New York City. Two of their performers, Martha and Marion Bull, who have performed since they were babies, relate well to the children in the audience, being children themselves. From October through May, on holidays and most Saturdays, there's a two-hour magic show at the **Larcom Theatre** (13 Wallis Street; same phone number) at 2:00 P.M. (doors open at 1:15 P.M.). Admission: $15 for adults, $10 for children 11 and under. Buy tickets at the Cabot Theatre box office, Monday through Saturday, 9:00 A.M. to 9:00 P.M.

Children's Theater

- **Neverland Express,** 284 Bay Road, Hamilton; (978) 468–1191

- **North Shore Music Theater,** 62 Dunham Road, Beverly; (978) 922-8500

- **Le Grand David and His Own Spectacular Magic Company,** 286 Cabot Street, Beverly; (978) 927–3677

- **Larcom Theatre,** 13 Wallis Street, Beverly; (978) 922–6313

- **Marblehead Little Theater,** Marblehead; (781) 631–9697

- **Firehouse Theater,** 1 Market Square, Newburyport; (978) 462–7336

Other Things to See and Do

Long Hill Sedgwick Gardens, *572 Essex Street; (978) 921–1944.* Five acres of rare and beautiful plantings managed by the Trustees of Reservations.

Where to Eat

Casa de Lucca, *145–148 Rantoul Street; (978) 922–7660.* Italian dining in a warm family atmosphere. Pasta specials, children's menu, and reasonable prices. $

The Beverly Depot and Saloon, *Park Street; (978) 927–0444.* Waiters dressed in engineer's uniforms serve your meal in noisy but festive surroundings. Still used as a train stop by the MBTA (be careful walking across the railroad track to get to this restaurant). An extensive salad bar and a variety of breads come with every meal. If it's your birthday, notify the waiter and you'll get a price break and a special cake. $$

Where to Stay

Lakeview Motor Lodge, *5 Lakeview Avenue, Route 1A, Beverly; (978) 922–7535.* Newly refurbished suites with kitchenettes; perfect for families. $$

Cape Ann Region

The towns in this region include Manchester-by-the-Sea, Magnolia, Gloucester, Rockport, and Essex. A great resource for information and brochures is the **Cape Ann Chamber of Commerce and Visitor Center,** 33 Commercial Street (978-283-1601), Gloucester. The Cape Ann area has a breathtaking coastline. An extremely pleasant way to meander along is by hooking up with Route 127 (Route 133 to Essex). For those more interested in getting there at a less leisurely pace, use Route 128.

The Jaffe Family's Favorite Beaches

- Crane Beach, Argilla Road, Ipswich

- Good Harbor Beach, Thatcher Road, Gloucester

- Parker River Natural Wildlife Refuge and Plum Island, Newburyport

- Singing Beach, Central Street, Manchester-by-the-Sea

- Wingaersheek Beach, Atlantic Street, Gloucester

Manchester-by-the-Sea

SINGING BEACH (all ages)
Beach Street. **Free**.

Manchester-by-the-Sea is home to one of the prettiest beaches on the North Shore, Singing Beach, a curving strip of sand that "sings" when the waves stroke it just right. Day-trippers from Boston take the train from North Station and walk the mile (a pleasant walk) to the beach. Between Memorial Day and Labor Day, beachside parking is strictly limited to residents only, so you'll have to drop the family at the beach, then drive back into town to park in one of the designated areas. At the beach you'll find a snack stand, rest rooms, and changing rooms. On the way to the beach, you'll pass a grocery store that's perfectly located for last-minute picnic fixings, and there's a good ice cream shop right next door, too, for postbeach snacking. *Directions:* Take Route 128 North from Boston, toward Gloucester. Take exit 15 (School Street) to the end. At the center of town, take a left through the village and follow Beach Street to the end.

Other Things to See and Do

HIKING SPOTS WITH VIEWS

Agassiz Rock, *School Street North toward Essex (exit 15).* **Free**.

Coolidge Reservation, *Summer Street (Route 127 North).* **Free**.

Where to Stay

The Old Corner Inn, *2 Harbor Street (off Route 127); (978) 526–4996.* Gracious Victorian, former summer home of Danish ambassador. Rate includes continental breakfast. Open year-round. $–$$$$

Magnolia

 HAMMOND CASTLE MUSEUM (all ages)

80 Hesperus Avenue; (978) 283–2080. Open daily from Memorial Day to Labor Day 10:00 A.M. to 5:00 P.M.; September and October, Thursday through Sunday 10:00 A.M. to 4:00 P.M.; November through May, weekends only, 10:00 A.M. to 4:00 P.M. Admission: $6.00 for adults; $5.00 for seniors and students; $4.00 for children ages 6 to 12.

Built in 1926 by John Hays Hammond, an inventor, Hammond Castle Museum is an odd combination of the very old—bits of medieval French houses are built right into the building's walls—and the modern, for its day: The eight-story, 8,600-pipe organ is the largest organ in a private home in the country. Most tours include a short demonstration of the organ, which is now played by a computer. There are lots of other sights here, from a huge fifteenth-century fireplace to a glass-enclosed courtyard to a swimming pool that Hammond regularly dove into from his bedroom window. The Castle's **Renaissance Fair** (second weekend in July) is always a high point.

Where to Stay

The White House, *18 Norman Avenue; (978) 525–3642.* Centrally located, charming inn with playground and sandy beach in walking distance. Rates in-season are $95 to $135 a night including continental breakfast. $$$–$$$$.

Gloucester

Gloucester is a grittier seaside village that's well known for its expert fishermen. Most members of the family will recognize the often-reproduced **Fishermen's Statue,** near the drawbridge. The statue, called **The Man at the Wheel,** was commissioned in 1923 to celebrate the town's 300th anniversary. Drive along the Harbor Loop to see the workings of a busy harbor.

Whale Watching

All of these whale-watching tours feature naturalists onboard and/or a touch tank. All are connected to research institutions.

- **Cape Ann Whale Watch,** *Rose's Wharf, 415 Main Street; (978) 283–5110 or (800) 877–5110; www.caww.com.* Also offers a day trip to Provincetown.

- **Captain Bill's Whale Watch and Deep Sea Fishing,** *Harbor Loop (near Capt. Carlo's Restaurant); (978) 283–6995 or (800) 33–WHALE; www.cape-ann.com/captbill.html.*

- **Seven Seas Whale Watch, Seven Seas Wharf,** *Rogers Street (Route 127); (978) 283–1776 or (800) 283–1776; www.cape-ann.com/7seas/whale-watch.html.*

- **Yankee Whale Watch and Deep Sea Fishing,** *75 Essex Avenue; (978) 283–0313 or (800) 942–5464.*

GOOD HARBOR BEACH (all ages)

Thatcher Road. Parking is $15 weekends and holidays, $10 midweek, (arrive early or you may not get a spot).

Good Harbor is the most popular swimming beach in Gloucester, and deservedly so.

1st floor by L+T
Rainforest Cafe 33B
U from 95/128 So.
Rt off ramp.
Mall is in R+.

WINGAERSHEEK BEACH (all ages)

Atlantic Street. Parking is $15 weekends and holidays, $10 midweek.
Wingaersheek is a sandy beach that's an especially good destination for families with young children: They love climbing on the smooth rocks and dunes. *Directions:* From Route 128, take exit 13.

MOBY DUCK AMPHIBIOUS SIGHTSEEING (all ages)

Harbor Loop and Rogers Street; (978) 281–DUCK. Operates seven days a week, weather permitting. Open weekends in May. Price: $13.00 for adults, $8.00 for children. No credit cards.

Same company as does the Salem Moby Duck tour (see separate entry). A unique tour of Gloucester combining land and sea highlights.

SCHOONER *THOMAS E. LANNON* (all ages)

Seven Seas Wharf, Rogers Street (Route 127); (978) 281–6634. Operates May through November; call for a schedule. Tickets cost $25 for adults, $22 for seniors, $17 for children.

Sail on a 65-foot schooner past fabulous beaches, estates, light-houses, and islands.

STAGE FORT PARK (all ages)

Route 127; (978) 281–9720. Open year-round. Visitor center open Memorial Day through October 9:00 A.M. to 6:00 P.M. Parking fee.

The settlers found life too harsh at this location and eventually moved to the Naumkeag Peninsula. Ironically, this area is now a serene location for picnicking, hiking, listening to summer concerts at the bandstand, or enjoying the beach and playground. Lovely harbor views.

Other Things to See and Do

Beauport, Sleeper McCann House (ages 10 and up), *75 Eastern Point Boulevard; (978) 283–0800. Open mid-May through mid-September, Monday through Friday 10:00 A.M. to 4:00 P.M.; mid-September through mid-October, Monday through Sunday 10:00 A.M. to 4:00 P.M. Admission: $6.00 for adults, $5.50 for seniors, $3.00 for children 6 to 12.* Whimsical summer home decorated with American and European finds by American designer Henry Davis Sleeper.

Ravenswood Park, *Route 127.* Owned by the Trustees of Reservations, a 500-acre park with cross-country skiing and hiking trails. Picnicking is allowed.

Rocky Neck, East Main Street. Oldest art colony in America, with many eateries and art galleries.

Where to Eat

Cameron's, *Main Street; (978) 281–1331.* A local favorite serving breakfast, lunch, and dinner. $–$$

Halibut Point Restaurant and Pub, *289 Main Street; (978) 281–1900.* Good chowder that attracts lots of locals. Open year-round. $–$$

McT's Lobster House and Tavern, *25 Rodgers Street; (978) 282–0950.* On the waterfront. Featuring steak, seafood, pasta, and large appetizer selection. $–$$.

The Rudder, *73 Rocky Neck Avenue; (978) 283–7967.* A family-run restaurant whose fun-loving owners often provide unorthodox entertainment along with their excellent food. Outdoor seating overlooking Smith Cove. Lunch and dinner served daily, spring through fall. $$–$$$

Schooners, *50 Rogers Street; (978) 281–1962.* Specializing in seafood. The Schooner's Sampler is a great deal. Open for lunch and dinner. $–$$$

Valentino's, *38 Main Street; (978) 283–6186.* Voted best pizza on the North Shore for seven years running. Try the Hawaiian pizza, a pan baked specialty, or one of the pasta dishes. $–$$

Festivals

St. Peter's Fiesta (held the last weekend in June) features a variety of events, including fireworks, races, and parades. The big attraction is the colorful "blessing of the fleet." Most events occur at the waterfront or in downtown Gloucester.

Where to Stay

Cape Ann Motor Inn, *35 Rockport Road; (978) 281–2900 or (800) 464-VIEW; www.cape-ann.com/motor inn.* Twenty-nine beachfront units overlooking Long Beach with views of Thatcher Island. $$–$$$$

Good Harbor Beach Inn, *Salt Island Road; (978) 283–1489.* Great location across from Good Harbor Beach. Wonderful views; family-style. Seasonal. $$$–$$$$

Harborview Inn, *71 Western Avenue; (978) 283–2277 or (800) 299–6696; www.harborviewinn.com.* Six rooms, most with views of the harbor. Rate includes continental breakfast. $$–$$$$

Ocean View, *171 Atlantic Road; (978) 283–6200 or (800) 315–7557.* Elegant resort facing the Atlantic; two outdoor pools. $$$$

Samarkand Guest House, *1 Harbor Road; (978) 283–3757.* Family-oriented B&B in operation for thirty years. $$–$$$

Rockport

BEARSKIN NECK (all ages)

Corner of Dock Square and South Road.

Browse in seaside shops, restaurants, and art galleries.

HALIBUT POINT RESERVATION (all ages)

Gott Avenue, Rockport; (978) 546–2997. Open daily year-round, 8:00 A.M. to sunset. Parking is $2.00.

Halibut Point is a lovely place for walking and picnicking by the sea. It's not a sandy beach, though; the shore here is rocky, and kids should be encouraged to keep their shoes on to avoid cutting their feet on rocks or shells. Take a twenty-minute walk around the old quarry (hang onto the kids' hands), then play in the tidal pools. Bring windbreakers and warm clothes—it's usually windy—and keep an eye out for poison ivy.

THE PAPER HOUSE (all ages)

50 Pigeon Hill Street; (978) 546–2629. Open daily April 1 through October 31, 10:00 A.M. to 5:00 P.M. Admission by donation.

Worth a stop, amazingly, everything in the house, from the walls to the furnishings, is made of paper.

Other Things to See and Do

Cape Shore Tours; *(978) 546–5281. One-and-a-half-hour tour of Rockport and Gloucester by air-conditioned van.* $–$$

Rockport Whale Watch Corporation, *9 Tuna Wharf; (978) 546–3377.* Whale watching and sunset cruises. $$$–$$$$

Where to Eat

Greenery Cafe and Restaurant, *15 Dock Square; (978) 546–9593.* Delightful view of harbor. Salads, pasta, and seafood. $$

My Place by the Sea Restaurant, *68 Bearskin Neck; (978) 546–9667.* Panoramic view of Rockport coastline; indoor and outdoor dining. BYOB. $$–$$$$

Where to Stay

Addison Choate Inn, *49 Broadway; (978) 546–7543 or (800) 245–7543; www.cape-ann.com/addison-choate.* Charming B&B minutes away from the heart of Rockport. $$–$$$$

Old Farm Inn, *291 Granite Street; (978) 546–3237.* Ten guest rooms in three buildings (a main house, a barn, and a cottage), all with private bath and some with a refrigerator. Most of the

rooms can be arranged in family-style suites, and cribs, cots, and rollaway beds are available. Rate includes continental breakfast plus. Open April through December. $$$–$$$$

Peg Leg Inn, *Beach and King Streets; (978) 546–2352 or (800) 346–2352; www.cape-ann.com/pegleg.* Close to shops, restaurants, art galleries, and Front Beach. $$–$$$$

Essex

THE ESSEX SHIPBUILDING MUSEUM (all ages)

28 Main Street/Route 133W; (978) 768–7541. Open May 15 through October 15, Thursday through Sunday, 11:00 A.M. to 4:00 P.M., and by appointment year-round. Admission: $5.00 for adults, $4.00 for students and seniors, $3.00 for children 6 to 12.

Reminiscent of the days when more wooden ships came from Essex than from anywhere else in the world, this excellent museum not only shows you how the ships were built but also gives you the context you need to understand the significance of the industry to the area. Real tools allow kids to try their hand at shipbuilding.

WHITE ELEPHANT (all ages)

32 Main Street; (978) 768–6901. Open daily year-round.

Essex is also known as an antiques-lover's haven. One of the more interesting shops is the White Elephant, next door to the Shipbuilding Museum. The stock changes often, but in the past it has included collections of wooden teeth, old train sets, and wasp-waisted dresses from a hundred years ago.

ESSEX RIVER CRUISES AND CHARTERS (all ages)

Essex Marina, 35 Dodge Street; (978) 768–6981 or (800) RIVER–06; www.essexcruises.com. Open April through October. Admission: $16.00 for adults, $8.00 for children 12 and under. Reservations suggested.

The ninety-minute tour cruise on the *Essex River Queen* takes you past beaches, marshes, "old money" estates, and shipbuilding yards. This is a relaxing and informative tour from a different perspective. Temperatures on the water can fluctuate, bring a jacket.

Other Things to See and Do

Agawam Boat Charters, *21 Pickering Street; (978) 768–1114*

Essex River Basin Adventures, *66R Main Street; (978) 768–ERBA or (800) KAYAK–04*

Stavros Reservation, *Island Road (off of Route 133).* Great views; hiking, picnicking, and bird-watching.

Where to Eat

Woodman's, *121 Main Street/Route 133; (978) 768–6451.* According to the Woodman family, this is where the first clam was breaded and fried (in 1916). $-$$

Periwinkles, *74 Main Street; (978) 768–6320.* Great spot overlooking a picturesque tidal river. $$

North of Cape Ann

The North Shore continues up the coast to the border of New Hampshire. Main access roads are Routes 1/95 and 495. Slower going is Route 133 from Ipswich, connecting to Route 1A toward Newburyport.

Ipswich

CRANE BEACH (all ages)

310 Argilla Road; (978) 356–4354 (recorded information) or (508) 356–4351. Open year-round 8:00 A.M. to sunset. Parking fee is $5.00 to $15.00 per car, depending on time of the year and day of week.

Crane Beach is a long, clean beach that's great for swimming, picnicking, and walking. During the summer there are lifeguards on duty and the bathhouse and snack bar are open. There are several pleasant, easy walks to take from the beach. One leads to Castle Hill; the other is a self-guided nature walk (trail map available) that leads you over boardwalks, through a swamp, and into a piney forest. *Caution:*

un events

- **Independence Day Celebration**—Castle Hill celebrates the Fourth of July with fireworks, music, and children's activities. Call (978) 356-4351 for more details.

- **Sand Blast**—Annual sandcastle contest in August at Crane Beach.

- **Concourse d'Elegance**—This annual classic car show in September at Castle Hill has been compared to the Concourse d'Elegance at California's Pebble Beach. For more information, call (978) 356-4351.

Greenbug season lasts for about two weeks in midsummer and can be annoying. *Note:* No dogs. *Directions:* From Route 1A south of Ipswich, take Route 133 East. Turn left onto Northgate Road. At the end of this road, turn right onto Argilla Road, which ends at the beach.

CASTLE HILL (all ages)
290 Argilla Road; (978) 356–4351

This former home of the Crane family, for whom Crane Beach is named. Now owned and managed by the Trustees of Reservations, a private land trust whose holdings include many other properties listed in this book, the beautiful old mansion is the summer home to an excellent performing arts series. Audiences sit on the sweeping lawn to hear the music or watch the play. There are other seasonal activities as well. Call or write for a schedule; tickets sometimes sell out.

CRANE ISLANDS TOUR (all ages)
Argilla Road, to the right of the Crane Beach Gate; (978) 356–4351. Open Memorial Day through October. Price: $12.00 for adults, $5.00 for children 3 to 12.

Tour Hog and Long Islands by hay wagon after crossing the Castle Neck River by boat. View wildlife and the Crane Wildlife Refuge. Very scenic.

NEW ENGLAND ALIVE (all ages)
189 High Street, Routes 1A: (978) 356–7013. Open May through November, weekdays 10:00 A.M. to 5:00 P.M., weekends 9:30 A.M. to 5:00 P.M. Admission: $5.00 for adults, $3.00 for children 2 to 12.

Kids can hold baby birds in their hands and learn about domestic and wild animals, including a black bear and several large reptiles. What makes this petting-zoo type of animal park unique is that it's also a wild animal hospital and orphanage. Picnicking is encouraged; there are plenty of outdoor tables on the shady grounds.

WOLF HOLLOW (all ages)
114 Essex Road, Route 133; (978) 356–0216. Open to the public on weekends only, 1:00 to 5:00 P.M., year-round. Admission: $4.50 for adults, $3.00 for children 17 and under.

Wolf Hollow is yet another wild animal refuge, this one dedicated to the gray wolf. There are presentations at 1:30 P.M. (and at 3:30 P.M. from March through November).

GOODALE ORCHARDS (all ages)

143 Argilla Road, Ipswich; (978) 356–5366.

More than an orchard, Goodale has a swing in the barn, animals in the barnyard that are accustomed to being petted, and hayrides during the fall. In season pick your own strawberries, blackberries, blueberries, raspberries, apples, and pumpkins. Don't leave without buying a few of the delicious homemade doughnuts, or a bottle of their vintage fruit wine or hard cider. Open daily from mid-May through December 1, 9:00 A.M. to 6:00 P.M.

FOOTE BROTHERS CANOE RENTAL (ages 3 and up)

230 Topsfield Road; (978) 356–9771. Open April 1 through October 31, 8:00 A.M. to 6:00 P.M. Price: $19 per canoe midweek, $23 per canoe weekends and holidays.

Provides canoes and advice for families who enjoy paddling on a calm river. Shuttle trips for longer journeys; overnight trips can be arranged.

Where to Eat

The Clam Box of Ipswich, *206 High Street; (978) 356–9707.* Local icon since 1935 shaped like a clam box; known for its burgers, clams, fries, and scallops. $–$$

White Farms Ice Cream, *266 High Street; (978) 356–2633.* Winner of the Best of Boston 1996 Award. Known for creative ice cream flavors like Expresso Explosion, Key Lime Pie, Reverse Chip, and Caramel Cow. $

Newburyport

PARKER RIVER NATIONAL WILDLIFE REFUGE (all ages)

Northern Boulevard; (978) 465–5753. During the plovers' nesting season (early April through early June), the beach is usually closed. Otherwise open daily year-round, dawn to dusk. Parking is $5.00 per car.

Covering about two-thirds of Plum Island, the Wildlife Refuge is a favorite destination for Boston-area families. The refuge is operated by the U.S. Fish and Wildlife Service; it is one of the very few natural barrier beach, dune, and salt marsh complexes left on the coast of New England. Along with the abundant wildlife on view here in its natural habitat, the great attraction of Plum Island (which is what the locals call it) is the beach. Those who are in the know arrive at the refuge very early (before 8:30 A.M.), since only a few parking spots are available. There are several observation towers that are well-used by bird-watchers in March and April, the peak migration periods for ducks and other waterfowl; the views are always good, though, and there are always birds to see—300 or so species live in the area. The 6-mile-long beach is nearly always deserted. Because of the strong undertow, it's not a good place for families with young children; also, there are no lifeguards. At the extreme end is **Sandy Point,** which is owned by the town of Ipswich and is a more placid place for a swim. *Note:* Don't bring pets; do bring bug spray.

MAUDSLAY STATE PARK (all ages)
Curzon's Mill Road; (978) 465–7223. Open year-round 8:00 A.M. to sunset. **Free.**

When the mansion of this 500-acre estate was taken down in the 1950s, the landscaped grounds became a state park. It's a great place on a spring or summer afternoon—picnic spots abound, and there are lots of walking trails through formal gardens, rolling meadows, woods, and an enormous stand of mountain laurel.

Other Things to See and Do

Merrimac Street Shops. Browsing in the quaint shops of Newburyport is a pleasant pastime.

Newburyport's First Class Whale Watches and Dinner Cruises, *Hilton's Dock, 54 Merrimac Street; (978) 465–9885 or (800) 848–1111.* Whale watches and deep-sea fishing.

Where to Eat

The Black Cow, *54R Merrimac Street; (978) 499–8811.* Water views of the Merrimac; outdoor deck seating. Daily and nightly specials, popular Sunday brunch, kid's menu. $$

Ciro's, *1 Market Square; (978) 463–3335.* Pasta, salads, Italian specialties. Outdoor dining. $–$$

Michael's Harborside, *Tournament Wharf, (978) 462–7785.* On the water overlooking the harbor. Specializing in steak and seafood. $–$$$

Ten Center Street and Molly's Pub, *10 Center Street; (978) 462–6652.* Traditional dining. Fireplaces in some of the rooms, lighter fare in the pub. $–$$$$

Where to Stay

Clark Currier Inn, *45 Green Street; (978) 465–8363.* Classic 1803 Federal building not far from the main shopping area of Newburyport. Request a family-style room; though they're all large, not all bedrooms are appropriate for children. There's a comfortable lounge/TV room, and backyard and garden. Open year-round. $$$–$$$$

Salisbury

SALISBURY BEACH STATE RESERVATION AND CAMPING AREA (all ages)

Beach Road off Route 1A; (978) 462–4481. Salisbury Beach State Reservation is open year-round and charges a $2.00 parking fee for cars.

Close to the border of Massachusetts and New Hampshire, Salisbury Beach State Reservation, on 520 acres, abuts both the Atlantic Ocean and the mouth of the Merrimack River. A long stretch of pristine, sandy beach is lifeguarded for safe swimming from Memorial Day to Labor Day. Beautiful vistas abound, and it's a haven for boating and fishing. Rest rooms and shower facilities are available near the campground area. The 483 campground sites have a limited number of trailer and RV hookups available. Look for the harbor seals on the rocks.

Amesbury

 ### AMESBURY SPORTS PARK (ages 4 and up)

12 Hunt Road (exit 54 off Route 495); (978) 388–5788. Open Christmas through mid-March, weekends 9:00 A.M. to 10:00 P.M., midweek 3:00 to 9:30 P.M.; extended hours during vacation period. Price based on day of week and time of day.

Managed by former Boston Bruins player Brad Park, this is a great place for winter tubing fun. The park has four rope tows to handle the crowds and to give you a boost up the hill. There are ten different runs at various levels; children ages four to seven must be accompanied by an adult. Helmets are **Free** of charge, and young children are required to wear them. There is a snack bar and cafeteria. Groups are welcome, so keep that in mind if you decide to visit during peak times. The Sports Park does snowmaking to ensure snow coverage on the hill.

Where to Eat

Hodgies, *Haverhill Street; (978) 388–1211.* Homemade ice cream, big scoops.

Lowell and the Merrimack Valley

The Merrimack River winds through the valley, flowing past large cities like Lowell and Haverhill and small, picturesque towns like Westford and the Andovers. The major highway connecting the region is Route 495.

Jaffe Family Farm Favorites The following is a list of area farms that have pick your own fruits and flowers, picnic areas, food stands, hayrides, batting cages, mini golf, farm animal viewing, or a combination of any of the above:

- **Brooksby Farm,** 38 Felton Street, Peabody; (978) 531–1631.

- **Homestead Farm and Orchard,** 13 Birch Meadow Road, Merrimac; (978) 346–4811.

- **Ingaldsby Farm,** 22 Washington Street, West Boxford; (978) 352–4440.

- **Long Hill Orchard,** 520 Main Street, Route 113, West Newbury; (978) 363–2170.

- **Richardson Farms Inc.,** 156 South Main Street (Route 114), Middleton; (978) 777–6368.

- **Smolak Farms,** 315 South Bradford Street, North Andover; (978) 688–8058.

Haverhill

BRADFORD SKI AREA (ages 3 and up)

South Cross Road (off Salem Street); (978) 373–0071; www.SkiBradford.com. Open mid-December to mid-March, Monday through Saturday 8:30 A.M. to 10:00 P.M., Sunday 8:30 A.M. to 4:30 P.M. Price: $18 midweek from 8:30 A.M. to 6:00 P.M., weekends $25 from 8:30 A.M. to 4:30 P.M., $17 for night skiing Monday through Saturday 6:00 to 10:00 P.M.

A great place to break a child into the sport of skiing or snowboard-ing, (oops, no pun intended!), Bradford with a 250-foot vertical drop is a family oriented hill. Bradford has 13 trails accessed by two triple chairs and three rope tows. For the snowboard enthusiast there is a snowboard park

Facilities include a lodge, equipment rentals, a snack bar, and a ski school.

Andover/North Andover

Recreation Opportunities

- **Harold Parker State Forest,** *1951 Turnpike Road, North Andover; (978) 686–3391.* State forest covering Andover, North Andover, and North Reading. Hiking, biking, fishing, horseback riding, nature study, picnicking, swimming, camping, and interpretive programs.

- **Ward Reservation,** *Prospect Road, Andover; (978) 682–3580.* Nice trails on 694 acres used for cross-country skiing, snowshoeing, hik-ing, and horseback riding.

- **Stevens-Coolidge Place and Gardens,** *139 Andover Street, North Andover; (978) 682–3580.* Historic house/museum on ninety-five acres.

- **Weir Hill,** *Stevens Street, North Andover; (978) 682–3580.* Activities include pond skating, nonmotorized boating, hiking, cross-coun-try skiing, picnicking, and horseback riding.

Lowell

The main tourist attraction of the Merrimack Valley is Lowell, the country's first planned Industrial City, in whose enormous brick mills the world's first mass-produced cotton cloth originated. Stop by the **Greater Merrimack Convention and Visitors Bureau** at 22 Shattuck Street (978–459–6150) for area information.

LOWELL NATIONAL HISTORICAL PARK (all ages)

Visitor center at Market Mills, 246 Market Street; (978) 970–5000. Visitor center open Monday through Saturday 9:00 A.M. to 5:00 P.M., Sunday 10:00 A.M. to 5:00 P.M. Boott Cotton Mills Museum open Monday through Saturday 9:30 A.M. to 5:00 P.M., Sunday 11:00 A.M. to 5:00 P.M. Admission for Cotton Mills: $4.00 for adults, $3.00 for seniors, and $2.00 for children. The visitor center is Free.

Lowell National Historic Park provides excellent presentations and tours that bring Lowell's heyday to life, in some cases, deafeningly so. Lowell was named for Francis Cabot Lowell, the man who came up with the idea (and much of the money) for a planned industrial community. He also had the idea, highly radical in its time, of employing women, who made up the majority of the workforce. Kirk Boott headed up the group of people who planned, financed, and built Lowell. The largest of the cotton mills was named for him, and today the **Boott Cotton Mills Museum** is the star of Lowell. Restored in 1992, the museum re-creates the work environment that the "mill girls" experienced, complete with eighty-eight looms in full operation. Earplugs are available for tourists, but there was no such thing for the workers, who spent about seventy-two hours a week here, on their feet, without the benefit of ventilation, and earning a weekly wage of $2.25. History comes to life here in more ways than one: Be sure to listen to the recorded stories of some of the workers who ran the mills.

Lots of Locks Another highlight of a family trip to Lowell is the boat ride through the city's intricate canal-and-lock system. Reservations for these tours are strongly recommended; you wouldn't want to arrive in Lowell to find out that your family won't fit onto any boats that day. Tours leave from the visitor center (978–970–5000). The fee is $3.00 for adults, $1.00 for children six to sixteen, Free for children under five.

AMERICAN TEXTILE HISTORY MUSEUM (all ages)

491 Dutton Street; (978) 441–0400; www.athm.org. Open Tuesday through Friday 9:00 A.M. to 4:00 P.M., weekends and holidays 10:00 A.M. to 4:00P.M. Closed Mondays, Thanksgiving, Christmas, and New Year's Day. Admission: $5.00 for adults, $3.00 for children ages 6 to 16.

History comes alive at the American Textile Museum, with an extremely engaging and impressive array of spinning wheels, weaving machines, 300 years of clothing and textile history, and industrial machinery. The museum, located in a historic mill building, is very well done and will amaze children.

Performing Arts for Children Discovery Series, University of Massachusetts, Lowell, *One University Avenue; (978) 934–4444. Price: $9.00 per person; reservations encouraged. Ask about discount packages.* Performances have ranged from juggling, African dance, and puppetry to stories and songs and Chinese acrobats.

Other Things to See and Do

Children's Museum, *256 Market Street;* (978) 459–9899, opening in 2000.

New England Quilt Museum, *18 Shattuck Street; (978) 452–4207.* Ongoing changing exhibits (limited hanging time before the quilts start to stretch).

Passport to Boston, *(800) 256–7206 (groups of 10 or more).* Personalized tours of the Merrimack Valley and Boston.

The Sports Museum of New England, *25 Shattuck Street; (978) 452–6775.* Exhibits change on an ongoing basis.

Whistler House Museum of Art, *243 Worthen Street; (978) 452–7641.* Birthplace of artist James McNeill Whistler, known for his painting "Whistler's Mother." Paintings and prints from the nineteenth and twentieth centuries.

Lowell Festivals

- **Lowell Folk Festival** (last full weekend in July). Largest folk festival in the country; ethnic food, music and dance.

- **Cambodian Water Festival** (third Saturday in August). Native Cambodian dancing and music at Sampas Pavilion. Call (978) 454–4286 for more information.

- **Banjo and Fiddle Contest** (third weekend in September). Premier East Coast competition at Boardinghouse Park. Call (978) 970–5000 for more information.

Sports

- **Lowell Locks Monsters,** *77 Merrimack Street, Tsongas Arena, Lowell; (978) 458–PUCK.* Affiliated with the New York Islanders and the American Hockey League. Call for a schedule.

- **Lowell Spinners,** *Edward A. Le Lacheur Park, 450 Aiken Street (U. Mass/Lowell Campus).* Farm league team of the Red Sox playing in a new 4,700-seat stadium.

Where to Eat

Brewhouse Cafe and Grill (at the Brewery Exchange), *201 Cabot Street; (978) 937–2690 or (978) 452–6900 (movies).* Serving steaks, seafood, and homemade desserts. In the evening, visit the pub cinema. The kids are served a soda, and adults can have a stronger beverage while watching the movie.

The Old Worthen House, *141 Worthen Street; (978) 459–0300.* Lowell's oldest tavern and restaurant;

restored and preserved interior with down-to-earth, quaint atmosphere. Kids' specialties. The most expensive item on the menu is $5.25. $

For aficionados of diners, try the following:

The Club Diner, *145 Dutton Street; (978) 452–1679.*

Four Sisters Owl Diner, *244 Appelton Street; (978) 453–8321.*

Where to Stay

Doubletree Riverfront Hotel, *50 Warren Street; (978) 452–1200.* Offers 252 guest rooms near all major attractions; indoor pool. $$–$$$$

Radisson Heritage Hotel Chelmsford, *10 Independence Drive, Chelmsford; (978) 256–0800.* Five minutes from the historic heart of Lowell; indoor pool and fitness center. $–$$$$

Westford

BUTTERFLY PLACE AT PAPILLON PARK

120 Tyngsboro Park, Westford; (978) 392–0955. Open daily from mid-April through mid-October, 10:00 A.M. to 5:00 P.M. Admission: $5.00 for adults, $4.00 for children 3 to 12.

Papillon means "butterfly" in French, and that's what your family will see at the Butterfly Place, a highly unusual farm where hundreds of butterflies flutter above and through flowering plants and weeds in an enormous solar dome. It's fun to see how many different kinds of butterflies you can identify. There's a pleasant picnic spot, too.

Marcia's Top Annual Events
On the North Shore

- **Strawberry Festival,** June, Meatinghouse Green, Ipswich; (978) 356-3231
- **St. Peter's Fiesta,** late June, Gloucester; (978) 283-1601
- **Castle Hill Festival,** June through September, Ipswich; (978) 356-4351
- **The Children's Theatre at Maudslay State Park,** June through September, Curzon's Mill Road, Newburyport; (978) 465-7223
- **Marblehead Race Week,** late July; (781) 631-2868
- **Lowell Folk Festival,** late July, Lowell (978) 970-4161
- **Hammond Castle Medieval Festival,** July, Gloucester; (978) 283-2080
- **Gloucester Waterfront Festival,** August, Gloucester; (978) 283-1601
- **Cambodian Water Festival,** late August, Lowell; (978) 454-4286
- **Essex Clamfest, September,** Memorial Park; (978) 283-1601
- **International Festival,** September, Peabody (978) 532-3000
- **Salem's Haunted Happenings,** October, Salem; (978) 744-0004
- **Topsfield Fair,** October, Topsfield; (978) 887-5000
- **Christmas on Cape Ann,** December, Rockport, Gloucester, Manchester, and Essex; (978) 283-1601

NASHOBA VALLEY
Powers Road; (978) 692–3033. Open November through March, 9:00 A.M. to 10:00 P.M. daily (weekends from 8:30 A.M.).

Offers nine lifts, thirteen trails. Facilities include a lodge, restaurant, and bar. Packages available.

Greater Boston

Chock-full of history, New England's largest city seems to have a significant site on every corner. Tourism has always been part of life in busy Boston, and residents don't mind sharing their beautiful city with visitors. They appreciate the smallness of the downtown area as much as you will. What's more, many of the older areas of the North End, Beacon Hill, and the Back Bay are surprisingly compact and therefore walkable for parents and kids alike.

Avoid restricting your journey solely to the sites along the well-trafficked red line of the Freedom Trail. Kids will also enjoy the museums of Boston, especially the Museum of Science, the New England Aquarium, and the Children's and Computer museums. Don't miss the bronze statues of Mrs. Mallard and her brood, the heroes of *Make Way for Ducklings,* near the pond in the Public Garden. And be sure to take a day or two to explore the nearby towns of Cambridge, Lexington, and Concord.

Some Practical Information

ACCOMMODATIONS

Boston is an expensive place to stay. If you won't be staying with friends, plan ahead to get the best prices. The hotels listed in this chapter offer family packages throughout the year, but you must reserve ahead of time. An alternative is **Bed & Breakfast Agency of Boston** (47 Commercial Wharf, Boston; 800–248-9262), which maintains an extensive list of B&B accommodations around the city. They'll match your requirements and price range with an appropriate room, suite, efficiency, or apartment in both Boston and Cambridge. Rates are $80 to $150, double occupancy; kids under six stay $\mathbf{Free}$. Winter packages are great: three nights for the price of two, based on availability.

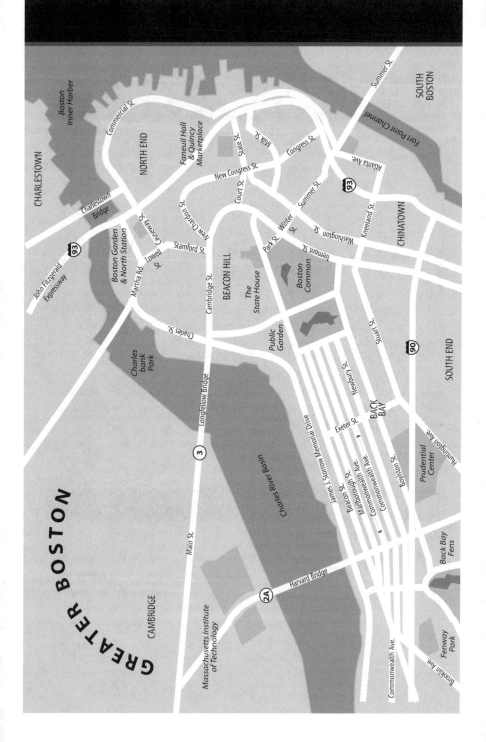

BABYSITTING

Town and Country Nannies Inc.; *(800) 94–NANNY.* Want to take a break from the kids? Town and Country Nannies is certified with Qanna, which is a set of standards set by the International Nanny Association for the teaching of nannies, and has more than twenty-five years of experience. The agency claims to carefully screen babysitters, so you can feel reassured while you have that well-deserved night out on the town.

MEDICAL

Inn-House Doctor; *(617) 859–1776. Payment: credit card, check, or cash.* It's no fun getting sick while you're on vacation, but lucky for you these dedicated doctors make house calls within one hour and come to more than one hundred hotels in the Boston area twenty-four hours a day. Staff includes general practitioners, pediatricians, and dentists who are affiliated with area hospitals.

Marcia's Top Family Adventures in Greater Boston

1. The Museum of Science Campus (the Science Museum, the Omni Theater, the Hayden Planetarium, and the Laser Light Show), Cambridge
2. Museum Wharf (Children's Museum, Computer Museum, and the Boston Tea Party Ship)
3. Duckling Statues and Swan Boat Ride at the Public Garden
4. New England Aquarium
5. John Hancock Observatory
6. Franklin Park Zoo, Jamaica Plain
7. Museum of Fine Arts
8. Boston Harbor Islands National Park and Recreation Area
9. Drumlin Farm, South Lincoln
10. Minute Man National Park, Lexington and Concord
11. Discovery Museums, Acton
12. Charlestown Navy Yard (Constitution Museum, the USS *Cassin Young,* and the USS *Constitution*)

PARKING IN BOSTON

Parking places are hard to come by in Boston. You'll enjoy your visit more if you leave the car in a parking garage and rely on public transportation, such as the MBTA (aka the "T"), and tour buses to get around.

TOURS

BEANTOWN TROLLEY TOURS (all ages)

14 Charles Street South at the Transportation Building; (617) 236–2148. Prices are $20.00 for adults, $16.00 for seniors and students, $6.00 for children 5 to 11, and **Free** *for children under five.*

An alternative to driving, the trolleys make twenty-three stops around the city, which will include most of the sites your family will want to see. Get on and off the trolley throughout the day, the entire narrated tour takes two hours and fifteen minutes. The trolleys are air-conditioned in the summer and heated in the winter. Tickets are sold on board as well as at outlets around the city. (*Note:* Only the transportation office accepts credit cards.)

CITYVIEW TROLLEY TOUR (all ages)

Board at the Boston Common Visitor Information Kiosk (Park Street MBTA Station) or by the Long Wharf Marriott Hotel; (617) 363–7899. Daily starting at 9:00 A.M. Tickets: $22. for adults, $20. for students and seniors, and $12. for children 12 and younger. Price includes **Free** *admission to the aquarium or a* **Free** *historic Boston Harbor cruise.*

Each trolley tour has a different spin on visiting Boston and Cityview Trolley is no exception. Cityview's hook is video-enhanced tours of Boston, with a multimedia presentation shown on onboard monitors. The tour takes approximately one hour, and there's a money-back guarantee if you don't enjoy it.

DISCOVER BOSTON MULTI-LINGUAL TROLLEY TOURS (all ages)

Custom House Block, 66 Long Wharf; (617) 742–1440. Offered year-round. Prices: $24.00 for adults, $22.00 for seniors and students, and $16.00 for children 3 to 12.

This trolley tour features a taped "Audiomate" of the Freedom Trail to carry with you on the walking portion of your tour as well as on board the trolley. The audio is available in six languages: English, French, German, Italian, Japanese, and Spanish. Discover Boston also includes a fifty-five-minute water tour of the USS *Constitution* and Rowes and Louis Wharfs. Special twilight and evening tours highlight little-known facts that focus on the darker side of Boston's history. This may frighten younger children, but rivet older ones.

THE DUCK TOUR (all ages)

101 Huntington Avenue (buy your tickets at the booth in the Prudential Center); (617) 723–3825 or (800) 226–7442. Offered daily mid-April through mid-November from 9:00 A.M. to a half hour before sunset. Tours leave every half hour. Prices (not including 5% Massachusetts sales tax): $21 for adults, $18 for seniors and students, $11 for children; **Free** *for children under 3.*

This eighty-minute land-and-sea tour is offered on a "duck," an amphibious World War II craft that travels both on land and in the Charles River. The rain-or-shine tour is lots of fun, and you will get many friendly stares as you wind your way through the streets of Boston. Once on the Charles River, the driver/narrator will ask for volunteers to pilot the duck. Both my daughter and her boarding-school roommate from Thailand found this to be the best part of the tour. *Tip:* A limited number of tickets are released two days prior but sell out by noon (there are no exchanges or refunds).

Boston Common and Beacon Hill

The best place to begin a Boston visit is at the corner of the Boston Common and Park Street. The Boston Common Information Booth is a few yards from here. At the booth you can collect **Free** maps, brochures, and information about sightseeing tours. The central stop of the "T" (subway), Park Street, is also right here.

Boston Common is the beginning of the Emerald Necklace, the largest continuous green space through an urban center in the United States. The park system was designed by Frederick Law Olmsted in 1895 (among other acclaimed projects, Olmsted also designed New York's Central Park). From Boston Common the Necklace stretches through the Public Garden to the Commonwealth Avenue Mall, the Back Bay Fens, through the Muddy River area, to Olmsted Park, Jamaica Park, and Jamaica Pond, and on to the Arnold Arboretum and Arborway before ending at the city's largest green space, Franklin Park. Sail, row, or fish at Jamaica Pond, bike and hike through any of the parks, play golf or visit the zoo at Franklin Park, or hear concerts; there's usually something going on at one of the parks along the Necklace. For daily updates, call the Parks and Recreation Activities Eventline (617–635–4006).

Amazing Massachusetts Facts

- Massachusetts has the oldest active constitution in the world. It was drafted in 1780.

- Massachusetts is one of only four commonwealths that are states (the others being Kentucky, Virginia, and Pennsylvania).

- In the first federal census (1790), Massachusetts was the only state in the Union to have no slaves.

- There are 351 cities and towns in Massachusetts.

- Symphony Hall turns one-hundred in October 2000.

- Harvard was founded in 1636 and was the first college in the nation, but the campus buildings date from the early eighteenth century.

MASSACHUSETTS STATE HOUSE, A FREEDOM TRAIL SITE (all ages)

Beacon Street; (617) 727–3676. State House hours are Monday through Saturday, 9:00 A.M. to 5:00 P.M.; tours, Monday through Saturday, 10:00 A.M. to 4:00 P.M. Closed Sundays, Thanksgiving, Christmas Day, and New Year's Day. Free.

Just up the hill from the Park Street end of the Common is the impressive gold-domed State House, built in 1778 on John Hancock's pasture. The original part of the building, which was designed by Charles Bullfinch, is in the neoclassical or federal style. Along with the legislative chambers, the state capitol holds a collection of flags, costumes, and other remnants of the state's history. Don't forget to ask for the handout and map that explain the function and location of the different rooms in the state house, and for the booklet *The Ladybug Story,* which clearly explains to children how a bill becomes law by using an example of schoolchildren who wanted the ladybug to be the official bug of Massachusetts. Walk up the capitol's front steps and turn around to see a terrific view of the Common and the tops of the taller buildings of the Financial District; then, with the building behind you, look over to the right. You'll see a fine statue of John F. Kennedy, whom the sculptor seems to have captured in mid stride as he left Boston for the U.S. Senate, where he served before his presidency. Of the many JFK monuments scattered around Boston, Massachusetts, and New England, this is the most human.

BOSTON COMMON, A FREEDOM TRAIL SITE (all ages)

Bordered by Beacon Street, Charles Street, Tremont Street, and Park Street. Open all day, every day. **Free.**

On a nice day a visit to Boston Common is worth a few hours. Tell the kids to imagine what it was like when Boston residents used this "common" area to graze their cattle, then discuss what it may have been like to live here when British soldiers used the Common as a training ground before the Revolutionary War. Nowadays, the Frog Pond is a big attraction year-round. On a hot summer's day, it's a great place for a cool dip. In the winter you can glide along on the ice. Forgot your skates? Don't worry; rentals are available for a nominal fee. At noon on any weekday, regardless of the weather, you're likely to share the park with many of the people who work in downtown offices. Bring a picnic lunch, or watch a softball game. A summer concert series attracts name talent and is popular with older kids, teens, and students. Charles Street separates the Public Garden from Boston Common.

PUBLIC GARDEN (all ages)

Bordered by Beacon Street, Arlington Street, Boylston Street, and Charles Street. Open year-round. **Free.**

Walk toward Beacon Street. Here the kids will find the bronze sculptures of Mrs. Mallard and her brood. Ask the kids to name the ducks (the first one is Jack, followed by Kack, Lack, Mack, Nack, Ouack, Pack, and Quack). Next, head for the lagoon, where your family may well see real-life cousins of the Mallard family. The **Swan Boat** ride is a must. The boats are on the lagoon from mid-April through mid-September, 10:00 A.M. to 5:00 P.M. The fare is $1.75 for adults, 95 cents for children under 13. It's a short twelve minutes or so—and people-powered; a boatswain pedals the boat from his or her perch behind a wooden swan. Remember to bring a bag of crumbs or peanuts along. Before or after your ride, be sure to check out the impressive statue of George Washington astride his horse, at the Commonwealth Avenue entrance to the Public Garden. The beautiful shrubbery, trees, and plantings, along with the picturesque bridge over the swan pond, attract many budding artists.

Duck, duck, duck, not goose! Historic Neighborhoods (99 Bedford Street; 617–426–1885; www.hnf@shore.net) runs a *Make Way for Ducklings tour* that follows the route taken by Mr. and Mrs. Mallard. During the week it's mostly school groups; however, on Friday and Saturday during the late spring, summer, and early fall, the general public can reserve a tour. **Ducklings Day** is an annual parade held on Mother's Day at Boston Common that reenacts the *Make Way for Ducklings* tale. Call for exact times.

AFRICAN MEETING HOUSE (all ages)

8 Smith Court, off Joy Street on Beacon Hill; (617) 742–5415. Open Memorial Day to Labor Day 10:00 A.M. to 4:00 P.M.; tours of the Black Heritage Trail are at 10:00 A.M., noon, and 2:00 P.M. daily. From Labor Day to Memorial Day the Meeting House is open from 10:00 A.M. to 4:00 P.M. Monday through Friday; tours are by reservation only. Suggested donations are posted.

The African Meeting House, owned by the Museum of African American History, is the oldest standing African American church in the country. Boston has a long history of abolitionism (Frederick Douglass spoke here); just after the Revolution, Massachusetts declared itself the first free state, with full citizenry extended to black residents. Before and during the Civil War, this was the headquarters of the Underground Railroad, which helped many escaped slaves leave the South and find new homes and livelihoods in the North. Puppet shows depict the Underground Railroad and the flight toward freedom.

BLACK HERITAGE TRAIL (all ages)

Tours meet at the Shaw Memorial across from the State House. Tours are conducted Monday through Friday at 10:00 A.M., noon, and 2:00 P.M. Suggested donation posted at the African Meeting House.

The Museum of Afro American History and the National Park Service operate the Black Heritage Trail. The trail, covering just over 1.5 miles, is a two-hour walking tour of Beacon Hill area buildings that are important to local and national black history. Along with the African Meeting House, sites include the **Hayden House,** an important stop along the Underground Railroad; the **Charles Street Meeting House,** where abolitionists Frederick Douglass and Sojourner Truth preached against slavery; and the **monument to Robert Gould Shaw and the Fifty-fourth Regiment,** which commemorates the first black division of the Union Army during the Civil War.

*B*lack Heritage Trail

- Site 1: Robert Gould Shaw and the Fifty-fourth Regiment Memorial, Park and Beacon Streets

- Site 2: George Middleton House, 5–7 Pinckney Street

- Site 3: The Phillips School, Anderson and Pinckney Streets

- Site 4: John J. Smith House, 86 Pinckney Street

- Site 5: Charles Street Meeting House, Mt. Vernon and Charles Streets

- Site 6: Lewis Hayden House, 66 Phillips Street

- Site 7: Coburn's Gaming House, 2 Phillips Street

- Sites 8–12: Smith Court Residences, 46 Joy Street

- Site 13: Abiel Smith School, 46 Joy Street

- Site 14: African Meeting House, 8 Smith Court

LOUISBURG SQUARE (all ages)

Between Pinckney and Mt. Vernon Streets on Beacon Hill. **Free**.

A site of interest to *Little Women* fans, Louisa May Alcott and her family lived at number 10 after her success with *Little Women* (long before Louisa's literary success, the Alcott family also lived at 20 Pinckney Street). Swedish Nightingale Jenny Lind who toured with P. T. Barnum's circus was married at number 14 Louisburg Square. *Make Way for Ducklings* fans will remember the book's superb overhead view of the square. Nearby is the House of Odd Windows, 24 Pinckney Street, whose facade boasts a wide variety of unusually shaped windows.

Where to Eat

Au Bon Pain, *22 AB Beacon Street; (617) 248–6876; or 52 Winter Street (617) 338–8304 (1 block south of Tremont Street).* Made-to-order sandwiches on freshly baked bread. $

Bull & Finch Pub (Cheers), *84 Beacon Street; (617) 227–9605.* Open daily, 11:00 A.M. to 1:30 A.M. The bar in the television show *Cheers* was modeled after the Bull & Finch. There's a souvenir gallery selling "Cheers" paraphernalia. Upstairs is the Hampshire House housing the Liberty Grill. $–$$$

Souper Salad, *82 Summer Street; (617)*
426–6834; or 103 State Street (617)
227– 9151. A good choice, especially if
you can't face one more sandwich. $

Where to Stay

The Eliot & Pickett Houses, 6 Mt.
Vernon Place; (617) 248-8707. Twenty-
room B&B in two brick town houses;
nice roof deck. Guests have use of the
kitchens. Rates are $85 and up per
night; children under 18 stay **Free**
in their parents' room. There is no
parking on site.

Beacon Hill Bed & Breakfast, 27
Brimmer Street; (617) 523-7376. This
brick rowhouse overlooking the Charles
River has large bedrooms with fireplaces and private baths. There are cots
and sofabeds, but no cribs. Rates are
$160 to $220 per night, including a full
breakfast. Parking is in a nearby
garage.

Downtown and Financial District

If your family is hungry for information about the city, or if you'd like to join a
Free ninety-minute guided tour of highlights of the Freedom Trail, walk over
to the **National Historical Park Visitor Center,** 15 State Street (next to the
Old State House; 617-242-5642). You'll find maps, books, and helpful staff.
The small bookstore has an excellent collection of reasonably priced books
about lesser known people and events in Boston and New England history.

 THE FREEDOM TRAIL (all ages)
Pick up a map of the trail at the National Historical Park Visitor Center. Only
three of the sites charge a fee: the Old State House, the Old South Meeting House,
and the Paul Revere House. A fee is sometimes charged at the Charlestown Navy
Yard for the Constitution Museum (the fee is currently being underwritten by an
anonymous donor); the USS Constitution *and the USS* Cassin Young *tours are*
Free.

The Freedom Trail, a 2.5-mile walking tour of the city's colonial and
revolutionary landmarks, begins at Boston Common and ends at the
Bunker Hill Monument. Only three of the sites are owned by the Federal
government; the rest are owned and operated by the city of Boston or
by the state of Massachusetts, or are privately owned. The Freedom Trail
is easy to follow; just look for the red line on the sidewalk. If your children are young, the walk as a whole may be too long; instead, you may
wish to visit just a few of the landmarks.

reedom Trail Sites

- Boston Common
- State House
- Park Street Church
- Granary Burying Ground
- King's Chapel and Burying Ground
- Franklin statue and site of the first public school
- Old Corner Bookstore
- Old South Meeting House

- Old State House
- Boston Massacre site
- Faneuil Hall at Quincy Marketplace
- Paul Revere House
- Old North Church
- Copp's Hill Burying Ground
- USS *Constitution* at the Charlestown Navy Yard
- Bunker Hill Monument

BOSTON BY LITTLE FEET (ages 3 and up)

77 North Washington Street; (617) 367–2345; www.bostonbyfoot.com. Tours are offered from May through October. Freedom Trail and downtown: Monday and Saturday 10:00 A.M., Sunday 2:00 P.M. The Boston Underground and the Big Dig tours (recommended for ages 6 and up): Sunday 2:00 P.M. $–$$. Reservations are suggested but not required. Meet at Fanueil Hall, the Congress Street side, in front of the Samuel Adams statue.

Covering part of the Freedom Trail as well as other sites that are of particular interest to kids, Boston by Little Feet (operated by Boston by Foot) is a family-oriented, one-hour tour of the downtown area that gives kids a great introduction to Boston's history and architecture. Boston by Underground is a one-and-a-half-hour tour offered once a week by Boston by Foot that focuses on the underground utilities, the way the city has grown down as well as up, and the "Big Dig," the depression of the central artery into Boston, the largest and most expensive construction project in the country.

OLD STATE HOUSE AND THE BOSTON MASSACRE SITE, A FREEDOM TRAIL SITE (all ages)

Corner of Washington and State Streets; (617) 720–3291. Open daily 9:00 A.M. to 5:00 P.M. (last tourists are encouraged to be here by 4:00 P.M.); closed Christmas. Admission: $3.00 for adults, $2.00 for seniors and students, $1.00 for children 6 to 18.

The brick Old State House built in 1713 is the oldest surviving public building in Boston. It manages to hold its own against the glass sky-scrapers that surround it. Kids enjoy looking at the lion and unicorn on the building's gables. When the building was erected, it was the seat of the British government in the colonies, and these symbols of the Crown indicated that fact. The current lion and unicorn aren't the originals; when the Declaration of Independence was read from the building's rooftop in July 1776, Bostonians removed these symbols of the Crown and burned them. The lion and unicorn weren't replaced until recently. In the middle of the intersection in front of the building (Congress and State Streets) is a star inside a ring of cobblestones, marking the site of the **Boston Massacre.** On March 5, 1770, a frightened group of British soldiers fired into a crowd of colonists who had gathered to protest recent crackdowns on customs duties and taxes. Though it was hardly a massacre, five people were killed on this spot, including a former slave, Crispus Attucks. Thereafter Sam Adams used the incident as a rallying point in his frequent speeches against the British.

OLD SOUTH MEETING HOUSE, A FREEDOM TRAIL SITE (all ages)

Corner of Washington and Milk Streets; (617) 482–6439. Open daily, year-round, from April through October, 9:30 A.M. to 5:00 P.M., and from November through March, 10:00 A.M. to 4:00 P.M. Admission: $3.00 for adults, $2.50 for seniors and students, $1.00 for children 6 to 18.

The Old South Meeting House began its life in 1729 as a church but quickly became a gathering place for political and revolutionary activity. The band of colonists who participated in the Boston Tea Party in 1773 dressed as "Indians" here before they sneaked down to the harbor. Today the meeting house serves as a museum to the colonial and revolutionary period, with recordings of dramatized versions of public speeches during the period, a good gift shop, and an interesting model of Boston. Incidentally, Old South still has a political life: During campaign years politicians often use it as a venue for announcing their candidacies.

GRANARY BURYING GROUND, A FREEDOM TRAIL SITE (all ages)

Next to the Park Street Church on Tremont Street, near the corner of Tremont and Park. Open year-round. **Free.**

The Granary Burying Ground is the final resting place of Paul Revere, John Hancock, Sam Adams, the five victims of the Boston Massacre, and the famous storyteller who was known as Mother Goose. No rubbings, please.

FLEET CENTER (all ages)

100 Causeway Street. Open year-round; check the schedule of events and games.

 The Boston Celtics and Boston Bruins play at the Fleet Center, which replaced the venerable Boston Garden in 1995. For Celtics and Bruins tickets, call Ticketmaster (617–931–2000). The Ice Capades are an annual favorite, as are other ice show extravaganzas. Concerts for the preteen and teen set are also held here.

NEW ENGLAND SPORTS MUSEUM (all ages)

100 Causeway Street at the Fleet Center; (617) 787–7678. Open 11:00 A.M. to 5:00 P.M. Tuesday through Saturday, Sunday noon to 5:00 P.M. Closed Monday and major holidays. The sports museum closes one hour earlier when there is an event or game. Admission: $5.00 for adults, $4.00 for seniors and children 6 to 17.

The museum has two floors of New England sports memorabilia, covering the Boston Red Sox, the Boston Bruins, the Boston Celtics, the New England Patriots, and the Boston Marathon. Special exhibits have featured old ballparks and women's Olympic hockey. The most satisfied visitors are kids who follow the Red Sox, Celtics, or Bruins, but enthusiastic sports fans will probably enjoy looking at the collections of memorabilia, such as one-hundred-year-old baseball spikes and the life-size carved statues of Boston idols Larry Bird, Carl Yastrzemski, and Bobby Orr. Budget some time to watch several of the videos of big-game highlights. Other sites of the New England Sports Museum are in Providence, Rhode Island, and Lowell, Massachusetts.

Where to Eat

Fajitas & 'Ritas, *25 West Street; (617) 426–1222. Open Monday through Wednesday 11:30 A.M. to 9:00 P.M., Thursday 11:30 A.M. to 10:00 P.M., Friday 11:00 A.M. to 11:00 P.M., Saturday noon to 10:00 P.M.; closed Sunday.* A good place for an informal Tex-Mex lunch. Features make-your-own fajitas, as well as chili and tacos. $

Where to Stay

The Omni Parker House, 60 School Street; (617) 227-8600 or (800) 843-6664. An old hotel in a great location; everything is within a few minutes' walk from the front door, including the Common. The mini-suites are perfect for families. $$$$

Quincy Marketplace and Government Center

Since it's rebirth twenty years ago, Quincy Marketplace has been a mecca for both locals and tourists. Upscale shops, historic buildings, street performers, and a wide variety of restaurants add to the intrigue. Nearby Haymarket is a colorful bargain open-air market that is reminiscent of a European street market. Government Center, with its tall, modern buildings, adds architectural interest to the landscape.

FANEUIL HALL (all ages)
Merchants Row; (617) 635–3105 or (617) 242–5675 (National Park Service). Open daily 9:00 A.M. to 5:00 P.M. **Free**.

Faneuil Hall is a historic site, a pedestrian zone, the entry to a massive shopping area, and a food market. Faneuil Hall itself was the site of many pre–Revolutionary War meetings, which is why it's called the "cradle of liberty." National Park Service guides give a twenty-minute historic talk of the hall and of the painting *Webster's Answer to Haynes,* depicting Daniel Webster with Senator Haynes of South Carolina. Tell the kids to look for the gold-plated grasshopper weathervane atop the building. Made in 1742, the grasshopper has become one of Boston's symbols.

QUINCY MARKET (all ages)
Between State and Congress Streets. Open Monday through Saturday 10:00 A.M. to 9:00 P.M., Sunday noon to 6:00 P.M.; closed Thanksgiving Day and Christmas. **Free**.

Beyond Faneuil Hall is copper-domed Quincy Market, in the center, and the North and South Market buildings on either side. The granite Greek Revival building has lived a long life as a marketplace. When it was built in 1826, the east portico was right on the edge of the harbor. The brick North and South Market buildings were built in subsequent years to accommodate the growing needs of the city's meat and produce wholesalers. In the 1970s the city hired an architectural firm to restore the buildings and their surrounding cobblestone streets into an area that would be suitable for a pedestrian shopping area. Obviously, the project was a success; many tourists now come to Boston just to see the market-place, and many locals come here to eat lunch and people-watch. The Quincy

*S*pecial Events at Faneuil Hall

- **Street Performers Festival,** last weekend in May.

- **Anniversary Party of Quincy Market,** August 22. **Free** cake for all.

- **Furnish the Future,** September. Artists donate furniture that they've decorated, proceeds going to the homeless.

- **Holiday Lighting Ceremony,** 5:00 P.M. weekend before Thanksgiving.

Market building itself is mostly devoted to take-out food vendors who sell everything from frozen yogurt to overstuffed deli sandwiches to pizza-by-the-slice to raw shellfish. Once you and your family have gathered your lunch fixings, head toward the large center area, which is full of tables, chairs, and benches. The North and South Market buildings hold shops and restaurants, from the kitschy to the upscale. Outdoors, regardless of the temperature, you're likely to see several street musicians, jugglers, mimes, and other performers. It's a fun place to spend an afternoon.

HAYMARKET (all ages)

Blackstone Street between North and Hanover Streets. Friday and Saturday 6:00 A.M. to 5:00 P.M. **Free**.

Walk along the east end of Quincy Market to Haymarket, an open-air market that's a sight in itself. Pick up the younger kids and walk along the narrow aisles between stands of fruit, vegetables, and seafood. Prices are excellent, and you'd have a tough time finding a better example of where the locals go: This is where many North End chefs buy their produce. Be sure to arrive early.

GOVERNMENT CENTER AND CITY HALL PLAZA (all ages)

Congress and Cambridge Streets. **Free**.

This is the home of the mayor of Boston and the location of several state and federal offices. It's also a great place to eat lunch on the steps or to listen to a nighttime concert sponsored by the city of Boston. The summer concert series features musical happenings on Wednesday (big bands) and Saturday evenings (oldies rock 'n' roll). Call (617) 635–3962 for more information and a schedule of events.

Other Things to See and Do

New England Holocaust Memorial,
Congress Street near Fanueil Hall
(617–457–0755).

Where to Eat

Durgin Park, *340 Fanueil Hall Market-place; (617) 227–2038.* Extremely noisy, bustling place that has had customers coming back for over 150 years. Real down-home New England fare—the original comfort food. $$

North End

North End is an Italian neighborhood with excellent restaurants, terrific cafes, and fun festivals on most summer weekends (particularly the Feast of Saint Anthony in August), as well as several of Boston's most famous historic sites, which is appropriate since it's the oldest surviving neighborhood in the city. It's an easy walk from Quincy Market (parking is tough to find on the narrow streets of North End); take the pedestrian passageway under the Fitzgerald Expressway (careful; this is a dangerous intersection!).

PAUL REVERE'S HOUSE (all ages)
19 North Square; (617) 523–1676; www.PaulRevereHouse.org. Open daily from April 15 through October 31, 9:30 A.M. to 5:15 P.M.; Tuesday through Sunday from November 1 through April 14, 9:30 A.M. to 4:15 P.M. Closed Thanksgiving Day, Christmas Day, and New Year's Day. Admission: $2.50 for adults, $2.00 for seniors and students with ID, $1.00 for children 5 to 17; Free *for children 5 and under.*

The oldest house in Boston, Revere left from here to make his famous ride. The Paul Revere House is a great place for kids to get an upclose view of domestic life during this period.

THE OLD NORTH CHURCH (all ages)

193 Salem Street; (617) 523–6676. Open daily, 9:00 A.M. to 5:00 P.M., except Thanksgiving and Christmas; Sunday services at 9:00 and 11:00 A.M. and 5:00 P.M. **Free***.*

In 1775 Robert Newman, the church's sexton, hung two lanterns from the belfry to alert Revere and his compatriots of the British troops' departure from Boston, by boat, on their way to Lexington and Concord to capture Sam Adams and John Hancock. This is the city's oldest remaining church. Across the street is Paul Revere Mall, with the famous statue of Revere.

 ### COPPS HILL BURIAL GROUND, A FREEDOM TRAIL SITE (all ages)

Hull Street (near Old North Church). **Free***.*

A great spot for a picnic, Copps Hill Burial Ground has the city's best view of the waterfront—Charlestown, the Navy Yard, the USS *Constitution,* and Boston Harbor. There's a nice playground here, along with picnic tables and a shaded grassy area. Enter from Hull Street, between Snowhill and Charter Streets. Pause and look across the street at the narrowest house in Boston (9 feet 6 inches wide), at number 44 Hull Street.

Where to Eat

Most Boston families think of the North End as one big restaurant. There's something for everyone here, from thin-crust pizza to fresh seafood to family-style Italian restaurants with large tables and friendly wait staff.

Pizzeria Regina, *11½ Thatcher Street; (617) 227–0765.* At the original Pizzeria Regina, you'll find high-backed booths, no-nonsense service, pitchers of soft drinks, and delicious thin-crust pizza. You may encounter a line when you get here, since there are no reservations. It's worth the wait. Open Monday through Thursday 11:00 A.M. to

11:30 P.M., Friday and Saturday 11:00 A.M. to midnight, Sunday noon to 11:00 P.M. $–$$

Pat's Pushcart, *61 Endicott Street; (617) 523–9616.* Upstairs is the better venue for families—the tables are larger. The red sauce is fantastic. Open for dinner only Tuesday through Saturday, 5:00 to 10:30 P.M. $–$$

The Daily Catch, 323 Hanover Street; (617) 523-8567. No reservations. The house specialty is calamari, but don't feel limited to squid dishes; everything's great. Open daily for lunch and dinner, 11:00 A.M. to 10:30 P.M. $–$$

Caffe Vittoria, 296 Hanover Street; (617) 227-7606. The decor is way over the top—faux marble tables, gilded mirrors, and garish murals of Italian seascapes—and that's all part of the scene. While the kids enjoy gelato, adults can savor espresso or cappuccino. Open daily, 8:00 A.M. to midnight Monday through Thursday, to 12:30 A.M. Friday through Sunday. $

Mike's Pastry, 300 Hanover Street; (617) 742-3050. Another North End institution. The kids will marvel at the selection of pastries and cookies. Open Sunday and Monday 8:00 A.M. to 9:00 P.M., Tuesday 9:00 A.M. to 6:00 P.M., Wednesday 8:00 A.M. to 9:30 P.M., Thursday and Friday 8:00 A.M. to 10:00 P.M., Saturday 8:00 A.M. to 11:00 P.M. $

Bova's, *134 Salem Street; (617) 523–5601.* Many North Enders say that Bova's is the best Italian bakery in town. Another reason why locals like it: It's open twenty-four hours a day. North Enders refer to Bova's as the "Beacon in the Night." $

Waterfront Area

The waterfront area can boast of a high concentration of kid-friendly museums and attractions. The New England Aquarium is one of the most progressive in the country; Museum Wharf clusters the Children's and Computer museums and the Boston Tea Party ship. If time allows, be sure to take in a whale watch or cruise to one of the Boston Harbor Islands maintained by the National Park Service.

 CHRISTOPHER COLUMBUS/WATERFRONT PARK (all ages)
Atlantic Avenue across from Quincy Marketplace. Open daily year-round.
    When the kids need a place to run off some energy, head to Christopher Columbus/Waterfront Park; it's one of the few places in Boston where people can actually relax on the waterfront without having to order something to eat. There's a nice playground (watch the little ones; the crow's nest is inviting, but the climb down is beyond most toddlers' abilities), as well as lots of room to stretch your legs. The rose garden is dedicated to Rose Fitzgerald Kennedy, the late matriarch

Cruising: For a short or long trip around the harbor or to nearby coastal towns, both Boston Harbor Cruises (1 Long Wharf; 617–227–4320) and Massachusetts Bay Lines (60 Rowes Wharf; 617–542–8000) offer inexpensive, regularly scheduled round-trips. Bring a lunch and a sweater or jacket; even on warm days the wind can make it chilly out on the open water.

of the Kennedy clan, who was born near here. A note of caution: Along Boston's waterfront area there's no physical barrier to prevent your children from tumbling into the water. Keep a sharp eye out.

NEW ENGLAND AQUARIUM (all ages)

Central Wharf; (617) 973–5200. Open Labor Day through June 30: Monday through Friday 9:00 A.M. to 5:00 P.M., weekends and holidays 9:00 A.M. to 6:00 P.M. July 1 through Labor Day: Monday, Tuesday, and Friday 9:00 A.M. to 6:00 P.M., Wednesday and Thursday 9:00 A.M. to 8:00 P.M., Saturday, Sunday, and holidays 9:00 A.M. to 7:00 P.M. Admission: $12.00 for adults, $10.00 for seniors, $6.00 for children 3 to 11; **Free** *for children under 3.*

One of Boston's greatest attractions is the New England Aquarium, and rightly so. Penguins, turtles, sea lions, and sharks share the stage with thousands of smaller fish, all contained in brilliantly designed tanks and pools. The four-story glass tank, wrapped by a spiral ramp, is the highlight of the aquarium. There's nothing like being eye to eye with a shark or walking up and down to follow a sea turtle's movements through the water. Plan to spend at least a couple of hours here, beginning with the harbor seal tank in front of the aquarium. Younger kids may be spooked, initially, by the dim lighting inside the aquarium; show them that the only illumination comes from the tanks, and they'll probably forget their fear and become interested in the fish. Feeding time (five times a day) in the main tank is worth waiting for: Scuba divers jump right in to feed the fish. The kids also get a kick out of the penguin feeding, and the penguin holding area is the first thing that one sees upon entering the aquarium building. On the third level is the ever-popular Edge of the Sea Tide Pool exhibit, which allows kids of all ages to touch and hold small marine creatures such as starfish, horseshoe crabs, and sea urchins. Don't miss the twenty-minute sea lion presentation (which is included in the price of admission) aboard the **Discovery Pavilion** that floats in the harbor *beside* the main building of the aquarium. The sea lion presentation is every hour and a half starting at 11:00 A.M. on weekdays, 10:30 a.m on weekends and holidays.

BOSTON HARBOR ISLANDS (all ages)

National Recreation Area managed by the National Park Service in Boston Harbor; (617) 727–7676; www.nps.gov/boha. Daily in-season departures from May through October from Heritage State Park in Lynn, Hewitts' Cove in Hingham, and Long Wharf (next to the aquarium), Boston.

Close to this urban area is a series of thirty islands, each of which has its own unique flavor. Only six of these islands are reachable by public ferry; the rest are accessed by private motorcraft. The six islands are part of a hub-and-spoke system that revolves around the main island, George's Island, where there is free water shuttle service to the other five.

- George's Island: Old fort, beach, rest rooms, snack bar

- Lovell's Island: Remains of a fort, lifeguarded beach, hiking and camping

- Gallop's Island: Inhabited by rabbits, myth about buried treasure, great views of Boston skyline

- Peddock's Island: Camping, hiking, and bird-watching

- Bumpkin Island: Ruins of a farmhouse and children's hospital; camping allowed in farmhouse orchard

- Grape Island: Varied wildlife; camping allowed

- Little Brewster Island: Home of one of the oldest lighthouses in the country

AQUARIUM WHALE WATCH (must be at least 3 years old and a minimum of 30 inches tall)

Central Wharf; (617) 973–5200 (general information). Offered in April, weekends only, departures at 10:00 A.M.; May 1 through June 30, 10:00 A.M. weekdays, 9:30 A.M. and 3:30 P.M. weekends; July 1 through September 6, departures at 9:30 A.M., 12:30 and 2:30 P.M. daily; September 7 through October 1 departures at 1:00 P.M. weekdays, 9:30 A.M., and 2:30 P.M. weekends; October 16 through November 7, departures at 10:00 A.M. weekdays. Price: $26 for adults, $21 for seniors and students with ID, $19 for children 12 to 18, $16.50 for children 3 to 11. Reservations are required in advance (617–973–5281); Monday through Saturday 9:00 A.M. to 4:00 P.M.

The aquarium operates a whale-watching tour from Central Wharf to Stellwagen Bank, the prime feeding grounds off the coast of Massachusetts; however this trip is long (about six hours, round-trip). An alternative for those who aren't keen on being on the water too long is to travel to Provincetown and make the shorter boat trip from there (see Chapter 3). For boaters, the trip down is lovely; it's a great way to cool off on a hot day while spotting whales and enjoying the harbor, coastline, and ocean.

MASSPORT'S WATER SHUTTLE AND CITY WATER TAXIS (all ages)

*Rowes Wharf and Boston Harbor Hotel; (800) 235–6426 (recorded informa-
tion). For information on Long Wharf to Logan Airport and Salem, call (978)
741–3442. For information on Long Wharf to Logan Airport and Quincy, call
(617) 376–8417. For information on City Water Taxis to various Boston destina-
tions call (617) 439–3131. Prices and times vary according to destination.*

Massport's Water Shuttle and the City Water Taxis arrives at and
leave from Rowes Wharf; they're a convenient way to get to and from
Logan Airport if you don't have much luggage. For the commuter,
they're a unique way to travel to the city. *Note:* There are no rest rooms
on board.

 THE COMPUTER MUSEUM (ages 3 and up)

*Museum Wharf; (617) 426–2800; www.tcm.org. Open daily during the sum-
mer, 10:00 A.M. to 6:00 P.M., Tuesday through Sunday during the winter, 10:00
A.M. and 5:00 P.M. Admission: $7.00 for adults, $5.00 for children over 5;*
ℱ𝓇𝑒𝑒 *for children under 5.*

Best for families with school-age children, the Computer Museum is
the only museum of its kind in the world. The standout exhibit is the Virtual Fishtank monitored by twenty-two computers which allow you to
program fish into an aquarium atmosphere. Your kids will love programming artificial life using simple rules to feed the fish and control their
behavior. Different stations are peppered throughout this very interactive exhibit. Another exhibit high on the must see list is the Walk-
Through Computer 2000, a house-size version of a PC, complete with a
keyboard and trackball that wouldn't be out of place on a playground.
Other exhibits include Tools and Toys, which gives visitors a glimpse into
the many worlds that are run by personal computers; People and Computers, a time machine that places the early computers and the people
who ran them in their historical contexts; The Networked Planet, an
explanation of how, when, and why the information superhighway
touches our lives; and the Best Offer for Kids Gallery, where you can log
on to play any of fifty software games. The museum store is an excellent
resource for families with computer-savvy kids; check out *The Computer
Museum Guide to the Best Software for Kids* (HarperCollins Perennial).

THE CHILDREN'S MUSEUM (ages infant to 10)

Museum Wharf; (617) 426–8855. Open summer: Saturday through Thursday 10:00 A.M. to 5:00 P.M., Friday 10:00 A.M. to 9:00 P.M.; September through June: closed on Monday, open Tuesday, Wednesday, Thursday, Saturday, and Sunday 10:00 A.M. to 5:00 P.M., Friday 10:00 A.M. to 9:00 P.M. Admission: $7.00 for adults, $6.00 for seniors and children 2 to 15, $1.00 for children 1 and under.

Families shouldn't miss the Children's Museum. It's a hands-on romp of a place with exhibits such as Playspace, a toddlers-only play area; the ever-popular two-story climbing structure, a vertical maze that stretches from the first floor to the second (don't let the little ones in here; you won't be able to fit yourself inside to get them out); and the New Balance Structure from the second to the third floors for kids 5 and over. The old standards include Grandma's House, for a taste of the past; the Super Mercado Grocery Store, where children can act as customers or cashiers/owners; and the Recycle Bin, which is a great resource for materials to take home for those rainy day art projects. Ask at the front desk about family-oriented activities; the museum serves as a clearinghouse for kids' activities around the city.

 ### BOSTON TEA PARTY SHIP AND MUSEUM (all ages)

300 Congress Street, off the Congress Street Bridge; (617) 338–1773. From March through Memorial Day and from Labor Day through November, open daily 9:00 A.M. to 5:00 P.M.; from Memorial Day to Labor Day, open daily 9:00 A.M. to 6:00 P.M.; closed December, January, and February. Admission: $8.00 for adults, $7.00 for students with ID, $4.00 for children 5 to 12.

Of course, it's not the real ship, but it's a good facsimile of the *Beaver,* and the "colonists" on board will retell the story that everyone knows: In 1773, to protest the high taxes imposed on tea, ninety Boston revolutionaries gathered at Old South Meeting House, and, accompanied by a large group of sympathizers, made their way to the *Beaver,* the *Dartmouth,* and the *Eleanor.* They slipped aboard and threw the ships' contents—342 chests of tea—into the harbor. The Beaver is the only Boston Tea Party ship that has been reconstructed. If you do go on board, the kids will be able to toss "tea chests" overboard themselves.

Where to Eat

The Milk Bottle, *Museum Wharf; (617) 451–2226.* Excellent salads, sandwiches, soup, and, of course, ice cream and frozen yogurt. The bottle on display was donated to the Children's Museum in 1977 by the H. P. Hood Company, a large dairy. It can hold 50,000 gallons of milk. Open daily spring and summer, 7:00 A.M. to 9:00 P.M. $

Bethany's, *332 Congress Street; (617) 423–4042.* Deli catering to workers in nearby businesses and staffs of the Children's and Computer museums. There are a few tables inside, but the emphasis is on take-out. $

South Station, *corner of Summer Street* and *Atlantic Avenue.* Recently restored and renovated, South Station has a pleasant food court area and lots of tables. $

Where to Stay

Marriott Long Wharf, *296 State Street; (617) 227–0800.* A stone's throw from the aquarium and close to Quincy Market and other area attractions. Cookies served every evening; pool and health club. $$$$+

Boston Harbor Hotel, *70 Rowes Wharf; (617) 439–7000 or (617) 856–7700.* Prestigious hotel with a good location on the waterfront. Upon check-in chocolate chip cookies and

milk are sent to the room for the children. $$$$++

The Harborside Hyatt, *101 Harborside Drive; (617) 568–1234 or (800) 233–1234.* The 270-room Harborside, located just beyond Logan Airport, has beautiful views of the Boston harbor and skyline with slightly better pricing than downtown Boston hotels. Water shuttle service is available to Rowes Wharf. $$$$

Chinatown, the Theater District, and Downtown Crossing

Indulge your family's senses with Chinatown's foods, smells, and sights; take in a topnotch performance in the Theater District, then head over to Boston's main shopping district, known as Downtown Crossing. Wander down the bricked-over section of the busy Washington Street shopping district, a pedestrian zone, past street vendors and performers. You're likely to see a mounted police officer or two. They're accustomed to kids' questions and the horses are very gentle, but ask first before allowing your kids to pat the horses' noses.

Women of History The Women's Heritage Trail (get maps at Boston Common) includes the homes of Elizabeth Peabody, founder of the kindergarten movement, and Sarah Hale, the reputed author of "Mary Had A Little Lamb."

 ### CHINATOWN (all ages)

Between Stuart and Essex Streets.

Walk through the ornate arch with the four marble Foo dogs into Boston's Chinatown for a gastronomic treat. It's hard to choose among the many restaurants. If you like to cook Chinese, this area is a great resource for Asian ingredients. Most signs in front of the shops are in both English and Chinese. A great time to expose the kids to a different culture is at the Chinese New Year Celebration in late January or early February.

(all ages)

426 Washington Street at Summer Street; (617) 357–2100. Open Monday through Saturday, 9:30 A.M. to 7:30 P.M., Sunday 11:00 A.M. to 7:00 P.M. Closed Thanksgiving Day, Christmas Day, Easter, and Fourth of July.

The original Filene's Basement is in the basement of Filene's, naturally. It's as good as you've heard; prices run the gamut from plain-old markdowns to rock-bottom, although the quality of the merchandise often suffers from overhandling. This isn't a place for young children or for anyone who isn't a die-hard shopper: Aisles can be narrow and shoppers downright rude, even to cute kids.

Other Things to See and Do

The Boston Globe Book Store, *1 School Street; (617) 523–6658.* Specializing in travel books. Children's section.

Jack's Joke Shop, *172 Tremont Street; (617) 426–9640.* Fun stop for practical jokes.

Where to Eat

Bruegger's Bagel Bakery, *7 School Street; (617) 367–4702.* Bagels are baked on the premises. Try one of their cream cheese mixtures; the fresh berry varieties are particularly good. Soups and salads also available. Open Monday through Friday 6:30 A.M. to 6:00 P.M., Saturday 7:30 A.M. to 6:00 P.M., Sunday 7:30 A.M. to 5:00 P.M. $

Chau Chow, *52 Beach Street; (617) 426–6266.* One of the best restaurants in Chinatown. Specializes in seafood, but everything's good. Open daily from 10:00 A.M. to 2:00 A.M. $-$$

Jacob Wirth, *31–37 Stuart Street; (617) 338–8586.* An unexpected treat in the Theater District is Jacob Wirth, a surprisingly genuine German restaurant that has high ceilings and long tables and features a broad menu with weekly specials. Open daily, 11:30 A.M. to 11:00 P.M. $$-$$$

Year-round Performances That Children Enjoy

- **Blue Man Group/Charles Playhouse (ages 6 and up).** *74 Warrentown Street in the Theater District; (617) 426–6912. Schedule varies week to week; call for tickets and schedule (Ticketmaster: 617–931–2787).* $$$$ It's hard to explain this unusual avant-garde production with a little bit of everything (literally) thrown in except to say that it's an enjoyable treat for the whole family. *Warning:* If you sit in the front rows, be sure to wear the raincoats that are provided.

- **Shear Madness/Charles Street Playhouse (ages 5 and up).** *74 Warrentown Street in the Theater District; (617) 426–5225. Call the box office for tickets and schedule.* $$$$ Boston's smash comedy "who done it" is in its nineteenth year. The kids will think that it's awesome that the audience votes on the guilty party and thus influences the play's outcome.

Where to Stay

Le Meridien Boston, *250 Franklin Street; (617) 451–1900 or (800) 543–4300.* Offers 326 nicely appointed rooms, a gourmet restaurant, and a pool club. A big hit with the kids is the Chocolate Buffet at Meridien's Cafe Fleuri every Saturday from 1:00 to 3:00 P.M. September to May. The buffet costs $16.95 for adults, $7.75 for kids. $$$$

Copley Square and the Back Bay

It's hard to imagine now, but until 1857 this part of the city was a smelly tidal flat, fronted by a failed dam, called the Back Bay (Boston itself was actually a peninsula). By the mid-nineteenth century, the city had grown so much that the marshy tidal flats became an advantageous area for expansion and the landfill operation began. When it ended in 1890, the 450-acre area was crisscrossed with Boston's only grid system, and well over 1,000 new buildings had been built to house more people and businesses. While you're in the Back Bay area, be sure to stroll over to Commonwealth Avenue and cross into the green area, called Commonwealth Mall, that runs from the Public Garden to the Fenway. You'll see other families here, mostly locals walking their dogs and stretching their legs. As you walk west (away from the Public Garden), note that the eight streets between here and Massachusetts Avenue are named in alphabetical order: Arlington, Berkeley, Clarendon, Dartmouth, Exeter, Fairfield, Gloucester, and Hereford. The **Boston Convention and Visitor's Bureau** is located at 2 Copley Place, Suite 105; (888) See BOSTON or (617) 536–4100.

JOHN HANCOCK TOWER (all ages)

200 Clarendon Street; (617) 247–1977. Open Monday through Sunday, 9:00 A.M. to 10:00 P.M. Admission: $5.00 for adults, $3.00 for seniors and children 5 to 15.

The Hancock building is a sixty-two-story rhomboid, an unusual shape for a building and one that makes it change in appearance when you see it from different angles. From Copley Square, it's a sharp, slim jab of reflective glass; from downtown, it's a wide mirror for the older Hancock building next to it. The interior of the building is nothing like the exterior; the atmosphere is dreary and rather disappointing. But the real attraction of the tower is at its top. The sixtieth-floor observatory provides stunning views of Boston. Try to go on a clear day, when you may be able to see as far as Vermont.

Pass It On If you're thinking of doing a lot of touring, the **Boston City Pass** includes five sites for one low price: the Hancock Observatory, the Isabella Stuart Gardner Museum, the Museum of Science, the Museum of Fine Arts, and the John F. Kennedy Library. Prices for the Boston City Pass are $26.50 for adults, $20.50 for seniors, and $13.50 for children 12 to 17.

THE BOSTON ATHLETIC ASSOCIATION'S BOSTON MARATHON SITES (all ages)

Finish line on Boylston Street just in front of the Boston Public Library and Copley Square. Open daily. **Free**.

This is the most popular viewing spot during the Boston Marathon's 26-mile Hopkinton to Boston Race; on any day but Patriots Day, you too can cross the finish line. Runners come from all over the world to compete in this prestigious marathon. The Tortoise and the Hare bronze sculptures are in the Copley Square Plaza in front of Trinity Church, a heartbreaking setting for the nonwinners of the race.

THE SKYWALK OBSERVATORY (all ages)

Prudential Tower, 800 Boylston Street, 50th floor; (617) 859–0648. Open 10:00 A.M. through 10:00 P.M. daily. Admission: $4.00 adults, $2.00 for children.

The observatory offers fabulous 360-degree views of Boston. The Top of the Hub Restaurant on the fifty-second floor is open to 1:30 A.M. and is a fantastic place for mealtime views of Boston. The shops and carts below in the Prudential Complex run the gamut from trendy to "old money" conservative.

BOSTON BALLET

19 Clarendon Street; (617) 695–6950.

Boston Ballet is the largest dance center in New England. The Boston Ballet's version of *The Nutcracker* is the most popular in the country; for the best seats, buy your tickets months in advance. One of the rehearsal studios is the same size as the Wang Center stage (where the troupe performs), which is one of the largest stages in the world. (The company also performs at the Shubert Theatre.) Tours are given by advance reservation. *Note:* The **Wang Center** is at 270 Tremont Street and the Shubert Theatre at 265 Tremont Street. Informances, given by the artistic director or the music director prior to the performance, deepen children's understanding and appreciation of the ballet. Call the Boston Ballet for a schedule of Informances. For Boston Ballet tickets, call Telecharge (800–447–7400), purchase online at www.telecharge.com.

NEWBURY STREET SHOPS, ART GALLERIES, AND RESTAURANTS (all ages)

Newbury Street from Arlington Street to Massachusetts Avenue.

Newbury Street is Boston's boutique row. Designers' shops rule the roost here, though there are plenty of other businesses, running the gamut from art galleries to several excellent secondhand clothes shops. Whether or not you enjoy window shopping, it's also a nice street for walking, since the sidewalks are slightly wider and there are lots of sidewalk cafes that will tempt you to rest for a while over a drink or a light meal.

Other Things to See and Do

Boston Public Library, *700 Boylston Street; (617) 536–5400.* Ongoing programs include a kid's cinema, magician performances, and storyteller hours. Call for a schedule.

Trinity Church, *Copley Square; (617) 536–0944.*

Institute of Contemporary Art; *955 Boylston Street; (617) 266–5152.*

F.A.O. Schwarz, *440 Boylston Street; (617) 262–5900.* Extravagant toy and book store.

Waterstone Booksellers, *26 Exeter Street; (617) 859–7300.*

Tower Records/Video, *360 Newbury Street; (617) 247–5900.*

Where to Eat

Hard Rock Cafe, *131 Clarendon Street; (617) 424–7625.* A fun place to have lunch—the burgers are excellent. The souvenir shop sells T-shirts, pins, hats, sweatshirts, and jackets commemorating your visit. Open 11:00 A.M. to midnight Monday through Thursday, 11:00 A.M. to 1:00 A.M. weekends.

Emack and Bolio's, *290 Newbury Street; (617) 247–8772.* This local chain of ice cream shops specializes in unusual homemade flavors. Winter hours are Sunday through Thursday noon to 10:30 P.M., Friday through Saturday noon to 11:00 P.M.; summer hours (May to September) are 11:00 A.M. to midnight daily.

Where to Stay

The Back Bay Hilton, *40 Dalton Street; (617) 236–1100 or (800) 874–0663.* Offers excellent family packages that include discount admission passes to many city attractions (request the discount book), a lending desk of children's books and videos, and a kids' menu in the hotel restaurant and through room service. $$$$

Boston Park Plaza Hotel, *64 Arlington Street; (617) 426–2000 or (800) 225–2008.* A grande dame of a hotel. Family package rates are available. $$$$

Beacon Guest Houses, *248 Newbury Street; (617) 266–7142.* A small, nononsense place that's perfect if you're a self-sufficient type of family. No TVs or room service, but excellent rates and a superb location. Ask about their efficiency apartments. $$$–$$$$

Huntington Avenue to the Fenway

When your family is ready for another bout of museum-hopping (don't do it all in one day or you'll never have the energy for all the don't-miss exhibits), check out the Christian Science Church Campus, the Museum of Fine Arts, and the Isabella Stewart Gardner Museum. Looking for family entertainment instead? Take the kids to a performance of the Boston Pops at Symphony Hall, a baseball game at Fenway Park, or a play at Wheelock Family Theatre.

CHRISTIAN SCIENCE CHURCH (all ages)

175 Huntington Avenue. The Mother Church and the Mapparium (slated to reopen spring 2000) are closed for renovations; call to check opening dates (617–450–2000).

This, the international headquarters of the Christian Science Church, has several buildings of architectural note, including the 1894 Mother Church. The twenty-acre plaza incorporates a long reflecting pool (no wading), with a wonderful circular fountain at its eastern end. But your kids should feel free to pull off their shoes and wade in the fountain's sprinkler; that's what it's there for. The plaza is a great place for the kids to work off any excess energy that they haven't lost during the day. When the kids have satisfied themselves with the delights of running around in the plaza and splashing in the fountain, walk through the passageway between the Colonnade building and the church to the bronze-doored Christian Science Publishing Society (where the *Christian Science Monitor* is published). Inside is the world-famous **Mapparium**. It's a 30-foot glass globe that you can walk into—one of the best geography lessons you'll ever see. The front lawn is a great place for a picnic or a Frisbee toss.

SYMPHONY HALL (ages 5 and up)

301 Massachusetts Avenue; (617) 266–1492.

Home of the Boston Symphony Orchestra (popularly known as the BSO), Symphony Hall is the most acoustically perfect auditorium in the United States. Tours are given as part of the BSO Youth Concert Series during the spring and fall. Plan ahead if you wish to attend the series: The tickets go on sale each spring for the following fall/spring series (call the Youth Activities Office, (617–638–9375). You can get same-day discounted tickets for the BSO Tuesday and Thursday evening performances and the Friday afternoon performance at the rush ticket window: Arrive by 5:00 P.M. on Tuesday and Thursday and by 9:00 A.M. on Friday. To order tickets by phone, call Symphony Charge (617-266-1200 or 888-266-1200); for online orders, check out www.bso.org. A **Free** annual open house in the spring celebrates the BSO and the musical life in Boston. Also, the BSO has **Free** weeklong performances at the Hatch Shell timed around July 4, just before the summer series at Tanglewood.

 ## THE MUSEUM OF FINE ARTS (all ages)

465 Huntington Avenue; (617) 267–9300. The entire museum is open Monday through Sunday, 10:00 A.M. to 5:00 P.M., until 10:00 P.M. on Wednesday, with a voluntary donation for admittance after 4:00 P.M. The West Wing and various other galleries are open on Thursday and Friday from 5:00 to 10:00 P.M. with an admission of $8.00 for adults, $6.00 for seniors and students with ID; **Free** *for children 17 and under. The museum is closed Thanksgiving and Christmas.* **Free** *tours (included with the price of admission) are given Monday through Saturday at various times. General admission: $10.00 for adults, $8.00 for seniors and students,* **Free** *for children 17 and under.*

The Museum of Fine Arts is one of the country's great city museums, holding collections of fine art, antiquities, furniture, silver, and ceramics. Highlights include the Monet collection and the works of Corot, Renoir, Manet, Pissaro, Gauguin, and van Gogh; the famous portraits of Sam Adams and Paul Revere by John Singleton Copley; several excellent portraits by John Singer Sargent; and mummies, altars, and hieroglyphics in the Egyptian rooms (the classical Egyptian collection is the second largest in the world). Don't try to see the museum without a plan; you'll get lost and the kids will get bored. *Tip:* A good idea is to determine a meeting place before exploring the building. The museum is large and complex, and there is no paging system to find stray parents. When you arrive, go, to the Information Center and ask the staff about the day's family-oriented activities (there are usually several). If your family is particularly interested in seeing certain works of art, have a staff member mark the location on a map as well as the shortest way to get there. The museum shop is an excellent source of gifts and souvenirs; allow some time for this. There is a Family Place Program on weekends (like a treasure hunt throughout the museum) geared to kids during the school year.

THE ISABELLA STEWART GARDNER MUSEUM (all ages)

*280 The Fenway; (617) 566–1401. Open Tuesday through Sunday, 11:00 A.M.
to 5:00 P.M.; closed on Thanksgiving and Christmas. Park at the Museum of Fine
Arts garage and lot on Museum Road. There is a guided tour on Friday at 2:30
P.M.; an audio guide on selected pieces is available. The cafe is very popular, as well
as the gift shop. Admission: $10.00 for adults on weekdays and $11.00 on weekends, $7.00 for seniors, $5.00 for students with ID except on Wednesday, when
it's $3.00;* **Free** *for children under 18.*

The museum was once the home of Isabella Stewart Gardner, who
built Fenway Court to house her personal art collection. A New York
native, Gardner shocked Boston with her short-sleeved dresses and her
unorthodox habits (local lore has it that she walked her pet lions down
Beacon Street, on leashes, like poodles; in reality, she never owned
lions). Her legacy to her adopted city is this museum. When Gardner
died in 1924, she left the museum in a public trust. The heart of this
1903 Venetian-style palazzo is a glass-ceilinged, three-story courtyard
that holds a lovely indoor garden. Every painting, sculpture, and piece of
furniture is in the same spot where she chose to place it, nearly a hundred years ago. Much of the art collection is from the Italian Renais-
sance and Dutch seventeenth-century master period, but there are
several fine late-nineteenth-century pieces too, notably the portrait of
Gardner painted by her friend John Singer Sargent and a beautiful small
seascape by James McNeill Whistler. Despite the grandness of the building and the breathtaking art collection, the museum's staff manages to
preserve the museum's origins: Flowers and plants are tastefully placed
throughout the museum, and staff members talk of Gardner as if she
were still in charge. Art-loving families should budget at least two hours
to explore the museum. To keep their interest, suggest to the kids that
they try to spot the animals in many of the paintings and sculptures,
and ask for the "Small Wonders" guide.

FENWAY PARK (ages 3 and up)

*4 Yawkey Way; (617) 267–1700 (tickets), (617) 482–4SOX (touch-tone), or
(617) 267–8661 (information); www.redsox.com. The box office is open from
9:00 A.M. to 5:00 P.M. Ask about discounted family days.*

Fenway Park, home of the Boston Red Sox, is a great place to take in
a ballgame. Even after a recent refurbishment, it's still a bit rickety, but

its size (smallest in the Major League) and genuine old-time charm make it the best place in the country to watch a game. Since you're never far from the field, there's not a bad seat in the house. Opening Day is very popular with Bostonians, who start the season with high hopes for their beloved Red Sox.

JILLIAN'S (ages 7 and up)

145 Ipswich (behind Fenway Park). Open daily to children under 18 until 7:00 P.M. Price: Charges are per game.

The arcade features every high-tech gadget and game to keep your child immersed for hours. This "entertainment mecca" includes 250 video games, virtual reality games, and rides, as well as a 3-D flight sim-ulator. Adult supervision is necessary to rent darts, play Ping-Pong, or use the pool table. Good luck convincing the kids to leave.

WHEELOCK FAMILY THEATRE (all ages)

180 The Riverway; (617) 734–4760. Productions are Friday at 7:30 P.M., Satur-day and Sunday at 3:00 P.M., and selected school matinees. Price: $10 to $15 per person, depending on seat location. Reservations required.

The 650-seat theater has an excellent reputation for unusual produc-tions and nontraditional casting. Musicals and plays are offered from October through May on Friday night and Saturday and Sunday after-noon.

Brookline and Jamaica Plain

Brookline is a separate city in government only; everything else about it is very much part of Boston city life. To the south of Brookline, Jamaica Plain is part of Boston proper.

LARZ ANDERSON PARK AND THE MUSEUM OF TRANSPORTATION (all ages)

 15 Newton Street, Brookline; (617) 522–6547 (Transportation Museum). Open year-round, Tuesday through Sunday, 10:00 A.M. to 5:00 P.M. Closed on major holidays; open on Monday during vacation weeks. Admission: $5.00 for adults, $3.00 for seniors and children 6 to 16; Free *for children under 5.*

A pleasant family outing can be had at **Larz Anderson Park** (a sixty-acre park in Brookline). On the hill behind the Transportation Museum is a wonderful picnic spot that is also one of the best kite-flying hills in Greater Boston. Off to the left at the bottom of the hill are soccer fields and a baseball diamond. Next to the playing fields is a great playground with an unusual seesaw made from old telephone poles. Continue on past the playground down the hill to the duck pond and more choice picnicking sites. Housed in an 1888 carriage house that looks for all the world like a castle, the **Museum of Transportation** (Carriage House, Larz Anderson Park) boasts an impressive collection of restored antique carriages and classic cars. Don't miss the children's activity room with a climb-in car. Held most Sundays from May through October is the Outdoor Lawn Show, which includes bicycles, motorcycles, and automobiles of the past. Family programs are scheduled from January to April on Sundays at 2:00 P.M.

FRANKLIN PARK ZOO (all ages)

Franklin Park, Jamaica Plain; (617) 442–2002. Open October through March from 10:00 A.M. to 4:00 P.M., April through September from 10:00 A.M. to 5:00 P.M. weekdays, 10:00 A.M. to 6:00 P.M. weekends and holidays. Admission: $6.00 for adults, $3.00 for children 2 to 15; admission is **Free** *from 10:00 to 11:00 A.M. Sunday and 9:00 to 10:00 A.M. Tuesday. Call for directions and parking instructions.*

The Tropical Rain Forest, the Australian Outback Trail, the Kalahari Kingdom, and the Savanna Exhibit of Giraffes are the highlights of the seventy-two-acre Franklin Park Zoo, which is undergoing a long-term revitalization program along with the enormous Franklin Park. The three-acre rain forest is the largest of its kind in North America. It holds pygmy hippopotamuses, gorillas, big cats, crocodiles, and thousands of exotic birds. The Children's Zoo has a contact area with farm animals. At the Hooves and Horns area, your children can see zebras, camels, and addax. Special events at the park and the zoo include the Kite Festival at Franklin Park, the third Saturday in May, and Zoo Howl, around Halloween.

THE ARNOLD ARBORETUM (all ages)

125 Arborway, Jamaica Plain; (617) 524–1718. The grounds are open dawn to dusk year-round; the main building is open Monday through Friday 9:00 A.M. to 4:00 P.M., noon to 4:00 P.M. on weekends. **Free**.

Harvard University established the 265-acre Arnold Arboretum in 1872. It was to become the first arboretum in the country. Designed by Frederick Law Olmsted, the arboretum specializes in trees, shrubbery, and vines displayed in a beautiful parklike setting. Two peak visitation times are the spring, when everything is in bloom and the air is heady with the aroma of budding trees and plants, and the autumn, for the vibrant colors. Passive recreational activities that are allowed on the property are cross-country skiing, snowshoeing (no groomed trails), walking, jogging, rollerblading, and biking. Dogs on a leash are allowed, but you are requested to pick up after them. To keep the arboretum pristine, there is no picnicking or food allowed on the grounds.

Other Things to See and Do

Children's Bookshop, *237 Washington Street, Brookline Village; (617) 734–7323.* Appearances by local and famous authors and illustrators.

Boston's Children's Theatre, *647 Boylston Street, Chestnut Hill; (617) 424–6634.*

John F. Kennedy Birthplace National Historic Site, *83 Beals Street, Brookline; (617) 566–7937.*

Puppet Showplace Theatre, *32 Station Street, Brookline; (617) 731–6400.* Puppet workshop held before selected shows.

Where to Eat

J. P. Licks, *659 Centre Street, Jamaica Plain; (617) 524–6740; and 311 Harvard Street, Brookline; (617) 738–8252. Open 11:30 A.M. to midnight year-round.* Great ice cream

Biking in Boston and Cambridge

One of the city's many fine green spaces is the Charles River Reservation (for information call the Metropolitan District Commission (617-727-5250), which borders the Charles, in both Boston and Cambridge, from Science Park all the way up to Harvard. A nice riverside bike ride (too long to walk) begins on the Boston side at the Community Boating boathouse, next to Massachusetts General Hospital. Continue along the riverside area called the Esplanade, which runs below Beacon Hill and the Back Bay, past the Hatch Shell. This is where the Boston Pops perform Free concerts during the summer (the Fourth of July concert and fireworks program regularly attracts half a million people) and, on summer Friday evenings, it's where Free movies are shown (imagine several thousand people gathered on blankets to watch *The Wizard of Oz* outdoors). You'll find several good playgrounds in this area, too. Continue along past the lagoon up to the bridge at Massachusetts Avenue—just to confuse you, this is called the Harvard Bridge (a good spot to view the head of the Charles Regatta). On the Cambridge side, ride along the Charles between MIT and Harvard. On Sundays from April through October, Memorial Drive is closed to auto traffic between the Western Avenue Bridge and the Eliot Bridge. The drive fills with walkers, strollers, bikers, skateboarders, and in-line skaters.

Cambridge

As home to two of the country's most illustrious universities, Harvard and MIT, bustling Cambridge owes much of its vibrancy to the schools' students, faculty, and staff, who are ruthless judges of food, bookstores, museums, art galleries, fashion, film, and the performing arts. As a result, the cultural life in this relatively small city is as good as that in any other city in America. You'll find enough shopping in and around Harvard Square to satisfy the most demanding teenager, and the range of food will thrill everyone. Don't leave Cambridge without walking through Harvard Square (location of the Discovery Information kiosk) and Harvard Yard (the best place to begin a trip to Cambridge), or without driving along Massachusetts Avenue until you reach MIT. These places give you the essence of the flavor of Cambridge. Step down to the Charles River along Memorial Drive and the graceful Weeks Bridge. You'll see the Radcliffe and Harvard boathouses here, and, if you're lucky, a few oarsmen and-women will carry their sculls out to the river while you're watching. Walk along the river, you'll pass the graceful sycamore trees that line Memorial Drive. Do yourself a favor and leave the car in a garage; parking is nearly impossible to find, and if you're lucky enough to find a spot, you'll have to keep running back to feed quarters into the meter (Cambridge meter maids have a sixth sense about every meter that runs out, and they are impervious to protests). For tourist information on Cambridge, contact **Cambridge Visitor's Information,** 18 Brattle Street (617-441-2884).

Let Me Entertain You
The street entertainers in Harvard Square are easy on the pocketbook (they depend on tips from the crowd) and diverse. Performing in the wide pedestrian area between Brattle and Mt. Auburn Streets, they offer a range of acts that can be pretty good (tell the kids that this is where singer Tracy Chapman got her start). On a warm afternoon it's nice to sit on the low brick walls, have a snack, and let the street life entertain the family for a while.

HARVARD MUSEUM OF NATURAL HISTORY (all ages)

26 Oxford Street; (617) 495–3045; www.hmnh.harvard.edu. Open Monday through Saturday 9:00 A.M. to 5:00 P.M., Sunday 1:00 to 5:00 P.M. Admission: $5.00 for adults, $4.00 for seniors and students, and $3.00 for children 3 to 13.

This is the umbrella name for the Museum of Comparative Zoology (with taxidermied animals from all over the world and dinosaur fossils and skeletons), the Botanical Museum (with the world-renowned Blaschka glass flowers), and the Mineralogical and Geological Museum (a varied and in-depth collection of gemstones and meteors). The Peabody Museum of Archeology and Ethnology is across the street and has some interesting totem poles and peace pipes.

*B*ookstore-hopping in Harvard Square

- **Wordsworth,** 1 JFK Street; (617) 498-0062.

- **Harvard BookShop,** 1256 Massachusetts Avenue; (617) 661-1515.

- **The Boston Globe Store,** Church and Palmer Streets; (617) 497-6277. An annex of the downtown shop, which specializes in travel books.

- **Schoenhof's,** 6A Mt. Auburn Street; (617) 547-8855. For foreign language books.

- **Starr Book Company,** 29 Plympton; (617) 547-6864. Used books and great atmosphere (it's in the funky building that houses the *Harvard Lampoon* offices).

MT. AUBURN CEMETERY (all ages)

580 Mt. Auburn Street; (617) 547–7105. The main gate is open from 8:00 A.M. to 5:00 P.M. seven days a week. The Green House is open from 8:00 A.M. to 3:30 P.M. Monday through Friday, 9:00 A.M. to 1:00 P.M. Saturday. The office is open Monday through Friday 8:30 A.M. to 4:30 P.M., Saturday from 8:30 A.M. to 12:30 P.M. **Free**.

Mt. Auburn Cemetery may sound like a strange place for a family outing, but when you arrive there, you'll see why so many Cambridge and Boston families make this a weekend destination: Its 174 acres are planted with 1,000 varieties of trees, shrubs, flowers, and other plants. This was the first garden cemetery in America when it was founded in 1831; the best time to visit is during the spring, when it seems as though every plant is in bloom. Stop at the office at the main gate for a map, and ask about the day's special activities and horticultural tours. Mt. Auburn Cemetery includes the resting places of Henry Wadsworth Longfellow, Isabella Stewart Gardner, and Winslow Homer.

MIT MUSEUM (all ages)

265 Massachusetts Avenue; (617) 253–4444. Open Tuesday through Friday 10:00 A.M. to 5:00 P.M., Saturday and Sunday noon to 5:00 P.M.; closed Monday and holidays. Admission: $3.00 for adults, and $1.00 for students and seniors.

The museum offers family programs the last Sunday of every month from 2:00 to 4:00 P.M. (the Sunday we were there students were racing robots that they had designed and built). It has a fantastic holographic collection from the 1940s to the present, a Mathspace, 3-D sculptures, and interactive exhibits.

MUSEUM OF SCIENCE CAMPUS

Science Park; (617) 723–2500; www.mos.org. The campus is closed on Thanksgiving and Christmas.

The museum campus consists of the **Museum of Science,** the **Hayden Planetarium,** the **Omni Theater,** and the **Laser Show.** If you want to see the museum exhibits as well as other attractions, you'll have to buy combination tickets. Buy your Omni tickets early, since it often sells out quickly, especially on winter weekends. If you get hungry, check out the cafe, and pizza and burger stations on the main floor.

MUSEUM OF SCIENCE (all ages)

Open from Memorial Day through Labor Day, Monday through Thursday and Saturday and Sunday 9:00 A.M. to 7:00 P.M., Friday 9:00 A.M. to 9:00 P.M.; between Labor Day and Memorial Day, Monday through Thursday and Saturday and Sunday, 9:00 A.M. to 5:00 P.M., Friday 9:00 A.M. to 9:00 P.M. Admission: $9.00 for adults, $7.00 for seniors and children 3 to 11; Free *for children under 3.*

Straddling a dam at the mouth of the Charles River, the Museum of Science deserves its reputation as a favorite field trip for Boston-area school kids. The museum is enormous, with more than 600 interactive exhibits; bring a stroller if you have toddlers. Young kids may not want to leave the Discovery Center, which was designed (and recently renovated) with them in mind. Other favorite exhibits include the Transparent Woman, which lights up to display organs; the Live Animal Show; and the Special Effects Stage, where, with the help of audiovisual technology, you can fly over Boston or walk on the moon.

THE MUGAR OMNI THEATER (all ages)

For a schedule of films, call (617) 333–FILM. Admission: $7.50 for adults, $5.50 for seniors and children 3 to 11.

The five-story theater has stadium seating, digital screens, and Surround Sound. The fifty-minute films are extremely realistic and can cause motion sickness or acrophobia. Tell your kids to close their eyes if something is upsetting to them.

HAYDEN PLANETARIUM (Not recommended for ages 4 and under)

Call for a schedule. Admission: $7.50 for adults, $5.50 for children.

Forty-five-minute presentations give you an introduction to the stars.

LASER LIGHT SHOW (all ages)

Open Thursday through Sunday nights. Admission: $7.50 for adults, $5.50 for seniors and children 3 to 11.

Laser light show set to rock music.

Harvard Art Museums

All museums are open Monday through Saturday 10:00 A.M. to 5:00 P.M. Admission is $5.00 for adults, Free for children under 18. Saturday mornings and all-day Wednesday are Free. Phone: (617) 495–9400.

- **Arthur M. Sackler,** *485 Broadway Street.* Art of Asia, the Mideast, and India.

- **Busch-Reisinger Museum,** *32 Quincy Street.* Central and Northern European art.

- **The Fogg,** *32 Quincy Street.* French and Italian art.

Other Things to See and Do

Cybersmith, *42 Church Street (Harvard Square); (617) 492–5857.* High-tech games intermingled with virtual reality pods

Longfellow National Historic Site, *105 Brattle Street; (617) 876–4491.* Home of poet Henry Wadsworth Longfellow while he taught at Harvard and former headquarters of George Washington.

Minuteman Bikeway Trail, *start at Alewife "T" stop in Cambridge; (617) 727–3180.* Ten-and-a-half-mile bike/hike trail from Cambridge through Arlington to Lexington.

Where to Shop

Jasmine and Sola, 37 Brattle Street; (617) 354–6043. Excellent clothing.

Urban Outfitters, 11 John F. Kennedy Street; (617) 864–0070. For clotheshound teenagers.

HMV, 1 Brattle Street; (617) 868–9696. An enormous music store with an especially good selection of classical and jazz recordings.

LearningSmith, 5 Brattle Street; (617) 661–6008. One of the most innovative toy/book/gadget stores you'll ever see; just try to leave without playing with something.

Serendipity, 1312 Massachusetts Avenue; (617) 661–7143. Teenage girls' shopping.

Oona's Experienced Clothing, 1210 Massachusetts Avenue; (617) 491–2654. One of Cambridge's best secondhand stores.

The Garment District, 200 Broadway in Kendall Square; (617) 876–5230. Used and vintage clothing of the 1960s and '70s.

Cambridgeside Galleria, 100 Cambridgeside Place; (617) 621–8666. Shopping plaza.

Where to Eat

Bartley's Burger Cottage, 1246 Massachusetts Avenue; (617) 354–6559. Features burgers and other simple fare. Students congregate here for the large helpings and low prices. $

Full Moon, 344 Huron Avenue; (617) 354–6699. A Parent's Paper award-winning choice: great food, children's menu, a kids' play space, and special events and lectures on child raising. $-$$.

Herrell's Ice Cream, 15 Dunster Street; (617) 497–2179. Opened by Steve Herrell after he sold his wildly successful chain, Steve's. $

Red Bones, 55 Chester Street in Somerville; (617) 628–2200. Real southern barbecue. $-$$

Where to Stay

The Charles Hotel, 1 Bennett Street; (617) 864–1200 or (800) 882–1818. Great location near Harvard Square; indoor heated lap pool (special children's hours), children's bedtime story line, and children's menu. $$$$

The Royal Sonesta, 5 Cambridge Parkway; (617) 491–3600 or (800) SONESTA. Across from the Cambridgeside Galleria and near the Museum of Science Campus. Ice cream is served in the lobby, bicycles can be requested from guest services (no fee charged), and you can sign up for boat rides on the Charles River. $$$$

Charlestown

Charlestown has reinvented itself in the last twenty years and the cornerstone has been both the Charlestown Navy Yard (with its crown jewel, the USS *Constitution*) and the Bunker Hill Monument and Museum. The lovely brownstone homes off City Square Park have been snapped up by the economically successful set. *A heads-up warning:* Streets and directions change at a fast pace here, with the Big Dig project (see page 113) happening right in Charlestown's backyard.

THE CHARLESTOWN NAVY YARD (all ages)

Constitution Road; (617) 242–5601 (visitors center) or (617) 426–1812 (Constitution Museum). The USS Constitution *is open daily from 9:30 A.M. to sunset (tours stop at 3:30 P.M.).* **Free***. The USS* Cassin Young *is open from 10:00 A.M. to 4:00 P.M. winter, 10:00 A.M. to 5:00 P.M. summer.* **Free***. The Constitution Museum is open September through mid-May from 10:00 A.M. to 5:00 P.M., summer from 9:00 A.M. to 7:00 P.M.* **Free***.*

The Charlestown Navy Yard is an on-site memorial to the thousands of warships that were built here between 1800 and 1974. The highlight is a visit to the **USS *Constitution.*** "Old Ironsides," as it's known (for its resilience rather than its materials; it's an all-wood ship), began its service in 1797; it's still commissioned, though it leaves the dock only once a year for a turnaround so that it ages evenly. The tour of the triple-decked ship, given by navy crew members, runs approximately twenty-five minutes and is well worth planning for (try to arrive early in the day to avoid being part of a too-large group). To orient you to the Navy Yard, start at the **Visitor's Center/Bookstore.** Don't miss the **Constitution Museum;** the wonderful **playground at Shipyard Park** (beyond the Constitution Museum), which features a shiplike climbing structure; and the **USS *Cassin Young,*** decommissioned in 1960, representing the ships that were produced at the Charleston Navy Yard.

BUNKER HILL MONUMENT AND MUSEUM (all ages)

Monument Square; call the National Park Visitor's Center at the Charlestown Navy Yard at (617) 242–5601. The monument is open daily from 9:00 A.M. to 5:00 P.M.; closed Thanksgiving, Christmas, and New Year's Day. **Free***. The museum is open from 9:00 A.M. to 5:00 P.M.* **Free***.*

In the center of Charlestown, the Bunker Hill Monument rises from the spot where, in June 1775, Colonel William Prescott or General Israel Putnam (there is some controversy over who uttered this famous phrase) told his revolutionary militia, "Don't fire until you see the whites of their eyes." As most schoolchildren know, the British eventually won the battle, but not until they had lost well over 1,000 soldiers to Prescott's forces; the battle was an effective morale booster to the revolutionaries in the early days of the war. Climb the grassy hill, which is actually called Breed's Hill (the Bunker part of the name comes from the bunker that the colonists built atop the hill), to reach the base of the monument. (Be forewarned: There are 295 winding steps, about a fifteen-minute climb, not an appropriate ascent for younger kids or for parents who don't want to carry them most of the way.) The museum at the monument's base has good dioramas of the battle and a toy soldier display. A park ranger is available for talks on request.

Other Things to See and Do

The Red Wagon, 26 Common Street; (617) 242–7402. Designer kid labels at budget prices.

Where to Eat

Barrett's Restaurant on Boston Harbor, 2 Constitution Plaza; (617) 242–9600. Outdoor deck gives whopping views of the harbor, the USS Cassin Young, and the USS Constitution. Serving lunch, dinner, and Sunday brunch. $-$$$

Fig's, 67 Main Street; (617) 242–2229. A trendy spot that serves creative pizzas and pasta dishes. $$

Dorchester

Columbia Point has the showcase John F. Kennedy Library, the University of Massachusetts Boston campus, and the Commonwealth Museum, with views of the Boston Harbor and skyline. Close by are the offices of the Boston Globe and the Bayside Exposition Site. The area can be somewhat daunting for walking (especially at night); a car is best here.

JOHN F. KENNEDY LIBRARY AND MUSEUM (age 4 and up)
*Columbia Point; (617) 929–4500. Open daily from 9:00 A.M. to 5:00 P.M.;
closed Thanksgiving, Christmas, and New Year's Day. Admission: $8.00 for
adults, $6.00 for seniors and students with ID, $4.00 for children 13 to 17;*
Free *for children under 12.* **Free** *to everyone President's Day and JFK's
birthday (May 29th).*

The John F. Kennedy Library and Museum is the busiest of all the
presidential libraries. The library itself is rarely visited by tourists, however; for most visitors the attraction here is the museum's excellent exhi-
bition program about JFK and his brother Robert, complete with
reminiscences taped by several close friends of the Kennedy clan. Other
exhibits of interest include the famous televised tour of the newly redec-
orated White House by Jacqueline Bouvier Kennedy and a mock White
House Cabinet room with documents and pictures of Kennedy and civil
rights leaders of the 1960s. The building itself, designed by I. M. Pei and
completed in 1979, remodeled and rededicated in 1993, is an extraordi-
nary sight from the expressway: Its sweeping shape captures JFK's love of
the ocean and of sailing. Combine a trip to the JFK Museum with a tour
of the *Boston Globe.*

BOSTON GLOBE (must be at least 12)

*135 Morrissey Boulevard; (617) 929–2653. Sixty-minute tours are given on Tues-
day and Thursday.* Note: *Reservations should be made at least two weeks in
advance, since tour sizes are limited to thirty people.* **Free**.

Start your tour with a ten-minute film depicting the daily workings of
a newspaper. Then find out what's involved in publishing a daily paper;
see the room where the presses roll (the *Globe* is published at night),
check out the newsroom and the advertising and classified departments,
and ask lots of questions.

Other Things to See and Do

Dorchester Heights Monument,
Thomas Park (617) 242–5642. Site of
General George Washington's first vic-
tory over the British.

Commonwealth Museum, 220 Morrissey Boulevard, Columbia Point
(between UMass and the Kennedy
Library); (617) 727–9268. History of
different industries and the labor that
supplied the workforce.

Quincy and Milton

Just a few miles south of Boston proper is Quincy, which has the unique claim to fame of being both the birthplace and the burial place of two U.S. presidents: John Adams, the second president, and his son, John Quincy Adams, the sixth president. Milton is home to Milton Academy, one of the preeminent private secondary schools in this country. Milton is close to Boston and is more of a bedroom community.

ADAMS NATIONAL HISTORIC SITE

135 Adams Street, Quincy; (617) 773–1177. Open daily mid-April through mid-November 9:00 A.M. to 5:00 P.M. Admission: $2.00. Note: You can visit the birth-places only as part of a guided tour, which lasts about two and a half hours. A **Free** *trolley from the Visitor Center goes to the birthplaces and the Old House.*

The Adams National Historic Site, run by the National Park Service, is the house and gardens of the Adams family. When John and Abigail Adams moved here in 1787, fifty-six years after the house was built, there were only seven rooms. As their fortune grew, they expanded the house until it had twenty rooms. Of special note here are the library, with its 14,000 volumes in twelve languages, and the study where John Adams died on July 4, 1826, fifty years to the day after the Declaration of Independence was signed. Here also are the small saltbox houses where the Adams presidents were born (1250 Hancock Street, Quincy; (617) 770-1175).

UNITED FIRST PARISH CHURCH (all ages)

1306 Hancock Street, Quincy; (617) 773–1290.

This church holds the remains of the two Adams presidents and their wives.

BLUE HILLS RESERVATION AND BLUE HILLS TRAILSIDE MUSEUM (all ages)

Hillside Street, Milton; (617) 333–0069, (617) 698–1802, or (617) 727–1300. **Free***; call for hours and prices for downhill skiing at Blue Hill Ski Mountain (781–828–7490 or 781–828–7490).*

The Blue Hills Reservation and State Park is operated and managed by both the Massachusetts Audobon Society and the Metropolitan District Commission (MDC).

The Blue Hills Trailside Natural History Museum at the foot of Blue Hill has a collection of live native animals and offers a natural history program. The reservation allows hiking, biking, horseback riding, boating; picnicking, swimming, fishing, cross-country, and downhill skiing. There are programs such as maple sugaring and hayrides; ask at the visitor center.

Other Things to See and Do

Quincy Quarries Historic Site,
Riccciuti Drive, Quincy; (617) 698–1802.

Where to Eat

La Paloma, *195 Newport Avenue;
(617) 773–9512.* Voted "Best Mexican Restaurant" in the metropolitan Boston area. Open Tuesday through Saturday 11:30 A.M. to 10:00 P.M., Sunday 3:00 to 9:00 P.M. Closed Monday. $-$$

West of Boston

Just a few miles to the northwest of Cambridge are the historic towns of Lexington and Concord. The "shot heard round the world" was fired in Lexington, and the subsequent first battles of the Revolutionary War were fought there and in Concord. During the nation's first century, Concord attracted thinkers and writers such as Nathaniel Hawthorne, Ralph Waldo Emerson, Louisa May Alcott, and Henry David Thoreau, whose homes are now open to the public. Thoreau's beloved Walden Pond is a terrific spot to learn a little about Thoreau or to picnic, sun, and swim. The DeCordova Museum and Sculpture Park is another great picnic spot as well as an innovative contemporary art museum in Lincoln. Waltham is still the home of several industries, although the emphasis now is on high tech. Acton, Framingham, and Natick still manage to maintain open spaces and promote family activities. For more information, contact the Lexington Chamber of Commerce and Visitor Information, 1875 Massachusetts Avenue (781-862-2480), and the Concord Chamber of Commerce, 2 Lexington Road (978-369-3120).

LEXINGTON BATTLE GREEN/LEXINGTON VISITOR CENTER

1875 Massachusetts Avenue, Lexington; (781) 862–1450. **Free**.

Battle Green is the site of the first battle of the American Revolution. The visitor center has a diorama of the battle as well as an interesting display of recently excavated artifacts.

MUSEUM OF OUR NATIONAL HERITAGE (all ages)

33 Marrett Road (Route 2A), Lexington; (781) 861–6559. Open daily. **Free**.

Exhibits on American history and culture.

MINUTE MAN NATIONAL HISTORICAL PARK (all ages)

Battle Road, Route 2A, Lexington/Lincoln line; (781) 862–7753. Open daily from 9:00 A.M. to 4:00 P.M. **Free**.

Minute Man National Historical Park extends along Battle Road from Lexington to Lincoln to Concord. It was established to commemorate the events that took place along the winding, hilly road on April 19, 1775. Stop at the visitor center for an excellent twenty-five-minute multimedia presentation that will orient you to the history and sights of the area. There's a nice 1-mile walk (follow the markers) to the ruins of the Fiske House, a farmhouse that was in the midst of the battle area.

Path of Glory

The **Minuteman Bike Path** is a fun way to travel from northern **Cambridge through Arlington, Lexington, and Bedford.** It's a 10.5-mile path that begins at the Alewife station in Cambridge (the northernmost stop on the Red Line) and follows some unused railroad tracks, ending in suburban Bedford. For more information about this trail and others in the Boston area, contact the Department of Environmental Management, 100 Cambridge Street, Boston 02202 (617–727–3180).

OLD NORTH BRIDGE/OLD NORTH BRIDGE VISITOR CENTER (all ages)

Monument Street (old North Bridge), and 171 Liberty Street (Visitor Center), Concord; (978) 369–6993.

Begin your trip to Concord at the Old North Bridge. This is the spot where the "shot heard round the world" was fired. The current bridge is actually the fifth reproduction since the historic event. Nearby (a ten-minute walk) is the North Bridge Visitor Center on Liberty Street. Park rangers answer questions at the center and also offer good presentations at the bridge itself (from June to October, daily; spring and fall, weekends only; winter, by advance request only).

ORCHARD HOUSE (all ages)

399 Lexington Road, Concord; (978) 369–4118. Open from April through December, Monday through Saturday, 10:00 A.M. to 4:30 P.M., Sunday, 1:00 to 4:30 P.M.; November through March, Saturday 10:00 A.M. to 4:30 P.M., Sunday 1:00 to 4:30 P.M. Admission: $5.50 for adults, $4.50 for seniors and students with ID, $3.50 for children 6 to 18, **Free** *for children 6 and under. Family rates are available.*

Near the middle of Concord is the home of *Little Women* author Louisa May Alcott and her family. The house is remarkably homey and informal; there are no ropes or fences, and there are enough recognizable items on view to make Alcott's fans feel as though she and her sisters have just left the room. Be sure to take the tour here.

SLEEPY HOLLOW CEMETERY (all ages)

Bedford Street and Court Lane, Route 62, Concord.

Remains of Ralph Waldo Emerson, Henry David Thoreau, Nathaniel Hawthorne, Louisa May Alcott, Daniel Chester French, Ephraim Wales Bull (developer of the Concord grape), and Elizabeth Peabody (founder of the kindergarten movement), among other notables.

GREAT MEADOWS NATIONAL WILDLIFE REFUGE(all ages)

Monson Road/Concord; headquarters and visitor center on Weir Hill Road/Sudbury; (978) 443–4661. Trails are open dawn to dusk year-round. **Free**.

Walking trails for bird-watching and hiking along pools, rivers, and uplands. Environmental and educational programs can be set up for groups.

WALDEN POND STATE RESERVATION (all ages)

Route 126, Concord; (508) 369–3284. Open daily; seasonal hours. Price: $2.00 parking fee in the summer; rest of the year by donation.

Walden Pond can be a crowded place, especially when the water is warm enough for swimming. It's best to come here in the off-season; otherwise, it's hard to imagine the peace that Thoreau found when he lived here alone. His cabin was taken down long ago, but in its place is a large pile of rocks that visitors have placed here as a simple tribute.

Ungroomed trails for cross-country and snowshoeing, canoeing, fishing, and kayaking are allowed on Walden Pond. No pets.

DISCOVERY MUSEUMS: CHILDREN'S DISCOVERY MUSEUM (under age 10) AND SCIENCE DISCOVERY MUSEUM (ages 6 and up)

177 Main Street, Acton; (978) 264–4201 or (978) 264–4222 (storyphone); www.ultanet.com/-discover/. Open Tuesday, Thursday, and Friday 1:00 to 4:30 P.M., Wednesday 9:00 A.M. to 6:00 P.M., Saturday and Sunday 9:00 A.M. to 4:30 P.M. Admission: $6.00 per museum or $9.00 for both, children under 1 get in Free.

The **Children's Discovery Museum** encourages touch and exploration. A favorite is the Water Discovery exhibit, where kids can create huge bubbles and play with water. The Duplo Room is Lego paradise; the Discovery Ship, located in the attic of the Victorian house, is great fun for improvisations of walking the plank. Interactive exhibits throughout the Science Discovery Museum encourage hands-on experimentation and invention. Children particularly enjoy the Inventor's Workshop woodworking shop.

DECORDOVA MUSEUM AND SCULPTURE PARK (all ages)

Sandy Pond Road, Lincoln; (781) 259–8355. Open year-round, Tuesday through Sunday, 11:00 A.M. to 5:00 P.M. The cafe is open daily from 11:00 A.M. to 4:00 P.M. Admission to the gallery: $4.00; Free *admission to the sculpture park.*

Housed in the castlelike brick mansion of a wealthy, early-twentieth-century Boston businessman, the DeCordova Museum is dedicated to promoting appreciation of contemporary art by American artists, particularly those working in the New England area. An ambitious schedule of exhibitions attracts a large, loyal audience. Outdoors on the museum's beautiful grounds, the sculpture park features permanent and temporary sculptures, some of which are musical and most of which will intrigue the kids. A fine concert series called Art in the Park is held in the outdoor amphitheater the second Sunday in June. Check the museum for a schedule of events.

DRUMLIN FARM (all ages)

South Great Road, South Lincoln; (781) 259–9807. Open year-round, Tuesday through Sunday and on Monday holidays (except Thanksgiving, Christmas, and New Year's Day), 9:00 A.M. to 5:00 P.M. Admission: $6.00 for adults, $4.00 for seniors and children 3 to 12, and Free *for children under 3.*

Drumlin Farm is a magnet for Boston-area families with young children. It's the headquarters of the Massachusetts Audubon Society as well as a "demonstration farm," which means that the exhibits are built around what you might find on a typical New England farm: kitchen gardens, flower gardens, meadows, ponds, and, of course, lots of animals, including cows, pigs, horses, birds, and forest creatures. Excellent kid-oriented demonstrations, discussions, and walks are given on weekends at 11:00 A.M. and 2:00 P.M. *Note:* Picnicking is allowed in designated areas only; no dogs allowed. Special programming includes in-season sleigh rides and hayrides for $1.00 and maple sugaring from mid-February through March.

Marcia's Top Annual Events
in Greater Boston

- **Chinese New Year,** late January or early February, Chinatown, Boston; (617) 536–4100

- **New England Boat Show,** February, Bayside Exposition Center, Boston; (617) 536–4100

- **New England Flower Show,** March, Bayside Exposition Center, Boston; (617) 536–9280 or (617) 474–6000

- **Saint Patrick's Day Parade,** March 17, South Boston; (617) 536–4100

- **Boston Marathon,** Patriots Day (the Third Monday in April), Hopkinton to Boston; (617) 236–1652

- **Paul Revere and Billy Dawes' Ride Reenactment,** Patriots Day, Lexington; (781) 862–1450

- **Battle of Lexington and Concord Reenactment,** Patriots Day, Lexington; (781) 862–1450

- **Big Apple Circus,** April, Boston; (617) 426–8855

- **Ducklings Day,** Mother's Day, Boston Public Garden; (617) 426–1885

- **Lilac Sunday,** May, Arnold Arboretum, Jamaica Plain; (617) 524-1718

- **Kite Festival,** May, Franklin Park, Jamaica Plain; (617) 442-2000

- **Dragon Boat Festival,** June, Charles River near Harvard; (617) 441-2884

- **Bunker Hill Day,** June 17, Charlestown; (617) 242-5628

- **Boston Globe Jazz and Blues Festival,** June, Newbury Street; (617) 267-2224

- **Art in the Park,** June, DeCordova Museum, Lincoln; (781) 259-8355

- **Harborfest,** July, Boston; (617) 227-1528

- **Feste (Saint's Festival),** nearly every weekend in July and August, North End; (617) 536-4100

- **Boston Pops Fourth of July Concert,** July 4, Esplanade, Boston; (617) 536-4100

- **USS *Constitution* Turnaround,** July 4, Charlestown Navy Yard, Charlestown; (617) 242-5601

- **U.S. Pro Tennis Championship,** August, Longwood Tennis Club, Chestnut Hill; (617) 731-2900

- **Art Newbury Street,** September, Boston; (617) 267-7961 or (617) 267-2224

- **Head of the Charles Regatta,** October, Charles River Cambridge/Boston; (617) 864-8415

- *The Nutcracker,* November through early January, Boston Ballet, Boston; (617) 482-9393 or (800) 447-7400

- **Christmas Tree Lighting,** late November, Prudential Center, Boston

- **Black Nativity,** December; (617) 442-8614

- **Boston Tea Party Reenactment,** December, Old South Meeting House to Boston Harbor; (617) 338-1773

- **Newbury Street Holiday Stroll,** December; (617) 267-2224

- **First Night,** December 31, Boston; (617) 542-1399

LONGFELLOW'S WAYSIDE INN (all ages)
72 Boston Post Road, Sudbury; (978) 443–1776.

The historic Longfellow's Wayside Inn is a pleasant place to spend a night. The red clapboard building, the oldest operating inn in the country, was built in 1702; the Ford Foundation bought it and renovated it in the early 1920s. There are ten guest rooms, two of them (original to the house) reached by a narrow staircase, all with private bath. The dining room serves lunch, and dinner (reservations required for dinner). On the Wayside Inn's one-hundred-acre grounds is the Red Schoolhouse, famous as the school that Mary and her little lamb attended; the Ford Foundation moved the building here from nearby Sterling, Massachusetts, during the 1920s renovation project (the schoolhouse is open daily April through November, weather permitting, noon to 5:00 P.M.).

GARDEN IN THE WOODS/NEW ENGLAND WILDFLOWER SOCIETY (all ages)
180 Hemenway Road, Framingham; (508) 877–6574. Open daily April 15 through June 15, 9:00 A.M. to 5:00 P.M. (until 7:00 P.M. in May); June 16 through October 31, Tuesday through Sunday 9:00 A.M. to 5:00 P.M. (last admission one hour before closing). Admission: $6.00 for adults, $5.00 for seniors, $3.00 for children 6 to 16.

Largest landscaped collection of wildflowers in New England spread over 45 acres. Over 1,600 plants, including more than 200 rare species. Informal tours at 10:00 A.M.

FOXBORO STADIUM
Route 1, Foxboro; (508) 543–0350, (617) 931–2000 or (800) 543–1776 for tickets.

Home to both the New England Revolution and the New England Patriots. Venue site for concerts and special events.

THE NEW ENGLAND PATRIOTS
Foxboro Stadium, Route 1, Foxboro; (508) 543–0350 or (800) 543–1776 for tickets.

New England's professional football team. The team has been threatening to relocate.

THE NEW ENGLAND REVOLUTION

Foxboro Stadium, Route 1, Foxboro; (508) 543–0350 or(877) GET REV for tickets.

Professional soccer team that has a growing following.

Other Things to See and Do

Beaver Brook Reservation, *Mill Street, Waltham; (617) 484–6357.*

Cochituate State Park, *Route 30, Natick; (508) 653–9641.*

Girl Scout Museum at Cedar Hill, *Patriots' Trail Girl Scout Council, 265 Beaver Street; (781) 891–8717.*

Great Brook Farm State Park, *Lowell Road, Carlisle; (978) 686–3391.*

Old Manse, *Monument Street, Concord; (978) 369–3909.* Trustees of Reservations Property, historical sight.

Waverly Oaks Playground, *Trapelo Road, Belmont; (617) 727–5380.* Spraying fountains and pool, climbing structures, picnic tables, and hiking trails.

Historic Haunts (ghost walks), *Concord Center; (978) 369–1890.* Open mid-April through October, reservations required.

South River Boat House, *496 Main Street/Route 62, Concord; (978) 369–9438 or (978) 371–2465.* Canoe and rowboat rentals, lunch and dinner service on a pontoon boat.

Charles River Museum of Industry, *154 Moody Street, Waltham; (781) 893–5410.* Open Monday through Saturday, 10:00 A.M. to 5:00 P.M. Explores the textile, watch (the Waltham Watch Company had an international reputation), bicycles, automobile, and tool industries.

Gore Place, *52 Gore Street, Waltham; (781) 894–2798.* Open mid-April through mid-November, Tuesday through Saturday, from 11:00 A.M. to 4:00 P.M. A historic mansion, farm, and gardens spread over forty-five acres. Small animal farm.

Cardinal Spellman Philatelic Museum, *235 Wellesley Street, Weston; (781) 894–6735.* Open Thursday through Sunday noon to 5:00 P.M. Admission: $5.00 for adults; Free for children 16 and under. Three million stamps from all over the world. Features a children's activities center, museum store, post office,and library.

Where to Eat

Mario's Italian Restaurant, *1733 Massachusetts Avenue; (781) 861–1182.* Family-style restaurant serving pasta and pizza. $–$$

Michael's Restaurant, *Route 117, Concord; (978) 371–1114.* Specializing in Italian dishes. $$

Rain Forest Cafe, *Burlington Mall, Burlington; (781) 272–7555.* You don't need raingear to eat here, but there are thunderstorms every twenty minutes, waterfalls, electronic jungle animals, and fish tanks. $-$$

Vinnie Testa's, *20 Waltham Street; (781) 860–5200.* Huge portions, laid-back family atmosphere, and great Italian food. $-$$

Walden Grill, *24 Walden Street, Concord; (978) 371–2233.* Casual atmosphere, Mediterranean dishes. $$

Where to Stay

Battle Green Motor Inn, *720 Massachusetts Avenue, Lexington; (781) 862–6100.* Family-style motel just down the street from the Battle Green; heated swimming pool and **Free** continental breakfast. $$-$$$

Colonial Inn, *48 Monument Square, Concord; (978) 369–9200.* On National Register of Historic Hotels; rumored to have one haunted room, which they don't rent out without the consent of the earthbound client. Close to sights, shopping, and restaurants in charming Concord Center. $$$$

Doubletree Guest Suites, *550 Winter Street, Waltham; (781) 890–6767 or (800) 222–TREE.* Indoor pool and sauna, game room, cookies at check-in, and kid's menu. $$$$.

Plymouth and the South Shore

More than a million tourists pass through "America's Hometown" each year, and for good reason. The *Mayflower II,* Plymouth Rock, and Plimoth Plantation tell the well-known story of our country's first permanent European settlers vividly, with only minor embellishments. Of the many tourist attractions that are packed into this tiny town, the rock, the boat, and the outdoor museum are by far the most interesting to kids. If you can, try to visit Plymouth during the spring or late fall—Thanksgiving is best, of course—when there are fewer tour buses. Also of interest in the area are New Bedford and Fall River, which were whaling capitals and leaders in the maritime industry. For more information, contact the Plymouth County Convention and Visitors Bureau (800–231–1620; www.Plymouth-1620.com) and the Bristol County Convention and Visitors Bureau (800–288–6263; www.bristol-county.org).

Marcia's Top Family Adventures
in Plymouth and the South Shore

1. Plimoth Plantation, Plymouth

2. *Mayflower II,* Plymouth

3. Duxbury Beach, Marshfield/Duxbury

4. New Bedford Whaling Museum, New Bedford

5. Battleship Cove and the Fall River Carousel, Fall River

6. Horseneck State Beach, Westport

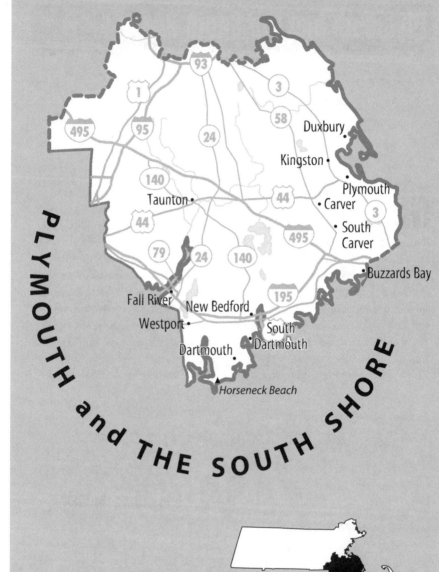

PLYMOUTH and THE SOUTH SHORE

Duxbury

Kingston

Plymouth

Carver

Taunton

South
Carver

Buzzards Bay

Fall River

New Bedford

Westport

South
Dartmouth

Dartmouth

Horseneck Beach

Hull, Hingham, and Northern Plymouth County

Shaped like an elbow, the west side of Hull has a commanding view of Boston Harbor and the Boston Harbor Islands, as does the neighboring more high-brow town of Hingham. World's End in Hingham was designed by Frederick Law Olmsted and is a calming respite after an active week. Lots of activities for families in this area are water-based fun. Try a canoe ride down the North River or a cruise to one of the Boston Harbor Islands.

NANTASKET BEACH (all ages)

Nantasket Avenue; (888) 925–HULL; www.Nantasket.com. Open year-round; $2.00 parking fee.

Seven miles of clear water and clean beach will attract your family, as will a vintage carousel (on Wharf Avenue) with hand-turned horses and chariots. Waterfront activities include a concert series, a Hull Heritage Days Festival, and the annual September Chowderfest. There is a new bathhouse, and the beach area has been restored.

WOMPATUCK STATE PARK AND WORLD'S END RESERVATION (all ages)

Off Route 228, Hingham; (781) 749–7160. Open daily dawn to dusk. Admission: $2.00.

Wompatuck State Park covers some 3,500 acres and offers over 400 campsites (some with trailer hookups) and shower facilities. Biking paths are threaded throughout the park, and there is a boat ramp for boating fun. Other popular forms of recreation are cross-country skiing, fishing, horseback riding, and hiking. Interpretive programs are offered. World's End Reservation at the tip of the park is managed by the Trustees of Reservations and has breathtaking panoramic views of Hingham Harbor, Hull, and the Boston skyline.

Other Things to See and Do

Hingham Ferry to Boston and Boston Harbor Islands; *(617) 727–7676.* See also the Boston Harbor Islands section in the Greater Boston Chapter.

King's Landing Marina, *Norwell; (781) 659–7273.* Canoe rentals on the North River.

Mary's On the North River, *Marshfield; (781) 837–2322.* Rent a powerboat and explore the North River.

South Shore Music Circus, *130 Sohier Street, Cohasset; (781) 383–9850.* Children's summer theater productions.

South Shore Natural Science Center, *Jacobs Lane, Norwell; (781) 659–2559.* Programs for children, nature trails, and animal exhibits. **Free.**

Winslow House, *Careswell and Webster Street, Route 139, Marshfield; (781) 837–5753.* Daniel Webster's law office at his former home is a national historic landmark.

Hull Lifesaving Museum, *117 Nantucket Avenue, Hull; (781) 925–LIFE. Open Friday through Sunday 10:00 A.M. to 4:00 P.M. Admission: $2.00 for adults, $1.50 for seniors;* **Free** *for children.* U.S. lifesaving station-turned-museum.

Amazing Massachusetts Facts

- America's oldest lighthouse is on Little Brewster Island off the coast of Hull.

- Old Ship Church is the oldest wooden church in the United States that has been in continuous use.

- The first canal in America was dug in the 1630s by the Pilgrims. It connected Plymouth Bay to Green Harbor in Marshfield.

- The first radio program in the world was broadcast in Marshfield on Christmas Eve 1906.

- The 1794 Court House Museum in Town Square in Plymouth is the oldest wooden courthouse in the country.

- The Forefathers Monument in Plymouth is the largest solid granite monument in the U.S.

Duxbury and Kingston

Heading south of Boston during the summer? In their Cape-bound haste, many people miss Duxbury Beach, one of the finest barrier beaches along the Atlantic Coast. On your way there, drive or walk across the Powder Point Bridge, the longest wooden bridge on the East Coast. The pedestrian portion of the bridge is wide, allowing room for walkers to pass behind the fishing enthusiasts who gather along the bridge. Famous Pilgrims buried at the Old

Burying Ground on Chestnut Street in Duxbury include Myles Standish and Priscilla and John Alden.

DUXBURY BEACH, aka BLAKEMAN'S PUBLIC BEACH (all ages)

At the end of Route 139 (accessed through the Green Harbor section of Marshfield); (781) 837–3112. Lifeguards are on duty from late May through early September. Parking is $8.00 on weekends, $5.00 on weekdays.

This 5-mile-long stretch of sand and beach grass is a favorite of locals. The old-fashioned, full-service bathhouse is a great find for car-bound travelers. For a quarter you can stow your clothes in a basket, spend the day on the beach, then wash the sand and salt water off the kids (and yourselves) before returning to the car. There's a good snack bar, too.

Herring Runs Sites to view the herring returning to their spawning grounds:

- Island Creek at Route 3A, Duxbury

- Jones River at Elm Street, Kingston

- Herring Run Park, Route 14, Pembroke

- Town Brook at Jenny Grist Mill, Plymouth

KING CAESAR HOUSE (ages 8 and up)

King Caesar Road, Duxbury; (781) 934-6106. Open mid-June through Labor Day, Wednesday through Sunday, 1:00 to 4:00 P.M. Admission: $5.00 for adults, $3.00 for children 6 to 18.

This is the Federal style home of Ezra Weston, a successful shipping magnate of the nineteenth century. Original wharves are located in Bumpus Park, where Ezra's ship, *The Hope*, was built. The main house has a children's room with period dolls and toys. A knot herb garden and a perennial garden are found on the property.

Other Things to See and Do

John Alden House, *105 Alden Street, Duxbury; (781) 934–9092.* Home of *Mayflower* Pilgrims John and Priscilla Alden.

Where to Eat

Farfar's Danish Ice Cream Shop, *Millbrook Station, St. George's Road, Duxbury; (781) 934–5152.* Delicious ice cream made daily on the premises. $

Persy's Place, *117 Main Street/Route 3A, Kingston; (617) 585–5464.* Diverse breakfast menu, from plain toast to catfish on eggs. Lunch also served daily. $

Plymouth

When you arrive in Plymouth, your first stop should be one of the two excellent tourist information centers. Adjacent to the highway, the **Massachusetts Tourist Information Center** (exit 5 on Route 3 South; 508–746–1150 or 746–1152) carries an excellent selection of books, maps, and brochures. The parking lot is large, and there are clean rest rooms and picnic tables. The hard-to-stump staff is happy to answer your questions and point you in the right direction. Open year-round, daily, 8:30 A.M. to 4:30 P.M. in the summer, 8:30 A.M. to 4:30 P.M. in the winter. The **Plymouth Visitor Information Center/Discover Plymouth** (508–747–7525 or 800–872–1620) and **Destination Plymouth** (508–747–7533; www.visit-Plymouth.com) are both located at 225 Water Street (right at the waterfront), near most of the sites your family came to Plymouth to see. The selection of tourist literature is good here, the staff is helpful, and the rest rooms are conveniently located (baby-changing stations in both). Open daily, 9:00 A.M. to 5:00 P.M.; extended hours in the summer and at other busy times.

PLYMOUTH ROCK TROLLEY (all ages)

Meets at the Information Center at 225 Water Street, Plymouth; (508) 747–3419. Operates weekends in May and November, daily Memorial Day to Halloween and Thanksgiving through the following Sunday. Hours: 9:30 A.M. to 5:00 P.M. Price: $8.00 for adults, $4.00 for children.

For families with very young children, or families who would rather see everything quickly without having to do too much walking, the Plymouth Rock Trolley is a convenient way to get around. The trolley stops at all the major sites, from Plymouth Rock to the *Mayflower II*, during each forty-five-minute trip. You can get on and off the trolley as many times as you like. During the summer the trolley ride is extended to Plimoth Plantation and Long Beach.

*B*oat Excursions in Plymouth

- **Andy Lynn,** *Town Pier, Plymouth; (508) 746–7779.* Fishing and whale-watching trips; naturalist on board. $$$-$$$$

- **Captain John Ferry and Harbor Cruises,** *State Pier; (800) 242–2469.* Operates daily from June through October. Ninety-minute boat ride from Plymouth to Provincetown, or forty-five-minute cruise of Plymouth Harbor. $$$-$$$$

- **Captain John Whale Watch and Deep Sea Fishing,** *Town Wharf; (800) 242–AHOY; www.captainjohn.com.* Floating classroom with naturalist on board. $$$-$$$$

- **Lobster Tales,** *Town Wharf; (508) 746–5342; www.lobstertales.com.* Harbor tour of historic Plymouth, followed by hauling of lobster traps and examination of the catch (crabs, fish, and lobster). Touch tank on board. $$-$$$

- **Lobster Tales Pirate Adventure,** *east end of Route 44, Town Wharf; (508) 746–5342.* Kids don pirate hats, bandanas, and makeup, follow a treasure map to find buried booty, have a battle at sea with an enemy pirate vessel, and eventually may win the treasure chest. The loot is divvied up, and a celebration ensues with buccaneer brew, dancing, music, and singing. $$-$$$

- **Pilgrim Belle,** *State Pier; (508) 746–2643; www.plymouthharborcruises.com.* Only authentic paddlewheeler in New England; meals served.

- **Splashdown Amphibious Tours,** *Harbor Place; (800) 225–4000; www.ducktoursplymouth.com.* One-hour land-and-sea tour of historic Plymouth. $$-$$$

- **Water Wheels,** *across from Town Pier, Plymouth; (800) 540–3495.* Historical land-and-sea tour. $$$-$$$$

COLONIAL LANTERN TOURS (ages 6 and up)

35 North Street Plymouth; (508) 747–4161 or (800) 698–5636; www.lanterntours.com. Offered from April 1 through the end of November. Two tours nightly; reservations recommended. Price: $8.00 for adults, $6.00 for children 6 to 18. Family rates available for four or more.

As you carry your punched tin lantern through the streets of Plymouth, you are given a glimpse of Plymouth past and present. This guided walking tour, given the much coveted AAA rating, covers about a mile circuit about town and lasts for an hour and a half. Special themed tours are given at Halloween and Thanksgiving; daily tours give the history of the town (The Lantern Tour) or recount spine-tingling tales of Plymouth (The Legends and Lore Tour).

Reading List: Recommended Children's books on Plymouth and the Pilgrim story

- *Sarah Morton's Day: A Day in the Life of a Pilgrim Girl*, by Kate Waters.

- *The First Thanksgiving*, by Jean Craighead George, illustrated by Thomas Locker.

- *The Pilgrims of Plimouth*, written and illustrated by Marcia Sewall.

PLYMOUTH ROCK (all ages)

Water Street. Open year-round dawn to dusk. **Free**.

As any schoolchild in America can tell you, the first European settlers in Plymouth stepped off the *Mayflower* onto this rock in 1620. Considering its prominence in American history, the size of the rock may disappoint you; it's a rather ordinary-looking boulder. Nevertheless, it's the number one tourist attraction in Plymouth.

MAYFLOWER II (all ages)

State Pier, (508) 746–1622; www. plimouth.org. Open April 1 through the Sunday following Thanksgiving. Admission: $6.50 for adults, $3.75 for children 5 to 12; **Free** *for children under 5. Special rates if you visit the boat and Plimoth Plantation on the same day ($19 for adults, $11 for children).*

Near Plymouth Rock is the *Mayflower II*, a reproduction of the original boat that brought the Pilgrims to Plymouth. The costumed staff knows all sorts of facts about the boat, which seems astonishingly small when you think about the 102 people who crowded onto it during its first journey from England to America. Self-guided tour.

PLIMOTH PLANTATION (all ages)

Route 3A/Warren Avenue; (508) 746–1622; www.Plimoth.org. Open end of March through November, daily, 9:00 A.M. to 5:00 P.M. Admission: $16.00 for adults, $9.00 for children 6 to 12; Free *for children under 6. Special rates if you visit the Mayflower II and Plimoth Plantation on the same day ($19 for adults, $11 for kids).*

One of New England's best living museums is Plimoth Plantation. Budget at least half a day to see this remarkable reproduction of a 1627 Pilgrim village. It is populated by authentically costumed people who play, convincingly, the parts of the residents. Ask them questions about their clothes, their chores, what they do for fun, what they eat, how they survive without indoor plumbing—whatever comes to mind.

Hobbamock's Homesite, comprising a longhouse and a weetu, is interpreted by native Wampanoag guides dressed in traditional garb. Massasoit, the Wampanoag chief, had sent Hobbamock and his family to live near the Pilgrims, to teach them to survive, and to keep track of their doings.

At the **Carriage House Craft Center,** artisans recreate crafts using the same materials and many of the same tools that were used in the 1600s.

The **Nye Rare Breeds Barn** features rare and minor breeds farm animals. Petting of the animals is allowed. Demonstrations include sheep shearing and cow milking.

The best day of the year to visit the plantation is Thanksgiving, of course; call ahead for a meal reservation. The gift shop has a large stock of books about Plymouth and the Pilgrims' lives and times. Call for the calendar of events and brochures; ask about children's activities and dining events.

 ## PILGRIM HALL MUSEUM (all ages)

75 Court Street, Plymouth; (508) 746–1620; www.pilgrimhall.org. Open daily, 9:30 A.M. to 4:30 P.M., closed in January. Admission: $5.00 for adults, $3.00 for children 6 to 16; (family rate of $13.00).

In operation since 1824, the Pilgrim Hall Museum holds the largest existing collection of Pilgrim possessions, including a portion of the *Sparrow-Hawk,* one of the ships that brought the earliest European migrants to Plymouth. The only known contemporaneous painting of a *Mayflower* passenger, Edward Winslow, is here, too.

CRANBERRY WORLD (all ages)

225 Water Street, Plymouth; (508) 747–2350. Open May through November 9:30 A.M. to 5:00 P.M. Free.

Ocean Spray sponsors this Free center of information about the history of cranberries and the cranberry industry. A scaled-down reproduction of a cranberry bog is among many exhibits, and there are lots of Free samples.

THE CHILDREN'S MUSEUM OF PLYMOUTH (younger ages)

46–48 Main Street, Plymouth; (508) 747–1234. Open from September through June, Monday through Saturday 10:00 A.M. to 5:00 P.M., Sunday noon to 5:00 P.M.; closed Tuesday. During July and August the hours are extended by one hour. Admission: $4.00 per person; Free *for children under 1.*

The Children's Museum of Plymouth allows kids to explore pint-size versions of several elements of everyday life in contemporary Plymouth, from operating a weather station at the lighthouse, to riding on a fire engine, to captaining one of Captain John's boats.

PLYMOUTH NATIONAL WAX MUSEUM (all ages)

16 Carver Street, Plymouth; (508) 746–6468. Open daily from March through December, with extended summer hours. Admission: $5.50 for adults, $2.25 for children 5 to 12; Free *for children under 5.*

This museum will probably seem cheesy to grown-ups, but kids love the life-size wax figures of prominent Plymouth residents. The over 180 characters tells the Pilgrim story from 1601 to 1627.

MAYFLOWER SOCIETY MUSEUM AND LIBRARY (all ages)

4 Winslow Street, Plymouth; (508) 746–2590 or (508) 746–3188; www.mayflower.org. The museum is open weekends from Memorial Day to the end of June, then daily through Labor Day. Hours: 9:00 A.M. to 4:30 P.M. The library is open year-round Monday through Friday from 10:00 A.M. to 3:30 P.M. Admission: $2.50 for adults, 50 cents for children (double the fee for both the museum and the library).

The museum, a beautiful white building with a sweeping double staircase, offers a mother lode of history. The original owner of the house (built in 1754) was Edward Winslow, who fled to Canada along with other Tories when the Revolutionary War began. The author and transcendentalist Ralph Waldo Emerson was married in the front parlor in 1835, and seven years later ether was discovered here. The Mayflower

Society Library, just down the driveway from the museum, is a wonderful resource if you're interested in researching your family's history. The building is the headquarters of the General Society of Mayflower Descendants, who have extensive archives and libraries of information that are open to the public.

Watch for the Pilgrim Progress every Friday in August at 6:00 P.M., when a costumed group, representing the Pilgrims that survived the first winter, parade through many historic locales in Plymouth.

RICHARD SPARROW HOUSE (all ages)

42 Summer Street; (508) 747–1240. Open April through December 10:00 A.M. to 5:00 P.M. Admission: $2.00 for adults, $1.00 for children 6 to 16.

Built in 1640, the Richard Sparrow House is now Plymouth's oldest surviving wooden frame house. The sparsely furnished house gives visitors a view of early Pilgrim life in an authentic setting.

THE JABEZ HOWLAND HOUSE (all ages)

33 Sandwich Street; (508) 746–9490. Open late May through mid-October, then weekends through Thanksgiving weekend, 10:00 A.M. to 4:30 P.M. Admission: $3.50 for adults, $1.00 for children age 6 to 12.

The Jabez Howland House is the only surviving house in Plymouth that is known to have been inhabited by *Mayflower* passengers.

PRISCILLA BEACH THEATRE (all ages)

Rocky Hill Road, Manomet; (508) 224–4888. Open June through mid-September. Performances on Friday and Saturday at 10:30 A.M.

The Priscilla Beach Theatre is the country's oldest summer-stock playhouse. Children's shows are presented from June through mid-September. The theater also runs a performing arts day camp (one- and two-week programs). Call ahead for show schedules and for more information about the day camp.

Other Things to See and Do

Middleborough Historical Museum, *Jackson Street, Middleborough; (508) 947–7120.* Mr. and Mrs. Tom Thumb of circus fame donated their collection of miniatures.

Little Shoes, *359 Court Street; (508) 747–2226.* Good selection of specially priced shoes below regular retail.

*B*eaches in Plymouth

- **Nelson Street Beach,** off Water Street, just north of Cranberry World. Good swimming, Free parking, and a playground.

- **Stephen's Field Park,** 1 mile south of Plymouth Center, just off Route 3A. Free parking, a small duck pond, a beach, tennis courts, picnic tables, and a playground.

- **Plymouth Beach,** Route 3A. Lifeguarded beach with snack bar and bathhouse.

Where to Eat

Iguana's, *170 Water Street, Plymouth;* *(508) 747–4000.* Mexican restaurant; children's menu, outdoor patio and deck. $

Peaceful Meadow's Ice Cream, *170 Water Street (Village Landing Marketplace), Plymouth; (508) 746–2362.* Homemade ice cream. $

Star of Siam, *Route 3A, Manomet;* *(508) 224–3771.* An excellent take-out Thai restaurant in the Manomet area of Plymouth, just a few miles south of Long Beach. $

Lobster Hut, *Town Wharf, Plymouth;* *(508) 746–2270.* Lobster in the rough with great views of the Plymouth Bay breakwater.

Where to Stay

The John Carver Inn, *25 Summer Street; (508) 746–7100 or (800) 274–1620; www.johncarverinn.com.* A large hotel/motel in the middle of town, with a pool and a restaurant. An indoor water park is being added. $$–$$$$

Pilgrim Sands, *150 Warren Avenue/Route 3A; (508) 747–0900 or (800) 729–SANDS; www.pilgrimsands.com.* On Long Beach, near the plantation. Call ahead to request an efficiency apartment. There are two pools—one indoor, one outdoors. $$–$$$$

Carver/South Carver

Along Route 58 in Carver (and on many back roads in the area as well), your family may see some of the state's cranberry bogs. Half of the country's cranberry crop comes from the marshy, sandy bogs in this area, and cranberries are Massachusetts's number one agricultural product. When it's harvest time (mid-September through early November), the farmers use machines to literally shake the berries from their vines. They corral the berries into large crimson islands, then use enormous vacuum hoses to scoop the harvest into trucks.

MYLES STANDISH STATE FOREST (all ages)

Cranberry Road, South Carver; (508) 866–2526. The fee of $6.00 per night includes showers. Directions: Take Route 3 to exit 5, turn south on Long Pond Road, then look for signs (approximately 2½ miles south).

Bike, hike, fish, or swim at Myles Standish State Forest, just a twenty-minute drive from Plymouth. The 14,635-acre park was Massachusetts's first state forest when it was created in 1916. There are miles of quiet walking trails, bike and horseback riding paths, fifteen ponds (two, Fearing Pond and College Pond, are designated for swimming; the rest are for fishing), and lots of picnic spots in the forests and meadows. Camping, too: The forest has 470 tent/RV sites (no hookups) with rest rooms and hot showers, plus fireplaces and picnic tables at each site.

Other Things to See and Do

Super Sports Family Fun Park (all ages). *108 North Main Street (junction of Routes 58 and 44) Carver; (508) 866–8000.*

Onset and Wareham

Onset, the "thermometer capital of the world," is a charming village that is part of Wareham. Onset Beach enjoys the warm waters that the Cape is known for and is a lovely spot to hear a musical concert at the bandstand on a warm summer's evening.

THE PORTER THERMOMETER MUSEUM (all ages)

49 Zarahemia Road, Onset; (508) 295–5504. Open daily year-round; call for an appointment (the museum is in Porter's home). **Free**.

Dick Porter's motto for his museum (the world's only) is "Always open and always **Free** with over 3,000 thermometers to see." This retired Lexington schoolteacher will amaze you with tidbits about his unusual collection, the largest in the world (he is in both the *Guinness Book of World Records* and *Ripley's Believe It or Not*). Porter has been featured on countless television shows and articles, and he is in great demand on the lecture circuit. Given his popularity, he is very interested in imparting his knowledge to every visitor and converting you into a "thermometermaniac." Some of the thermometers that he is most proud of are the pill-size thermometers swallowed by John Glenn on his NASA shuttle mission. This is a fun and educational experience. The Plymouth County Convention and Visitor's Bureau awarded the Thermometer man its Hospitality Award for Tourism in 1998.

Other Things to See and Do

Cape Cod Canal Cruises, *Onset Pier, Wareham; (508) 295–3883.* Narrated cruise on the canal.

Onset Beach, *Onset Avenue (Cranberry Highway/Routes 6 and 28 to Onset Avenue), Wareham.*

Water Wizz, Route 28, Wareham; (508) 295-3255. Water park.

Greater New Bedford and Greater Fall River

The entire downtown area of New Bedford seems to be a monument to the city's world-famous whaling days. The New Bedford National Historical Park includes the Whaling Museum and the schooner *Ernestina*. Though it's inland, Fall River is a major seaport, and Battleship Cove is a magnet for those who enjoy touring warships and other vessels.

NEW BEDFORD WHALING MUSEUM (all ages)

18 Johnny Cake Hill, New Bedford; (508) 997–0046. Open daily year-round, 9:00 to 5:00 P.M., Thursday until 8:00 P.M. Memorial Day through Labor Day. Admission: $4.50 for adults, $3.00 for children 6 to 14; ʄʳᵉᵉ *for children under 6.*

Kids are justifiably awed by the tools of the trade: enormous hooks, harpoons, and a 90-foot-long whaling bark that they are welcome to climb on. The scrimshaw collection is remarkable for its quality and depth—among the 2,000 items are a sled and a birdcage carved from whalebone. Be sure to watch the twenty-two-minute vintage silent film of an actual whale chase and capture. A new display is the 65-foot skeleton of a blue whale. The museum's annual Maritime Heritage Festival in May is fun for the entire family; also of interest is the annual reading of the classic tale of *Moby-Dick* by Herman Melville that takes place on January 3 (Melville was a crew member on a whaler that departed from New Bedford).

SEAMAN'S BETHEL

15 Johnny Cake Hill, New Bedford; (508) 992–3295. Donations accepted.

Chapel visited by Herman Melville and described in *Moby-Dick*. The chapel is a memorial to those who were lost at sea.

DEMAREST LLOYD STATE PARK (all ages)

Barney's Joy Road, South Dartmouth; (508) 636–3298 (seasonal phone). From Memorial Day through Labor Day, parking is $2.00 per car. Directions: Take Route 24 south to Route 195 east to the Faunce Corner exit. Turn right onto Faunce Corner Road; cross Route 6 onto Chase Road and follow the signs.

Not far from New Bedford is South Dartmouth and Demarest Lloyd State Park, a beautiful beach with calm water, long sandbars, great hiking trails, rest room facilities, and lots of picnic tables in a shady area. Considering how pleasant this beach is, there are surprisingly few people midweek (during the weekends the gates close as soon as the parking lot fills up—usually by 10:00 A.M.).

HORSENECK STATE BEACH (all ages)

John Reed Road, Route 88, Westport; (508) 636–8816. From Memorial Day through Labor Day, parking is $2.00 per car. Directions: Take Route 24 south to Route 195 east to Route 88.

Just to the west of Dartmouth is Westport, site of another gorgeous beach. Horseneck State Beach is a 3-mile-long stretch of sand. There's a bathhouse, a snack bar, picnic tables, a 100-site campground adjacent to the beach, hiking, and good swimming. Watch the kids at low tide, however; the sandbars drop off suddenly.

BATTLESHIP COVE (all ages)

Exit 7 off Route 24, Fall River; (508) 678–1905; www.battleshipcove.com. Open daily year-round, 9:00 A.M. to 5:00 P.M.; closed Thanksgiving, Christmas, and New Year's Day. Admission: $9.00 for adults, $4.50 for children 6 to 14; Free *for children under 6.*

Today Battleship Cove holds six, U.S. Navy warships from the World War II era, including a submarine. The USS *Massachusetts* is the biggest, by far, and probably the most interesting to the kids, who will avail themselves of the opportunity to clamber throughout the ship's nine decks (you don't have to take a tour in order to explore the ship). Start your tour with the introductory video film that is five to seven minutes long, or watch the twenty-minute orientation film. The *Massachusetts* was moved here in 1965 to stand as a permanent memorial to the more than 19,000 Massachusetts men and women who gave their lives in service during World War II, Vietnam, Korea, and Desert Storm. If your family wants to explore the ship independent of a tour, be sure to pick up a brochure when you arrive; it's easy to get lost. Try out the hammocks that served as the sailors' bunks, climb the turrets, and admire the enormous main deck. Next, check out the Russian Navy Crevette built in 1984 and acquired by Battleship Cove in 1997. A marvelous history lesson is an overnight encampment program offered to youth and school groups ($33 per person). The participants speak to former crew members, get a tour of all the ships, have a knot-tying lesson, eat sailor's grub, and sleep in the sailor's bunks throughout the ships.

THE FALL RIVER CAROUSEL (all ages)

(508) 324–4300. Open year-round; seasonal hours. Rides are $1.00 each; a companion ride is $1.50.

Also at Battleship Cove is the Fall River Carousel, a restored merry-go-round that was moved here from Dartmouth in the early 1990s. The horses are hand-carved and hand-painted. Bring a picnic lunch; there's a nice grassy area next to the carousel.

FALL RIVER HISTORICAL SOCIETY (all ages)

451 Rock Street, Fall River; (508) 679–1071. Seasonal hours. Admission: $5.00 for adults, $3.00 for children.

Lizzie Borden took an axe, gave her mother forty whacks, when she saw what she had done, she gave her father forty-one—every girl remembers this jump rope song. At the Fall River Historical Society, there are over 10,000 items related to the Lizzie Borden trial, the largest collection in the United States. The Lizzie Borden collection is just a small part of this museum, which offers a house tour of the former mill owner's mansion, nautical exhibits, paintings and furnishings, as well as 2,000 items of clothing and costumes in a revolving exhibit.

Other Things to See and Do

Children's Museum in Dartmouth, *276 Gulf Road, South Dartmouth; (508) 993–3361.* Large property abutting conservation land. Children's programs are ecology based.

Children's Museum in Easton, *The Old Fire Station, 9 Sullivan Avenue, North Easton; (508) 230–3789.* Located in an old firehouse. Hands-on arts-and-crafts and woodworking room, dress-up area, kids' clinic, firepole, laboratory for learning, and dinosaur table.

H.M.S. *Bounty,* Heritage State Park, *Fall River; (508) 673–3886.* Tour a tall ship.

Marine Museum at Fall River, *70 Water Street, Fall River; (508) 674–3533. Titanic* exhibits and artifacts.

New Bedford Fire Museum, *51 Bedford Street, New Bedford; (508) 992–2162.* Restored fire trucks and related exhibits.

Old Colony and Fall River Railroad Museum, *Battleship Cove, Central and Water Streets, Fall River; (508) 674–9340.* New England railroad memorabilia and historical displays.

Rotch-Jones-Duff House and Garden Museum, *396 County Street, New Bedford; (508) 992–4900.* Mansion of whaling magnate William Rotch, Jr.

Schooner *Ernestina,* *New Bedford State Pier, New Bedford; (508) 992–4900; www.ernistina.org.*

Where to Eat

Audrey's Restaurant, *Johnson and Wales Inn, 213 Taunton Avenue, Seekonk; (508) 336–8700.* Johnson and Wales students ply their craft in an award-winning setting. $$

Bittersweet Farm Restaurant and Tavern, *438 Main Road, Westport; (508) 636–0085.* Country setting for fine dining halfway between Fall River and New Bedford. $$-$$$

Where to Stay

Lizzie Borden Bed & Breakfast, *92 Second Street, Fall River; (508) 675–7333.* Five-room inn and museum (former home of the infamous Borden family). $$$$

Hampton Inn Hotel, *Hampton Way, Fairhaven; (508) 990–8500.* Pool and Jacuzzi. $$$

Johnson and Wales Inn, *213 Taunton Avenue, Seekonk; (508) 336–8700.* Run by students from Johnson and Wales University; the staff is eager to please. $$$

Marcia's Top
Annual Events

in Plymouth and the South Shore

- **Plimouth Plantation: Rare Breeds and Heirloom Seeds,** Memorial Day Weekend, Plymouth; (508) 745-1622

- **Farm Day at the Children's Museum,** June, South Dartmouth; (508) 993-3361

- **Tweeter Center for the Performing Arts,** Summerlong Concerts, Mansfield; (508) 339-2333

- **New Bedford Summerfest,** early July, New Bedford; (508) 999-5231

- **Waterfront Festival,** mid-July, Plymouth; (508) 830-1620

- **Onset Blues Festival,** August, Onset, Buzzards Bay; (508) 295-7072

- **Plymouth Lobster Festival,** August; (508) 746-8500

- **Marshfield Fair,** late August, Marshfield Fairgrounds; (781) 834-6629

- **Fall River Celebrates America Festival,** August, Fall River; (508) 676-8226

- **Feast of the Blessed Sacrament,** end of July/August, New Bedford; (508) 992-6911

- **King Richard's Faire,** late August–October, Carver; (508) 866-5391

- **Plimouth Plantation Dutch Days,** Columbus Day weekend; (508) 746-1622

- **Cranberry Harvest Festival,** October, South Carver; (508) 747-2350

- **Plimouth Plantation's Thanksgiving Celebration,** November, Plymouth; (508) 746-1622 or (800) USA-1620

- **La Salette Festival of Lights,** Thanksgiving through early January, Attleboro; (508) 222- 5410

Cape Cod, Martha's Vineyard, and Nantucket

CAPE COD

Shaped like a bent arm and stretching 60 miles into the Atlantic, the peninsula of Cape Cod offers nearly 300 miles of beaches, along with acres of nature preserves, dozens of pretty villages, and an abundance of top-notch inns and restaurants that welcome families. For **Free** information on the Cape, contact the Cape Cod Chamber of Commerce (888-33-CAPECOD). At the fist of the Cape's arm, pulsating Provincetown surrounds the Pilgrim Monument, a replica of the Campanile in Siena. The spectacular view of the curving Cape and the surrounding ocean and bay is worth the climb up the tower's 116 steps. Regardless of the season, visit one or more of the first-class beaches along the Cape's eastern edge. A fun way to keep kids interested during the short drives from town to town is to make the trip into a lighthouse tour. There are seven working lighthouses on the Cape, from Provincetown all the way to Woods Hole. Bed & Breakfast Cape Cod is a great reservation service connecting you to outstanding properties on the Cape (800-541-6226).

Bourne and Sandwich

When you drive over the Sagamore Bridge, you end up on Route 6 in Sandwich. Few visitors stop here; most zip on by on their way to the beaches and cottages of the outer Cape. You can travel to Sandwich by train from Hyannis, tour the village's family-oriented attractions, and travel back, all in an afternoon.

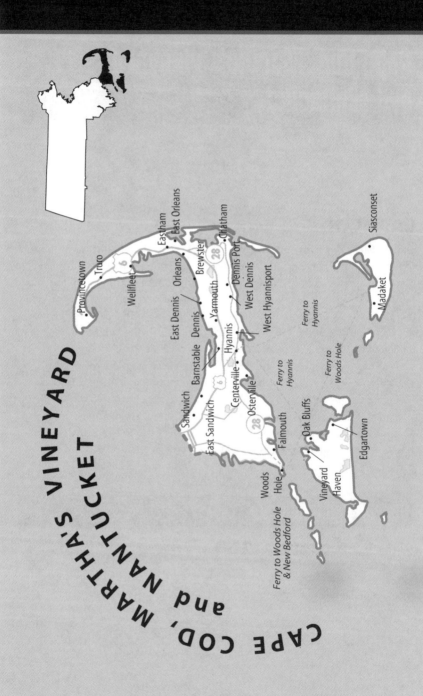

CAPE COD, MARTHA'S VINEYARD and NANTUCKET

Provincetown
Truro
Wellfleet
Eastham
East Orleans
Orleans
Brewster
Chatham
East Dennis
Dennis
Dennis Port
West Dennis
Yarmouth
West Hyannisport
Sandwich
Barnstable
Hyannis
East Sandwich
Centerville
Osterville
Falmouth
Oak Bluffs
Woods Hole
Vineyard Haven
Edgartown
Ferry to Woods Hole & New Bedford
Ferry to Hyannis
Ferry to Woods Hole
Ferry to Hyannis
Siasconset
Madaket
28
6
6
28

CAPE COD CANAL BIKE TRAIL (all ages)

Access points along the Cape side of the canal: in Sandwich, at the U.S. Engineering Station; in Sagamore, from Pleasant Street; from the Bourne Bridge; and at the Buzzards Bay Recreation area next to the Bourne Bridge; (508) 759–4431. **Free**.

The well-maintained Cape Cod Canal Bike Trail borders the canal on both banks. The 6.8-mile-long trail along the Cape side is less hilly and further removed from auto traffic than the 7.2-mile-long mainland-side trail. Families should avoid crossing either bridge with children, either on foot or on bicycle. If you must cross the canal on your bikes, use the Sagamore Bridge (its sidewalk is safer), and don't ride—walk. Because the bridges' auto lanes are so narrow, drivers aren't looking out for pedestrians or bikers—they're avoiding cars in adjacent lanes.

SCUSSET BEACH STATE RESERVATION (all ages)

Scusset Beach Road, Bourne and Sandwich. Located north of the Cape Cod Canal; (508) 888–0859. Open year-round 8:00 A.M. to 8:00 P.M. Parking is $2.00 per car.

Scusset Beach is a 380-acre park/beach area, which remains reasonably populated in the summer months. Facilities include rest rooms, a snack bar, picnic tables, and 103 campsites.

Marcia's Top Family Adventures
on Cape Cod Martha's Vineyard, and Nantucket

1. Cape Cod National Seashore

2. Nauset Beach, East Orleans

3. Cliffs at Gay Head, Martha's Vineyard

4. Jetties Beach, Nantucket

5. National Marine Fisheries Service Aquarium, Woods Hole

6. Flying Horses Carousel, Martha's Vineyard

7. Whale-watching trips from Provincetown

8. Chatham fish pier

9. Pilgrim Tower, Provincetown

GREEN BRIAR NATURE CENTER AND JAM KITCHEN (all ages)

6 Discovery Hill Road, East Sandwich; (508) 888–6870. Open year-round.
Free.

Two miles from the Burgess Museum (see entry below) is the Green Briar Nature Center and Jam Kitchen. The Nature Center comprises fifty-seven acres of gardens and forests laced with easy walking trails. The Thornton W. Burgess Society runs a full program of nature walks and natural history classes, mostly geared to kids, throughout the year. After you explore the Nature Center, stop in at the Jam Kitchen, an old-fashioned kitchen in a pondside building that looks like it's right out of one of Burgess's stories. The Jam Kitchen sells natural jams, jellies, and pickled goods. Ask about classes on the fine art of making jam.

HERITAGE PLANTATION (all ages)

Grove and Pine Streets, Sandwich; (508) 888–3300;
www.heritageplantation.org. Open daily from mid-May through mid-October, 10:00 A.M. to 5:00 P.M. Admission: $9.00 for adults, $4.50 for children 6 to 18, **Free** *for children under 5.*

Heritage Plantation holds an interesting collection of antique cars in mint condition exhibited in a replica of a round Shaker stone barn (if you want to see the real thing, visit the Hancock Shaker Village near Pittsfield; see the Berkshires chapter). Toy-soldier fans enjoy the collection of several thousand hand-painted miniature soldiers. Catch a ride on the restored antique carousel at the Art Museum. Gardening enthusiasts and kids with lots of energy love to roam the acres of meticulously tended paths that wind through fantastic flower gardens and blooming shrubs.

HOXIE HOUSE AND THE DEXTER GRIST MILL (all ages)

18 Water Street, Sandwich; (508) 888–1173. Open mid-June to mid-October, Monday through Saturday 10:00 A.M. to 5:00 P.M., and Sunday 1:00 to 5:00 P.M. Admission: $1.50 for adults, 75 cents for children 12 to 16; **Free** *for children under 12. A combination ticket for Hoxie House and the Dexter Grist Mill is $2.50 for adults, $1.00 for children 12 to 16;* **Free** *for children under 12.*

This Cape Cod saltbox, restored to its original 1675 interior, contains furnishings on loan from the Boston Museum of Fine Arts. The Dexter Grist Mill was built in 1640 and is still in operation. Demonstrations of corn being ground into flour are fascinating to children. Scenic Shawme Pond on the property attracts swans, ducks, and Canada geese (bring bread to feed them). For the past one-hundred-years, the town of Sandwich has celebrated the Illumination Boat Parade at Shawme Pond on the Fourth of July. The evening begins with an old-fashioned band concert. Participants affix Japanese lanterns to their boats to outline elaborate displays—pirates, dragons, or whatever they can conjure up.

SANDWICH GLASS MUSEUM (all ages)

129 Main Street, Town Hall Square, Sandwich; (508) 888–0251. Open daily year-round 9:30 A.M. to 5:00 P.M.; closed January. Admission: $3.50 for adults, $1.00 for children 6 to 16; **Free** *for children under 6.*

On a bright day the Sandwich Glass Museum is a colorful sight to behold. Since much of the museum's collection is displayed in front of windows, sunlight is very much a part of the installation. Sandwich is internationally known for its glassware, the making of which was most active during the nineteenth century. An excellent video and a diorama explain the glass-making process.

THORNTON W. BURGESS MUSEUM (under 10)

4 Water Street, Sandwich; (508) 888–6870; www.thorntonburgess.com. Open from April to October (and the first two weeks in December for the Victorian Christmas) Monday through Saturday 10:00 A.M. to 4:00 P.M., Sunday 1:00 to 4:00 P.M. Admission by donation.

The cottage by a duck pond is the Thornton W. Burgess Museum, which houses books and memorabilia of the renowned author (he wrote the *Mother West Wind* stories about Reddy Fox and Paddy the Beaver). The 10:30 A.M. story hour ($1.00 per person) takes place three days a week in July and August and on some holidays and school vacations on Monday, Wednesday, and Saturday. The Farmer's Market Festival is in October.

Other Things to See and Do

Pairpont Glass Works, *851 Sandwich Road, Sagamore; (508) 888–2344 or (800) 899–0953.* Watch glassware being made using methods that have been passed down for generations.

Yesteryears Doll Museum, *Main and River Street, Sandwich; (508) 888–6870.* Thousands of dolls every shape, size, national origin, and whimsical costume.

Where to Stay

Daniel Webster Inn, *149 Main Street, Sandwich; (508) 888–3622 or (800) 444–3566.* A traditional inn with four-poster beds and fireplaces in some of the rooms. Pool; restaurant. $$$$

Where to Eat

Bayberry's, *271 Cotuit Road, Sandwich; (508) 477–4094.* Log cabin setting with great food and large portions. Kid's menu and activity book. $–$$

The Marshland, *109 Route 6A, Sandwich; (508) 888–9824.* Picturesque views of the marshes, great food. Open Tuesday through Saturday for dinner, Sunday for breakfast from 6:00 A.M. to 1:00 P.M., Monday 6:00 A.M. to 1:00 P.M. for breakfast and lunch. $$

Falmouth and Woods Hole

West of the town of Barnstable is Falmouth, a pleasant New England village that pulses with visitors throughout the summer. Its Nantucket Sound coast is lined with guest houses, hotels, and summer homes. The downtown area has some good shopping and a few ice cream parlors, but the main attraction of Falmouth is its coastline: The beaches are terrific, and the many inlets provide lots of space for private boat mooring. Of the four beaches that are open to nonresidents, the best are South Cape Beach, Surf Drive Beach, and Old Silver Beach. Woods Hole is home to the Woods Hole Oceanographic Institute, the National Marine Fisheries Service Aquarium, and the Steamship Authority. The village of Woods Hole is part of Falmouth; it's a fun place for kids to watch the boats going in and out of Eel Pond, which serves as a harbor and town center, of sorts. Walk around the pond to see the village's sites: the aquarium, St. Mary's Bell Tower and Garden, the harbor, and the drawbridge. Many families see little more of Woods Hole, however, than the Steamship Authority parking lots and waiting area.

ASHUMET HOLLY WILDLIFE SANCTUARY (all ages)

286 Ashumet Road, East Falmouth; (508) 563–6390. Trails open dusk to dawn. Admission: $3.00 for adults, $2.00 for children 3 to 12; **Free** *for children under 3.*

Enjoy nature trails that wind among Holly trees (more than sixty-five varieties) on over forty-five acres. During the Holly Days Festival, held the first two weekends in December, you can buy fresh greens and holly. The sanctuary sponsors year-round ecology, seal, and sunset cruises to Cuttyhunk and other Elizabeth Islands; call for the schedule.

BARNSTABLE COUNTY FAIR (all ages)

Barnstable County Fairgrounds, Route 151, East Falmouth; (508) 563–3200.

In late July bring the kids to Barnstable for a real old-time county fair. You'll enjoy livestock shows, oxen pulls, baking contests, a midway, and lots of great food.

CAPE COD CHILDREN'S MUSEUM (under 10)

137 Tea Ticket Highway (Falmouth Mall on Route 28); (508) 457–4667; www.capecodchildrensmuseum.pair.com. Open Monday through Saturday 10:00 A.M. to 5:00 P.M., Sunday noon to 5:00 P.M. Admission: $3.50, $2.50 for children under 5.

The Cape Cod Children's Museum is a good place to spend a rainy day. It has a sand room and a 30-foot pirate ship, both especially popular with toddlers. Visit the toddler castle, the star lab planetarium, and the science workshops. The arts-and-crafts workshops, field trips, and monthly museum activities are fun for everyone.

ISLAND QUEEN

Falmouth Heights Road (off Route 28), Falmouth; (508) 548–4800; www.islandqueen.com. Operates May to October to Oak Bluffs. Price: $10.00 for adults, $5.00 for children 3 to 12; **Free** *for children under 3. Bicycles cost $6.00 to transport.*

If your family is in the mood for a pleasant boat ride, an alternative to the Steamship Authority ferries to and from Martha's Vineyard is the *Island Queen,* which departs from its own dock in Falmouth's Inner Harbor. Park the car at the *Island Queen* parking lot on Falmouth Heights Road, and take the ferry over to the Vineyard for the day; it's less expensive, and the boat is smaller and more comfortable than the Steamship Authority boats.

*S*neak This One In . . . If you're in the Falmouth–Woods Hole area in mid-August, cheer on the runners in the **Falmouth Road Race,** an annual 7-mile race that attracts participants from all over New England. For more information, call (508) 540-7000.

NATIONAL MARINE FISHERIES SERVICE AQUARIUM (all ages)

Water to Albatross Street, Woods Hole; (508) 548–7684. Open year-round, Monday through Friday 10:00 A.M. to 4:00 P.M., plus weekends in summer. **Free**.

The National Marine Fisheries Service Aquarium preserves living sea creatures that are native to the Cape's waters. The touch tanks are low to the ground so that even toddlers can reach in and feel the crabs, lobsters, turtles, and other sea creatures. The whole place is child-oriented, and the helpful staff love to answer kids' questions. A real treat is to watch the seal feedings at 11:00 A.M. and 4:00 P.M. at the seal tank in front of the building.

NOBSKA LIGHT (all ages)

Nobska Road. Open year-round.

Nobska Light sits on a bluff above winding Nobska Road between Woods Hole and Falmouth, overlooking Martha's Vineyard, Vineyard Sound, and the Elizabeth Islands. The lighthouse building that stands on this site today was built in 1876. Flashing every six seconds, Nobska's fixed-beacon light provides precise information to mariners: Seen head-on, the beam is white, indicating the safest route into Woods Hole Harbor; seen from either side, the red beam warns mariners against routes that could force them to go aground against the shoals. The light guides thousands of ships each year through the treacherous waters that lead to Woods Hole.

SHINING SEA BIKE PATH (ages 8 and over)

Depot Avenue in Falmouth to Locust Street, Woods Hole Harbor. Open year-round. **Free**.

The Shining Sea Bike Path is a 3⅓-mile trail between Falmouth and Woods Hole that's named for the last line of Falmouth native Katherine Lee Bates's beloved song, "America the Beautiful." The path can be crowded in the summer, and it's hilly in a few spots. Pick it up on Palmer Avenue in Falmouth. From here it winds through forests, goes past Nobska Lighthouse, and ends at Woods Hole Harbor.

Whisked Away The **Whoosh Trolley** operates between Falmouth and Woods Hole from late May to mid-October ($1.00 for adults, 50 cents for children 6 to 17).

POW-WOW The **Wampanoag Pow-Wow** is held the first weekend in July in the Upper Cape. This three-day event features native crafts and foods. Native drumming, dancing, and singing demonstrations and contests are key to this colorful festival. A highlight is the clambake dinner held on the last day. Admission is $7.00 for adults, $4.00 for seniors and children 12 and under. For more information, call the Mashpee/Wampanoag Indian Tribal Council Office (508–477-0208).

  ### SOUTH CAPE BEACH (all ages)

Great Oak Road, Falmouth; (508) 548–0495. Parking is $2.00.

South Cape Beach is part of a state park (South Cape Beach State Park) that has several nice nature trails. The beach is the attraction here, though: It's a 2-mile-long barrier beach with a bathhouse, a snack shop, and a big parking lot that rarely fills.

 ### STEAMSHIP AUTHORITY (all ages)

Woods Hole; (508) 477–8600. Directions: Follow the signs to the Woods Hole Steamship Authority off Route 28. Parking is $10 a day.

If you want to visit Martha's Vineyard without a car, park in one of the Steamship Authority's parking lots and take the **Free** shuttle bus to the harbor. You don't need a reservation if you're traveling without a car; simply purchase tickets for each person. The trip takes approximately forty-five minutes for Martha's Vineyard, and there are numerous ferry departures for both Oak Bluffs and Vineyard Haven. The vehicle reservations for the Steamship ferries go fast; the reservation lines open in mid-March, so plan early.

SURF DRIVE BEACH (all ages)

Off Main and Shore Streets, Falmouth; (508) 548–7611. Parking is $10.

On Vineyard Sound, Surf Drive Beach is popular with sailboarders and sea kayakers, some of whom have beachside "garages" for their boats and gear. It's west of the main part of Falmouth, which keeps much of the summer crowd away.

Other Things to See and Do

Edward's Boatyard and Waquoit Kayak Co., *1209 East Falmouth (Route 28), East Falmouth; (508) 548–2216 or (508) 548–9722; www.edwardsboatyard. com.* Canoe or kayak on the Child's River or Waquoit Bay. Guided tours are offered.

Spohr's Garden, *on Fells Road, off Oyster Pond Road, Falmouth.* A three-acre garden that's a lovely spot. Donations accepted.

Where to Eat

The Black Duck, *73 Water Street, Woods Hole; (508) 548–9165.* Charming spot on Eel Pond. Seafood dishes; kids' menu. $–$$$

Coonamessett, *311 Gifford Street, Falmouth; (508) 548–2300.* Fine dining in a country inn overlooking a pond. Appealing kids' menu. $$$

Pat's Pushcart, *339 Main Street, East Falmouth; (508) 548–5090.* Serves some of the best unfussy Italian food to be had on the Cape. $–$$

Pie in the Sky, *10 Water Street, Woods Hole; (508) 540–5475.* Great muffins, juice, coffee, and sandwiches, open year-round. $

Where to Stay

The Coonamessett, *311 Gifford Street, Falmouth; (508) 548–2300.* Fine country inn in picturesque setting; children welcome. $$$$+

Sea Crest Resort, *350 Quaker Road, Falmouth; (508) 540–9400 or (800) 225–3100.* Two hundred-room resort on the beach. $$$

Woods Hole Passage, *186 Woods Hole Road, Woods Hole; (508) 548–9575.* Quiet B&B in the northern part of Woods Hole. Rooms are spacious and comfortable, and breakfasts are delicious. Open May through October; rates range from $85 to $135, double occupancy. $$$–$$$$

West Barnstable, Centerville, and Hyannis

Barnstable is the Cape's largest town: Its 60 square miles include the villages of Barnstable and West Barnstable along Cape Cod Bay, and Cotuit, Marstons Mills, Osterville, Centerville, and Hyannis along Nantucket Sound. These villages differ greatly. Hyannis is the commercial center of the Cape, as well as its most crowded town. If you're coming to the Cape to get away from crowds, malls, and traffic, you should avoid Hyannis. If you like the bustle of a busy harbor town, however, you'll enjoy Hyannis—but be sure to get out into the quieter villages that border it on the north and west. By the way, while you're in Hyannis, don't bother looking for Kennedys: When they're at their private compound on the town's western edge, they're on vacation, too, and they keep well out of sight.

 ## Cape Sports Teams

- **Cape Cod Baseball League.** Looking for something to fill your family's summer vacation evenings? Between mid-June and early September, the Cape Cod Baseball League is just the thing. Ten towns on the Cape field teams made up of the country's top college baseball players, who play before enthusiastic small crowds and, more often than not, big-league scouts. Past players have included Carlton Fisk, Mo Vaughn, Nomar Garciaparra, Jeff Bagwell, Frank Thomas, and Will Clark. The league conducts weekly clinics for kids. For more information, contact the Cape Cod Baseball League at Box 164, South Harwich 02661 (508–996–5004; www.capecodbaseball.org).

- **Cape Crusaders Soccer Team.** The only professional sports team on the Cape since 1993, the Cape Crusaders are the farm team of the New England Revolution (the professional New England soccer team based in Foxboro at Foxboro Stadium). Preseason games are held in March and April; the season runs from May to September. Former Crusader players include Kevin Wiley and Francis O'Karoh. Games are played at Dennis/Yarmouth High School's Alan Carlson Field (tickets are $8.00 for adults, $5.00 for children 14 and under). The team also runs a summer soccer day camp for ages four to eight and ages nine to fourteen (Jr. Crusader/Jr. Renegades). For more information, contact the Cape Crusaders at 35 Winter Street, Suite 101, Hyannis 02601 (508–790–4782; www.capecodcrusaders.com).

CAPE COD CENTRAL RAILROAD (all ages)

The train leaves from the station at Main and Center Streets in downtown Hyannis; (508) 771–3800; www.capetrain.com. Operates May through October, Tuesday through Sunday, weekends the rest of the year. Call for a schedule and prices.
$$–$$$

The one-and-three-quarter-hour ride on the Cape Cod Central Railroad, an air-conditioned train from Hyannis to Sandwich, is fun for kids. Views of the Cape's forests and cranberry bogs line the route, and the small village of Sandwich is a nice place to stroll for a couple of hours before you catch the train back to Hyannis. *Tip:* A pretty time to take the tour is at sunset.

CAPE COD POTATO CHIP FACTORY (all ages)

Independence Drive, off Route 132 to Breeds Hill Road, Hyannis; (508) 775–7253. Open weekdays year-round, 9:00 A.M. to 5:00 P.M.; extended hours in the summer (Saturday 10:00 A.M. to 4:00 P.M.) **Free**.

One of the highlights of a trip through busy Hyannis is a self-guided tour of the Cape Cod Potato Chip Factory, followed by lots of **Free** samples. As you approach, you can smell the chips.

CRAIGVILLE BEACH (all ages)

Craigville Road, Barnstable; (508) 790–9888. Parking costs $8.00 midweek, $10.00 weekends.

On Nantucket Sound, Craigville Beach is a busy place that's popular with teenagers as well as families with young children. The water is warmer here than on the north or east coasts of the Cape. Craigville Beach has lots of parking, changing rooms and showers, rest rooms, and a snack bar (and plenty of clam shack–type eateries within a few minutes' walk of the beach).

KALMUS PARK BEACH (all ages)

End of Ocean Street, Hyannis; (508) 790–9884. Parking is $8.00 midweek, $10.00 weekends.

Wide scenic Kalmus Park Beach is a good spot for families. There are gentle waves, fine sand, fishing areas, lots of seashells to collect, and a sheltered area for toddlers, as well as rest rooms and a snack bar. Kalmus juts out into Lewis Bay and Nantucket Sound (one of the largest windsurfing areas on the Cape).

SANDY NECK BEACH (all ages)

Sandy Neck Road, off Route 6A, West Barnstable; (508) 862–4044. Parking is $10.

At Barnstable's lovely beach on Cape Cod Bay, the dunes of 6-mile-long Sandy Neck Beach protect Barnstable Harbor from heavy surf. They also form one of the Cape's finest barrier beaches, and one that's rarely crowded. There's an adjacent parking lot, rest rooms, changing rooms, and a snack bar. Parking is $10.

Hyannis Ferries

Hyannis Ferries Fast ferries from Hyannis to Nantucket take approximately one hour and can zip along at a faster rate because they are smaller vessels, carry fewer people (in a more luxurious setting), and don't accept vehicles. The traditional Martha's Vineyard and Nantucket ferries take approximately two hours, with only the Steamship Authority accepting vehicles. All of the ferries offer rest rooms, a snack bar, **Free** shuttle service from their parking lots in Hyannis, and onboard carriage of bikes for a fee. Arrive forty-five minutes before departure. Call for prices and hours.

- **Hyline Cruises,** *Main Street and Route 28, Ocean Street Dock, Hyannis; (508) 778–2600 or (888) 778–1132; www.hy-linecruises.com.* Fast ferry to Nantucket only, traditional ferry service to both Nantucket and Martha's Vineyard. No cars accepted.

- **Steamship Authority,** *corner of Pleasant Street and South Street, South Street Dock, Hyannis; (508) 477–8600 or (508) 693–9130; www.island-ferry.com.* Choice of traditional or fast ferry service to Nantucket, passage to Martha's Vineyard is from Woods Hole only. Cars are accepted with reservations on the traditional ferry.

VETERANS PARK BEACH (all ages)

Ocean Street, at the end of Gosnold Street, Hyannis; (508) 790–9885. Parking is $8.00 midweek, $10.00 weekends.

Adjacent to the John F. Kennedy Memorial, Veterans Park Beach has lots of picnic tables and other facilities.

Other Things to See and Do

Cape Cod Melody Tent, *West Main Street, Hyannis; (781) 383–9850.* Theater productions showcasing nationally known casts.

John F. Kennedy Hyannis Museum, *397 Main Street, Hyannis; (508) 790–3077.* Not as impressive as the one in Dorchester, but worth a look.

Sturgis Library, *Route 6A, Barnstable; (508) 362–6636.* Oldest public library building in the United States.

The West Parish Meetinghouse, *Corner of Route 149 and Meetinghouse Way, West Barnstable; (508) 362–4445.* Second oldest surviving meetinghouse on the Cape.

Old Indian Meetinghouse, *Meetinghouse Way near the Route 28 Intersection, Mashpee. (508) 477–0208.* Built in 1684 for the Mashpee/Wampanoag tribe, the Old Indian Meetinghouse is the oldest surviving meetinghouse on the Cape.

L and and Sea Tours in the Hyannis Area

- **Cape Cod Duckmobile,** *447 Main Street, Hyannis; (508) 362–1117 or (800) 225–3825.* Land-and-sea tour of Hyannis on an amphibious duckmobile.

- **Catboat Eventide,** *Ocean Street Docks, Hyannis; (508) 775–0222.* Harbor and sunset cruises; the price for children ninety pounds and under is $5.00.

- **Hyline Hyannisport Harbor Cruises,** *Ocean Street Dock, Hyannis; (508) 778–2600.* Specializing in Lobster Lunch cruises; Sunday Ice Cream "Float" cruises, and jazz and blues cruises. Children sail for Free on early morning and late afternoon family cruises.

Where to Eat

Four Seas, *360 South Main Street, Centerville; (508) 775–1394.* Rated #1 in New England by *Gourmet* magazine. Serves some of the best ice cream on the Cape, along with sandwiches and lobster rolls. Open spring and summer only. $

Gringo's, *577 Main Street, Hyannis; (508) 771–1173.* Features seafood, pizza, and Mexican dishes. Children's menu. $–$$

Paddock Restaurant, *25 West Main Street, Hyannis; (508) 775–7677.* Steaks and seafood specialties. $$$

Where to Stay

Anchor Inn, *1 South Street, Hyannis; (508) 775–0357.* The only hotel in Hyannis with its own boat-docking facilities; harborside pool. Family-friendly. $–$$$$

Captain Gosnold Village, *230 Gosnold Street, Hyannis; (508) 775–9111.* Large cottages with fully equipped kitchens. Pool, basketball hoop, lawn-

game equipment, and gas grills. Open May to October. $$–$$$$

Centerville Corners, *1338 Craigville Beach Road; (508) 775–7223 or (800) 242–1137.* Near Craigville Beach. Indoor pool, two saunas, large lawn, and croquet and badminton equipment. $$–$$$$

Yarmouth, Dennis, and Harwich

Yarmouth, Dennis, and Harwich cover both the Bay and the Sound coasts of the Mid-Cape, as well as the congestion of Route 28 and the peaceful residential areas north of Route 6A and south of Route 28.

THE CAPE COD RAIL TRAIL (all ages)

Running from Route 134 in South Dennis to Locust Road in Eastham. To pick up the trail, take exit 9 off Route 6 in Dennis, turn south on Route 134, and travel approximately ¼ mile. The trail ends in Wellfleet, just east of Route 6, near the Wellfleet Chamber of Commerce information booth. **Free**.

The Cape Cod Rail Trail is a 20-mile-long asphalt biking path that follows the old (discontinued) railroad tracks that cut a swath through six towns, Nickerson State Park, and the Cape Cod National Seashore. The trail is fairly flat and safe; however, there currently are some short sections of the trail that are on roads. There are lots of places to pull over for beach fun or to buy a hard-earned snack.

CAPE COD WATERWAYS (all ages)

Route 28 (¼ mile east of Route 134) on the Swan River in Dennis Port; (508) 398–0080. Rent by the hour; price depends on boat chosen and number of participants.

Paddleboat or canoe, which to choose? Luckily, the rental is by the hour and the owner allows you to change boats midstream. Our decision was to canoe the route to South Village Beach and change over to the paddleboat for the northerly trek to Swan Pond. The paddleboats can be electronically operated to help navigate the changing tidal currents, or you can switch over to manual and use feet power to propel you on your way.

DISCOVERY DAYS CHILDREN'S MUSEUM (all ages)

444 Route 28, Dennis Port; (508) 398–1600. Open daily mid-June through Labor Day, 9:30 A.M. to 7:30 P.M.; Labor Day through early June, open Wednesday to Monday, 10:00 A.M. to 5:00 P.M. Admission: $2.50 for adults, $4.50 for children over 1.

The 4,000-square-foot Discovery Days Children's Museum houses a variety of interactive educational (but fun) exhibits and offers organized activities.

mazing Massachusetts Facts

- It is the law in Massachusetts for children twelve and under to wear protective helmets when operating or riding as a passenger on a bicycle.

- The tallest all-granite structure in the United States is the Pilgrim Tower in Provincetown.

FREEDOM CRUISE LINE (all ages)

Saquatucket Harbor Dock, Harwichport; (508) 432–8999. Operates June through September 15, three times a day. Price: $35 for adults, $29 for children 2 to 12, $5.00 for children under 2. Parking is Free *for day-trippers only.*

Ninety-minute cruise from Harwichport to Nantucket. Reservations are recommended; bikes allowed onboard for an extra fee. No vehicles accepted.

GRAY'S BEACH (all ages)

Off Centre Street from Route 6A, Yarmouth; (508) 398–2231. Open parking, no fee.

A fine beach for families, Gray's Beach has another attraction—the long wooden Bass Hole Boardwalk, which stretches over a salt marsh. Kids love to scamper along the elevated walkway; it's also fun to peer out over the marshy grasses and flowers. The beach has calm water, picnic tables, rest rooms, and a playground. *Caution:* There is a strong current beyond the swimming area.

PIRATE'S COVE (all ages)

782 Main Street (Route 28), South Yarmouth; (508) 394–6200. Open daily April through November from 10:00 A.M. to 7:00 P.M., with extended hours from late-June through Labor Day (9:00 A.M. to 11:00 P.M.) Admission: $6.50 for adults, $5.50 for children 12 and under.

Among the many miniature golf courses that line Route 28, the most inventive is Pirate's Cove. The two courses are laid out around a pirate ship that sits in a lagoonlike pond, surrounded by cliffs and waterfalls.

SCARGO TOWER (all ages)

Route 6A, to Old Bass River Road, take the first left onto Scargo Hill Road, Dennis.

Scargo Tower isn't that tall a tower—only 28 feet—but the high hill it sits on makes it a great place to take in a terrific view of Cape Cod Bay and the Cape's midsection.

WEST DENNIS BEACH (all ages)

Off Davis Beach Road, West Dennis. Parking is $10.

One-mile-long West Dennis Beach, bordering a flat salt marsh and several tidal streams, is a busy place in the summer. The eastern end is for Dennis residents only; the rest of it is taken over by families who park in the enormous parking lot—so big that it rarely fills (unusual for a good Cape beach). Enjoy the beach and its many facilities—good swimming, lots of lifeguard stations, rest rooms, showers, play areas with swing sets, and a snack bar.

Other Things to See and Do

Cape Museum of Fine Arts, *Route 6A, Dennis; (508) 385–4477.* Work by Cape Cod artists.

Captain Bangs Hallet House, *11 Strawberry Lane (off Route 6A), Yarmouth; (508) 362–3021.* Fifty-acre sea captain's estate; hiking trails.

ZooQuarium, *674 Route 28, West Yarmouth; (508) 775–8883.* Marine animal shows, wildlife exhibit, aquarium, and barnyard animals.

Where to Eat

Black Rock Grill, *633 Route 28, South Yarmouth; (508) 771–1001.* Black Angus steaks, salads, game dishes. Western riding gear decor. $$$

Clancy's, *175 Route 28, West Yarmouth; (508) 775–3332.* Seafood, steaks, kid's menu. Irish music singalongs. $$

Lobster Boat, *681 Main Street, West Yarmouth; (508) 775–0486.* Lobster and other seafood dishes, as well as hot dogs, fried chicken, and the like. $$–$$$

The Sunday School, *387 Lower County Road (off of Route 28), Dennis; (508) 394–9122.* Homemade ice cream and sundaes. $

Where to Stay

All Seasons Motor Inn, *Route 28, South Yarmouth (508) 394–7600 or (800) 527–0359.* Indoor and outdoor pool; TV, VCR, and refrigerator in every room. $$$–$$$$

The Lighthouse Inn, *1 Lighthouse Road, West Dennis; (508) 398–2244; www.light-house inn.com.* Family-oriented resort on Nantucket Sound, near the Bass River.

Accommodations include single rooms and cottages scattered across nine well-maintained acres. On-site attractions include a working lighthouse, tennis courts, a pool, miniature golf, shuffle-board, a private beach, and lots of planned activities for kids. Breakfast included in rate. $$$$

Chatham

Chatham is a village of shingled cottages, with a delightful Main Street full of shops and cafes and a variety of top-level summer accommodations for families. There are several attractions that are in the don't-miss category for families: the Fish Pier, Chatham Lighthouse, the Friday-evening band concerts at Kate Gould Park, and the Railroad Museum.

Catch As Catch Can Watch the day's catch being unloaded from the observation deck at **Chatham Fish Pier** between 2:00 and 6:00 P.M. It's just north of town, on the corner of Bar Cliff Avenue and Shore Road.

CHATHAM LIGHT AND CHATHAM BREAK (all ages)

On Main Street between Shore Road and Bridge Street.

Chatham Light sits across from a small parking lot, several sets of coin-operated binoculars, and a breathtaking view of the Chatham Break. The Break occurred during a ferocious winter storm in 1987, when storm-pounded waves broke through the barrier beach that stretches south from Nauset Beach, forming a separate island (now called South Beach) and a break in the barrier that had protected Chatham's harbor and coastline from the full brunt of the Atlantic. The break is a spectacular example of the power of weather, wind, and ocean. The present structure is one of a pair of towers that was built in

1877 (the light's twin was moved to Nauset in 1923). Chatham's original lighthouses were built in 1808. Heavy erosion, which is still a problem in Chatham,

Safety Tip The road between Chatham and Orleans can be busy; take the time to drive the kids to the beach rather than allowing them to walk.

forced the Coast Guard to move the lights back from the coast to the spot where the light stands today. Chatham Light flashes two times every ten seconds.

CHATHAM RAILROAD MUSEUM (all ages)

Depot Road; no phone. Open mid-June through mid-September, Tuesday through Saturday, 10:00 A.M. to 4:00 P.M. **Free**; *donations accepted.*

The restored depot building of the Chatham Railroad Museum, with its Cheerio-like architectural details, holds an impressive collection of thousands of model trains. Thomas the Tank Engine fans will enjoy the old caboose, which is most kids' favorite object. *Tip:* There's a great playground across the street.

 ### HARDINGS BEACH (all ages)

Hardings Beach Road, Chatham; (508) 945–4014. Parking is $8.00 per day, $35 per week, and $60 for the season. Pay by the day at the beach, or obtain a sticker at the permit department at Town Hall.

The best family beach in Chatham is Hardings Beach. It's a long beach with small dunes, rest rooms, a snack bar, and a large parking lot (arrive early; it can fill up before noon in the summer).

Down by the Sea A variety of water tours in Chatham can be arranged by contacting one of the following boat tour operators:

- Beachcomber (508–945–5265)

- Chatham Water Tours (508–432–5895)

- Rip Rider (508–945–5450)

- Outermost Harbor Marine (508–945–2030)

*B*reaker's Beach If you're looking for a deserted beach, try **South Beach,** which is the part of Nauset Beach that was separated by the Chatham Break. There are no lifeguards and no facilities here; pack a lunch and plenty of water. You'll share the beach with lots of shorebirds, the overflow from Monomoy Island.

KATE GOULD PARK

On Main Street. Every Friday night from early July through early September.
Free.

Every Friday night there's a band concert at the bandstand in Kate Gould Park. Thousands of visitors and locals show up for these evenings to dance to old standards, Sousa marches, and the like.

MONOMOY ISLAND WILDLIFE REFUGE (all ages)

If your family would like to tour Monomoy, you'll need to arrange a guided tour with one of two organizations: either the Cape Cod Museum of Natural History (call 508–896–3867 for information and reservations) or the Wellfleet Bay Wildlife Sanctuary (508–349–2615).

One of the true adventures left for Cape visitors is a trip to Monomoy Island Wildlife Refuge, a 2,700-acre wilderness area on two islands that serve as a resting area for migratory birds and a home for as many as 285 species of seaside birds. In addition, there is an amazing number of gray and harbor seals that call the rocks off this island home. On your tour of the islands (North and South Monomoy), you'll see acres of true seaside wilderness: There are no roads, no buildings, and no electricity. If you don't have time for a guided tour, visit the **Monomoy Island Wildlife Refuge Visitor Center** on Morris Island. They don't offer tours, but the helpful staff will provide you with plenty of literature and will point you and the kids toward the ¾-mile self-guided interpretive tour around Morris Island. No dogs, please. *Directions to the Monomoy Island Visitor Center on Morris Island:* From Main Street in Chatham, between Bridge Street and Shore Road, take the first left after Chatham Light. Take the first right; follow Morris Island Road to the visitor center (508-945-0594).

Other Things to See and Do

Atwood Museum, *347 Stage Harbor Road, Chatham; (508) 945–2493.* Antiques, shell collections, artwork by local artists, and paraphernalia make for an eclectic museum.

Cabbages and King's Bookstore, *628 Main Street, Chatham; (508) 945–1603.* Toys, games, and adult and children's books are among the dizzying array found here.

Cape Cod Flying Circus, *240 George Ryder Road, Chatham Airport; (508) 945–2363.* Sightseeeing rides of Monomoy Island seals or Provincetown.

Grist Mill, *Chase Park, Shattuck Place, Chatham.* Original old mill.

Where to Eat

Break-Away Cafe, *240 George Ryder Road, at Chatham Airport, Chatham; (508) 945–3637.* Serving breakfast and lunch. Open mid-March to November. $

Buffy's Ice Cream, *456 Main Street, Chatham; (508) 945–5990.* Homemade ice cream made fresh daily. $

Chatham Bars Inn, *Shore Road, Chatham; (508) 945–0096 or (800)* 527–4884. Meals are served in spacious, elegant dining rooms; clambakes take place on the beach once a week. $$–$$$$

Chatham Candy Manor, *484 Main Street, Chatham; (508) 945–0825 or (800) 221–6497; www.candymanor.com.* Hand-dipped chocolates and unusual candies.

Where to Stay

Chatham Bars Inn, *Shore Road, Chatham; (508) 945–0096 or (800)* 527–4884. Select from suites, cottages, and rooms with balconies; there are 205 rooms in all on the twenty-two-acre property. The inn has a private beach just across Shore Road, with planned activities (including all-day children's programs). Room rates are $190 to $1,200 a night. $$$–$$$$

Horne Family Cottages, *off Morris Island Road; P.O. Box 174, Chatham 02633); (508) 945–0734.* Cottages on the nicest private beach in Chatham. Clean and beautifully maintained. Rates range from $1,250 to $2,200 per week. $$$–$$$$

Monomoy Point Lighthouse Keepers House/Monomoy Island Wildlife Refuge. *Reservations made through the Cape Cod Museum of Natural History (508–896–3867).* Open Saturday night in the spring and fall, Tuesday, Thursday, and Saturday night in the summer. A forty-five-minute boat shuttle takes you to Monomoy Island. Overnight accommodations are in the keepers' house (which sleeps up to eight people). Rate ($145 per night) includes dinner and breakfast. Children must be at least 12.

Pleasant Bay Village, *Route 28, Chatham; P.O. Box 772, Chatham 02633; (508) 945–1133 or (800) 547–1011.* Large complex of buildings set on beautifully maintained grounds. Efficiency units have well-equipped kitchens. Heated pool. Rates are $115 to $435 per night.

Brewster

Brewster was home to dozens of ship captains during the nineteenth century, many of whom built beautiful homes along what is now Route 6A. Today, when the tide is out, Brewster's beaches along the bay—Sea Street Beach, Paines Creek Beach, and Point of Rocks Beach—are fun spots for kids to explore the miles and miles of sun-warmed tidal pools and skittering seaside animals, birds, and bugs.

BASSETT WILD ANIMAL FARM (all ages)
620 Tubman Road, off of Routes 124, Brewster; (508) 896–3224. The farm is open daily from mid-May to mid-September, 10:00 A.M. to 5:00 P.M. Admission: $5.75 for adults and children over 12, $4.00 for children 2 to 12.

The Bassett Wild Animal Farm has a small collection of exotic and domestic animals—lemurs, peacocks, monkeys, unusual birds, ebus, llamas, goats, and more—that appeal to toddlers and young children. Pony and hayrides are 75 cents each, and there's a petting zoo. If you get the munchies, there's a snack bar as well as a picnic area.

CAPE COD MUSEUM OF NATURAL HISTORY (all ages)
869 Route 6A, Brewster; (508) 896–3867; www.ccmnh.com. Open year-round Monday through Saturday 9:30 A.M. to 4:30 P.M., Sunday 11:00 A.M. to 4:30 P.M. Admission: $5.00 for adults, $2.00 for children 5 to 12; Free *for children 4 and under.*

. The Cape Cod Museum of Natural History does a terrific job of teaching kids (and their parents) about the Cape's fragile ecology. The museum also runs tours of Monomoy Island Wildlife Refuge (see the description under Chatham in this chapter). There are three nature trails and marine tanks with live indigenous creatures. The touch tanks feature lobsters, crabs, mollusks, fish, turtles, frogs, and other local species. The museum also sponsors canoe and kayak day trips for a nominal fee.

 NEW ENGLAND FIRE AND HISTORY MUSEUM (all ages)
Route 6A, Brewster; (508) 896–5711. Open Memorial Day to Labor Day, weekdays 10:00 A.M. to 4:00 P.M., weekends only from Labor Day to Columbus Day. Admission: $5.00 for adults, $2.50 for children 5 to 12, $1.00 for children 4 and under.

The six buildings of the New England Fire and History Museum hold a variety of exhibits, including historic fire fighting equipment, a 50-foot exhibit entitled Boston Burns in 1852, a life-size reproduction of Benjamin Franklin's firehouse, a blacksmith shop, an apothecary, and a fireboat that kids can climb on. The museum claims to have the largest fire equipment collection in the world. Picnic sites are available.

 NICKERSON STATE FOREST (all ages)
3488 Main Street and Route 6A, Brewster; (508) 896–3491. **Free.**

If your family would rather not swim in salt water, Nickerson State Forest is a great place for you—it has several large freshwater ponds with a small beach at one of the ponds. The park also features hiking trails, fishing, bike trails, boating, summertime interpretive programs, and camping. Jack's Boat rental (508) 349–9808 is located right in the park. Skating and cross-country skiing (conditions permitting) are popular in the winter.

Where to Eat

Chillingsworth Bistro, 2449 Main Street, Route 6A, Brewster; (508) 896–3640. Don't confuse the bistro with the restaurant of the same name, unless you're up for a seven-course dinner in an antique-filled setting (not a good idea with kids). The bistro specializes in grilled food, has a contemporary setting with lots of glass and skylights, and will gladly do a pasta dish for the kids. $$$

Where to Stay

Ocean Edge Resort and Golf Club, 2907 Main Street, Brewster; (508) 896–9000 or (800) 343–6074. Located on a private beach with two indoor and four outdoor pools, four dining rooms (the most family friendly is The Reef and Mulligan's $$–$$$). You can opt to stay in a hotel room ($295 a night) or a one-, two- or three-bedroom villa (from $1,770 to $4,140 a week). $$$$+

Orleans and East Orleans

For families, Orleans's main attraction is actually in East Orleans—Nauset Beach. Other recreational opportunities take advantage of water locations. Orleans is bounded on the east by the Atlantic and on the west by Cape Cod Bay.

NAUSET BEACH (all ages)

Beach Road, East Orleans; (508) 240–3775 or (508) 240–3780. Nonresident's fee: $8.00; you can park at both Nauset and Skaket (see entry below). Directions: From exit 12 off Route 6, turn right onto Eldredge Park Way, right onto Tonset Road, right onto Main Street, then left onto Beach Road, which leads to Nauset Beach.

Nine miles long and backed by high dunes, this is one of the Cape's best beaches. If you're willing to walk a bit, Nauset Beach is so long that you will be able to stake out your own territory even on the busiest summer weekends. If you want to stay near the lifeguards, however, keep within the marked area. There's a large bathhouse with rest rooms, changing rooms, and showers; there's also a good snack bar with outdoor picnic tables. On Mondays in July and August from 7:00 to 9:00 P.M. there are bandstand concerts. Everything from folk to rock'n'roll can be heard. Children like to dance down front, and couples can walk the beach and still hear the music.

How to Eat a Lobster
For the uninitiated in the fine art of eating a lobster, we offer this primer.

1. Assemble your tools: a nutcracker, a lobster pick or fork, and a lobster bib (eating lobster can be a very messy undertaking).

2. Twist off the claws, crack them open with the nutcracker, and dip in drawn butter.

3. Separate the tail from the body (bend it until it breaks away), then split the tail down the middle to get to the meat. You may see a green or red line in the center of the tail meat. This is the liver or tomalley and is a treat to some lobster connoisseurs *Warning:* Eat the liver only if it is green.

4. Open the main body of the lobster and hunt down the lobster meat in the small pockets. Other sources of meat are the small claws (break them off the body) and the flippers of the tail.

SKAKET BEACH (all ages)

Skaket Beach Road, Orleans; (508) 240–3775. Nonresident's fee: $8.00; you can park at both Nauset (see entry above) and Skaket beaches for the same price. Directions: Take exit 12; turn right off the exit and take the first left onto West Road. Follow West Road until the end (facing Skaket Beach Road). Take a left onto Skaket Beach Road for Skaket Beach.

Skaket Beach, Orleans's bay beach, is popular with families who enjoy playing in tidal flats. Facilities include rest rooms, changing rooms, and a snack bar.

Other Things to See and Do

French Cable Station Museum, *corner of Cove Road and Route 28, Orleans; (508) 240–1735.* Rare collection of undersea telegraph cables, instruments, and memorabilia.

Kid's Kaboodle, *115 Route 6A, Orleans; (508) 240–0460. Unique clothing for infants and young children.*

Goose Hummock Kayak, *Route 62 on town cove, Orleans; (508) 255–2620 or (508) 255–0455; www.goose.com.* Canoe, kayak, and bicycle rental. *Note:* This is a challenging area to paddle.

Where to Eat

Hot Sparrow Chocolate, *85 Route 6A (Lowell Square), Orleans; (508) 240–2230.* Coffee and chocolate bar (specializing in drinks, deserts, and ice cream). $

Kadee's Lobster and Clam Bar, *212 Main Street, East Orleans; (508) 255–6184.* Seafood served any way you like it (steamed, broiled, or fried); indoor and outdoor seating, children's menu. $-$$$$

Land Ho!, *corner of Route 6A and Eldredge Park Way, Orleans; (508) 255–5165.* The kale soup is a specialty here, but everything's good. Open daily year-round. $$

Where to Stay

Kadee's Gray Elephant Guest Studio's, *Main Street, East Orleans; (508) 255–7608.* Charming rooms with queen-size beds and private baths. Not for large families. Rates: $95 to $110 a night year-round, breakfast basket included. $$$-$$$$

Eastham

Eastham is where Myles Standish and his band first met native tribes in 1620, after the Pilgrims' landing in Provincetown and before their settlement of Plymouth. The meeting spot is commemorated by a bronze marker at the top of the dunes of First Encounter Beach. Today most visitors go to Eastham to enter the Cape Cod National Seashore, which covers nearly 27,000 acres of the outer Cape. It is administered by the National Park Service.

FIRST ENCOUNTER BEACH (all ages)

Samoset Road, Eastham; (508) 240–5972. Directions: From Route 6, turn left on Samoset Road. Parking is $5.00 June through Labor Day, $\mathbf{Free}$ *the rest of the year.*

First Encounter Beach is named for the first site that the Pilgrims scoped out before determining that the soil was too sandy to support farming. Look for the bronze plaque erected to commemorate the event. Lifeguards and rest rooms add to your family's comfort and safety.

CAPE COD NATIONAL SEASHORE (all ages)

Off Route 6 on Nauset Road, Eastham; (508) 255–3421. Parking at Little Creek parking lot is $7.00 and includes a $\mathbf{Free}$ *bus shuttle to Coast Guard Beach. The National Park Service also provides tours of the original brick lighthouses during the summer; ask for a schedule at the Salt Pond Visitors Center information desk. A Cape Cod National Seashore Seasonal Pass is $20.*

Be sure to visit the Salt Pond Visitors Center in Eastham, where helpful guides offer complete information on the seashore and walking trails (the Nauset Marsh Trail is especially scenic), as well as orientation talks and guided field trips. Respect the rules set forth by the Park Service; they are designed to protect this unique and fragile area. Two major points of interest are Coast Guard Beach and the Nauset Lighthouse.

Coast Guard Beach is one of the best beaches along the National Seashore and can be reached by shuttle bus. The bathhouse is one of the Cape's best. To reach Coast Guard Beach from the Salt Pond Visitors Center, continue on to Doane Road or take the Nauset Trail bicycle path (a spur off the Cape Cod Rail Trail). Little Creek Road will be on the left.

Nauset Light, the red-striped lighthouse, has a complicated history. In 1923 the brick building was moved from Chatham, where it was one of two lights. Because of soil erosion, the building was moved again to its current location in 1997. The site it now occupies was also the site of the first of the three lighthouses that sat in a row on the cliffs of Nauset from 1838 until 1911. The original "Three Sisters" were moved to Cable Road at Cape Cod National Seashore, not far from the Salt Pond Visitors Center. Nauset Light's single red stripe helped mariners to distinguish it from other Cape Cod lighthouses during the day. The round ball at the top of the tower is called a ventilator ball; it allows air to circulate and cool the lantern room, where the lighthouse's beam rotates.

Other Things to See and Do

Oldest Windmill on the Cape, *Corner of Samoset and Route 6, Eastham.* Original grist mill built circa 1680.

Where to Eat

Lobster Pool, *Route 6, North Eastham; (508) 255–9706.* Rustic setting with great food; the seafood is especially fresh. Children's menu. $$–$$$

Where to Stay

Captain's Quarter's, *Route 6, Eastham; (508) 255–5686 or (800) 327– 7769.* Complimentary bicycles and continental breakfast, heated outdoor pool, tennis courts. Along the Bike Trail. Prices during the high season range from $96 to $126 a night. $$$–$$$$

Wellfleet

The focus in Wellfleet falls equally on the arts and the natural world. Many of the year-rounders and summer-house owners who live in or near Wellfleet's tiny, picturesque harbor are artists, writers, actors, and other arts-oriented people; under their influence several arts day camps are run each summer for children and families. Well over half of Wellfleet's area is conservation land. Much of it is in the care of the Cape Cod National Seashore; the rest is part of the 1,000-acre Wellfleet Bay Wildlife Sanctuary.

LONG POND (all ages)

Off East Main Street (take Long Pond Road), Wellfleet. Seasonal and **Free**.

If you're looking for freshwater swimming, try Long Pond, where you'll find a shady picnic area and a float in the middle of the pond.

Wellfleet Ocean Beaches

- **Marconi Beach**—part of the Cape Cod National Seashore. Great bathhouse. Parking: $5.00.

- **Cahoon Hollow Beach**—town beach with rest rooms. Parking: $10.

- **White Crest Beach**—town beach, broader than Cahoon Hollow; rest rooms. Parking: $10.

WELLFLEET BAY WILDLIFE SANCTUARY (all ages)

West side of Route 6, Wellfleet; (508) 349–2615; www.wellfleetbay.org. Visitor center open daily from May through October, 8:30 A.M. to 5:00 P.M.; November through April, Tuesday to Sunday, 8:30 A.M. to 5:00 P.M. Trails are open from dawn to dusk year-round. Admission: $3.00 for adults, and $2.00 for children. Excursion costs vary, usually $25 to $35 per day per program. If you've been a member of the Audubon Society for at least a year, you and your family can camp here.

Massachusetts Audobon Society's Wellfleet Bay Wildlife Sanctuary offers myriad nature-oriented activities for families: bird and bat watches; trips through salt marshes; guided trail walks at all hours of the day and night; and several excellent self-guided walking trails, where you'll see a variety of birds and coastal animals (watch for turtles). Write to P.O. Box 236, Wellfleet 02663, for schedules and reservation information.

THE WELLFLEET DRIVE-IN (all ages)

On Route 6 just north of the Eastham-Wellfleet line; (508) 349–2520 or (800) 696–FLEA.

The Wellfleet Drive-In wears two hats: From 8:00 A.M. to 4:00 P.M. on Wednesday, Thursday, weekends, and Monday holidays, April through fall, it's a flea market; in the evenings it's a 700-car first-run drive-in movie theater, with a playground and a snack bar. An indoor theater and an outdoor mini-golf course ensure that the whole crowd is pleased no matter what the weather.

Other Things to See and Do

Marconi Wireless Site, *South Wellfleet.* Site of first transatlantic communication.

Where to Eat

The Lighthouse, *317 Main Street, Wellfleet; (508) 349–3681.* Hearty breakfasts are particularly good. $$

The Bayside Lobster Hutt, 91 *Commercial Street, Wellfleet; (508) 349–6333; www.lobsterhutt.com.* Seating is family-style at long tables; predictably, the menu leans heavily toward seafood, including Wellfleet's famous oysters. There's take-out, too. $$

Painter's, *50 Main Street, Wellfleet; (508) 349–3003.* Good seafood, as well as creative linguica (Portugese sausage) dishes. $$$

Where to Stay

Wellfleet is a cottage colony mecca. One of the best is:

Surfside Colony, *Ocean View Drive, along the Cape Cod National Seashore, South Wellfleet; (508) 349–3959.* One-, two-, and three-bedroom cottages are available, all with kitchens, fireplaces, and screened-in porches; some have roof decks as well. Rates are $450 to $1,350 per week depending on cottage size and season. Write to P.O. Box 937, South Wellfleet 02663.

Truro

Truro is best known for its beaches and the plethora of summer houses and cottages that dot its high hills and dunes. For such a beautiful place (over half of the town is park or conservation land), it's remarkably untouristy. To reach the town center, as it were, of Truro, take the Pamet Road exit off Route 6.

BAYSIDE CORN HILL BEACH (all ages)

Castle Road, Truro; (508) 487–6426. Take Castle Road from the center of Truro (follow signs from Route 6), then follow it to Corn Hill Beach. Parking is $5.00.
Bayside Corn Hill Beach is the place where Miles Standish and his desperately hungry group "borrowed" their first corn from the natives. A marker on the cliff at the edge of the bay indicates the spot where the

event took place. This is also a great place for shelling. *Note:* No life-guards here.

CAPE COD LIGHT/HIGHLAND LIGHT AND THE HIGHLAND MUSEUM (all ages)

Off Highland Road, Cape Cod National Seashore, Truro. Interior tours of the light-house and the Highland Museum run by the Highland Museum and Lighthouse Inc., (508–487–3397). The lighthouse is open May through October, the museum daily June through September from 10:00 A.M. to 5:00 P.M. **Free** *for children under 12.*

The first light that sailors see when they make the trip from Europe to Boston is that of Cape Cod Light, the oldest lighthouse on the Cape. Because it was built on the highlands of Truro, it is also known as the Highland Light. The present buildings date from 1857, but the first lighthouse constructed on this spot went up in 1798. Highland Light's precarious position on eroded cliffs made it likely that it would tumble into the ocean, so the Truro Historical Society successfully spearheaded efforts to move it to its present site 450 feet back in 1997. Ownership of the Cape Cod Light was transferred from the Coast Guard to the Cape Cod National Seashore. At night children will enjoy looking for the light's bright white beam, which is visible during the drive on Route 6 from Truro to Provincetown. Highland is the highest (182 feet above sea level) as well as the tallest (66 feet) lighthouse on the Cape. The museum gives you a peek into the past and is operated by the Truro His-torical Society. Of special interest are native Wampanoag artifacts, Pil-grim tools and furniture, and mariner history.

HEAD OF THE MEADOW BEACH (all ages)

Head of the Meadow Road (off Route 6), North Truro. Parking is $7.00.

The part of the Head of the Meadow Beach that's maintained by the Cape Cod National Seashore (the town of Truro manages the remainder) has a beach house with rest rooms. There are no lifeguards here, but on a calm day this beach is one of the best along the National Seashore.

THE PILGRIM HEIGHTS AREA (all ages)

Off Route 6, North Truro.

The Pilgrim Heights area of the National Seashore has a nice trail to the place where the Cape's first European visitors found fresh water. Take the Pilgrim Spring Walk from the interpretive shelter. The Small Swamp trail is a short, fairly flat loop.

For bicycle enthusiasts, there's a 2-mile path from Head of the Meadow Beach stopping near High Head Road.

PILGRIM LAKE SAND DUNES (all ages)

Highhead Road off Route 6 at the south end of Pilgrim Lake. Park at the Highhead parking lot at the Cape Cod National Seashore, Truro; (508) 487–1256 (Province Lands Visitors Center, Provincetown).

The Pilgrim Lake area of the Cape Cod National Seashore is the only place along the National Seashore where visitors can legally walk over the enormous sand dunes that roll across this part of the Cape. Previous visitors have worn away much of the sand and, with it, the beach grass that covers and preserves the dunes; therefore, the National Park Service restricts foot traffic on the dunes to this area.

Where to Eat

Adrian's, *Route 6, North Truro; (508) 487–4360.* Casual dining, eat indoors or outdoors overlooking the bay. $–$$$

The Whitman House, *Route 6, Truro; (508) 487–1740.* Traditional Cape Cod setting. $$–$$$

Where to Stay

Kalmar Village, *674 Shore Road, North Truro; (508) 487–0585 or (617) 247–0211.* Cottage colony on private Beach Point; swimming pool, grills, and picnic tables outside each room; across from the National Seashore. In season weekly rates are $940 to $1,780.

Provincetown

At the fist end of the Cape, Provincetown is an eclectic collection of open-minded artists, fishermen, windworn buildings, and seaside moors. Go here for the beaches, the whale watching, and the people-watching, which is especially good in this, New England's most tolerant seaside community.

HERRING COVE BEACH (all ages)

Herring Cove Beach is at the end of Route 6, Provincetown; (508) 349–3785. Parking is a onetime day fee of $7.00 (accepted at all National Seashore beaches).

One of Provincetown's best beaches for families is Herring Cove Beach, which has gentler waves than Race Point (see entry below). A snack bar, showers, and rest rooms are available here. To be sure of a parking place in the summer, arrive early.

LONG POINT LIGHTHOUSE AND WOOD END LIGHTHOUSE (ages 12 and up)

Commercial Street, Provincetown. Not appropriate for young children or for anyone without sturdy footwear and good balance; best walked at low tide.

When it was built in 1827, Long Point was the center of a busy fishing community on the tip of the Cape. Now isolated at the end of a long breakwater, Long Point Lighthouse (and its companion, Wood End) can best be viewed from the rotary at the end of Commercial Street (while you're here, look for the plaque that commemorates the first landing place of the Pilgrims). If your family is up for a long walk along a rocky breakwater, park the car at the rotary and walk along the breakwater for about a half hour to reach Long Point. Another half-hour's walk, to the end of the breakwater, will lead to Wood End Lighthouse. The unusual tower is square; most lighthouses are circular. Wood End was built in 1873. It flashes a red light every fifteen seconds, whereas Long Point flashes a green light; together they mark Provincetown Harbor's entrance. *Caution:* It's a long walk—bring something to drink and watch the tides.

WHALE-WATCHING TOURS

The best of the many whale-watch cruises are:

- *Dolphin* **Fleet,** *McMillan Pier, Provincetown; (508) 340–1900 or (800) 826–9300; www.whalewatch.com. The ticket office is located in the Chamber of Commerce building.* The *Dolphin* operates from April through October. Rates, depending on the season, are $18 to $19 for adults, $15 to $16 for children 7 to 12; **Free** for children 6 and under. There is a $2.00 discount given to seniors and AAA members. Scientists and naturalists from the Center for Coastal Study guide every cruise and are available to answer questions.

- The *Portuguese Princess*, *MacMillan Wharf, Provincetown; (508) 487–2651 or (800) 442–3188. The ticketing center is located at 70 Shank Painter Road.* The *Princess* operates from April through October. Rates, depending on season, are $16 to $20 for adults, $15 to $16 for children 7 to 12; **Free** for children 6 and under. The *Portuguese Princess* is associated with WhaleNet, a data collection consortium of research and educational groups. A naturalist is on board with running commentary to help enhance the experience.

- **The *Ranger V*, MacMillan Wharf,** *Provincetown; (508) 487–3322 or (800) 992–9333. The ticket office is at the corner of Bradford and Standish Streets. The Ranger V operates from April to the end of November. Price: $20 for adults, $15 for children 7 to 12;* **Free** for children under 7. The *Ranger V* prides itself on being the largest and fastest whale-watch boat on the Cape. A naturalist is on board every cruise.

A Whale of a Trip You'll find whale-watching trips advertised everywhere along the Cape (and in Boston and on the North Shore too, for that matter), but the best place from which to take one is Province-town. Why? Because it's closest to Stellwagen Bank, the whales' feeding ground, which is only 6 miles from Provincetown; other trips take much longer to reach the same spot. Most of the whale-watching expeditions from Provincetown are about three and a half hours long, but some last all day. Regardless of the weather on shore, be sure to bring a warm sweater and long pants for everyone in your party—even at the height of summer, the wind on the open ocean can be downright cold.

PROVINCETOWN HERITAGE MUSEUM (all ages)

460 Commercial Street and corner of Center Street, Provincetown; (508) 487–7098.

Art collection and model of the vessel *Rose Dorothea*. The museum has been extensively renovated.

THE PROVINCETOWN MUSEUM AND PILGRIM TOWER (all ages)

High Pole Hill, Provincetown; (508) 487–1310. Open daily, April 1 through November 30, 9:00 A.M. to 5:00 P.M.; until 7:00 P.M. in July and August. The last admission is forty-five minutes before closing. Admission: $5.00 for adults, $3.00 for children 4 to 12; **Free** *for children under 4.*

The Provincetown Heritage Museum and Tower is worth a visit for the view from the 252-foot-high tower that was modeled after the Campanile, or bell tower, in Siena, Italy. The tower was built to commemorate the landing of the Pilgrims. On a clear day the view of the curving Cape is breathtaking. The museum focuses on maritime history and the whaling industry.

National Seashore Visitor Center While you're in the Province Lands area, stop at the **Province Lands Visitors Center** (508-487-1256). The center is open from 9:00 A.M. to 6:00 P.M. in the summer, 9:00 A.M. to 4:30 P.M. during the spring and fall.

RACE POINT BEACH (all ages)

End of Race Point Road, off Route 6, Provincetown; (508) 349–3785. Parking is a onetime day fee of $7.00 (accepted at all National Seashore beaches).

Race Point has large sand dunes and smaller crowds, making it a great family beach. Public showers and rest rooms are available. Arrive early to get a parking spot.

RACE POINT LIGHTHOUSE (all ages)

Race Point Beach, Provincetown; (508) 487–1256.

The 2-mile walk to reach Race Point Lighthouse is along Race Point Beach (bring refreshments, especially drinks; the long sandy walk back to the car can be tough for kids). Race Point Lighthouse was erected in 1816 to help ships navigate around the treacherous "knuckles" of the Cape to Provincetown. Between 1816 and 1946 more than a hundred shipwrecks were recorded in this area. Race Point Lighthouse has a white light and a foghorn that warns ships of low-visibility conditions. If your family doesn't have the energy to take the long walk to Race Point, the best view is from the Province Lands Visitors Center's observation deck. Race Point Lighthouse is also visible from Herring Cove Beach.

Other Things to See and Do

Expedition Whydah Sea Lab, *MacMillan Wharf, Provincetown; (508) 487–7955.* Authentic pirate treasure discovered from sunken ships.

Provincetown Off the Coast Kayaking, *Provincetown; (877) TT–KAYAK.* The name says it all.

Norma Glamp's Rubber Stamps, *357 Commercial Street, Provincetown; (508) 487–1870.* Wide variety of stamps and colorful ink pads.

Where to Eat

Michael Shay's, 350 Bradford Street, Provincetown; (508) 487–3368. Seventeen-foot salad bar, specializing in ribs and seafood; cozy decor with a wood-burning stove. Kid's menu. $$

Cafe Blasé, 328 Commercial Street, Provincetown; (508) 487–9465. Outdoor dining in a fun setting. $–$$

Lewis Brothers Ice Cream, 310 Commercial Street, Provincetown; (508) 487–1436. $

Where to Stay

Provincetown Inn, 1 Commercial Street, Provincetown; (508) 487–9500 or (800) WHALEVU; www.provincetowninn.com. Private beach and outdoor pool. Rates are $119 to $259 in-season. Kids under 12 eat and stay for **Free** from late June to mid-September. $$$$

Race Point Lighthouse Keepers House, Race Point Beach, Provincetown; (508) 888–9784. The property consists of a three-bedroom house with a kitchen, living room, and bathroom. Bring your own food and water (the running water isn't drinkable) and gas lanterns. Open April to November; rates are $95 to $150 a night per room. $$$–$$$$

THE ISLANDS: MARTHA'S VINEYARD AND NANTUCKET

The islands of Martha's Vineyard and Nantucket provide more spectacular beaches and seaside atmosphere with less stress and fewer visitors than you'll see on the Cape. The unique character of each island has much to do with their distance from the mainland—at its closest point, the Vineyard is only 7 miles from Falmouth, whereas Nantucket is a good 30 miles out to sea. The Vineyard is more populous and cosmopolitan; Nantucket is more traditional and much less crowded, even during the summer. Fertile Martha's Vineyard boasts large expanses of deep forest and acres of rolling farmland, whereas moors cover a large percentage of Nantucket. Nantucket's bike paths and long beaches make for wonderful family vacations; the colorful cottages and Flying Horses Carousel in Oak Bluffs, on the Vineyard, are beloved to the lucky children who live on the island as well as those who visit. Annual visitors treat their island vacations as sacred family rituals, booking their reservations as far as six or eight months ahead; try to make your family's ferry and accommodations plans as early as possible.

Martha's Vineyard

The Martha's Vineyard Chamber of Commerce has a sophisticated telephone messaging system for ordering visitor information. The Chamber can be reached at (508) 693-0085; www.mvy.com.

Vineyard Vacations has a reservoir of rooms and represents most hotels and inns. Contact them at (508) 693-1300 or www.vineyardvacations.com.

Children's Favorites Delightful children's books with Island settings are:

- *Morning Beach* by Leslie Baker. Set in Martha's Vineyard.

- *Nat, Nat the Nantucket Cat* by Peter W. Barnes, illustrated by Susan Arciero. Set in Nantucket.

Tisbury (aka Vineyard Haven)

Tisbury has great restaurants and shopping in a more relaxed setting than some of the other Vineyard towns. Vineyard Haven Harbor is a more romantic setting than bustling Oak Bluffs.

FELIX NECK WILDLIFE SANCTUARY (all ages)

Off Edgartown—Vineyard Haven Road, Vineyard Haven; (508) 627–4850. Open year-round. Trails open daily from dawn to dusk. The visitor center is open daily from June to October, and Tuesday through Sunday from October to May from 8:00 A.M. to 4:00 P.M. Admission: $3.00 for adults, $2.00 for seniors and children 3 to 12.

A preserve that's affiliated with the Audubon Society, Felix Neck Wildlife Sanctuary comprises 350 acres of forests, salt marshes, and fields, as well as beaches and an excellent interpretive center that conducts guided nature walks year-round. There are several pleasant 1½-mile hiking trails that leave from the sanctuary's exhibit building. A magnet for bird watchers, sightings have included ospreys and swallows.

NIP N'TUCK FARM (all ages)

Vineyard Haven (508) 693–1449. Open late spring through September.

Tours feature old farm buildings and farm animals. Buggy and hayrides are a treat for all ages. Seasonal farm stand sells farm-grown vegetables.

Other Things to See and Do

Black Dog General Store, *two locations: Water Street and State Road, Vineyard Haven; (508) 693–1991 or (800) 626–1991.* Here's where you can buy those Black Dog T-shirts, sweatshirts, and hats that everyone seems to be wearing.

Island Cove Mini Golf, *State Road, Vineyard Haven; (508) 693–2611.*

Where to Eat

Black Dog Bakery, *two locations: Water Street and State Road, Vineyard Haven; (508) 693–1991 or (800) 626–1991.* Delectable desserts and baked goods. $

Black Dog Tavern, *Vineyard Haven Harbor, Vineyard Haven; (508) 693–1991.* Fun and salty atmosphere. $$$

Where to Stay

Martha's Vineyard Family Campground, *569 Edgartown Road, Vineyard Haven; (508) 693–3772; www.campmvfc.com.* One mile from the Vineyard Haven ferry; only campground on Martha's Vineyard. A limited number of one- and two-room cabins are available from $80 to $90 a night. Tent sites are $30 a night (maximum of four people per site—extra charge of $2.00 per child); RV sites are $34 a night, complete with campfire area. The main building has showers, bathrooms, a laundry room, a rec hall, and a grocery store.

Oak Bluffs

The colorful gingerbread cottages of the Wesleyan Grove Campground were built here during the late nineteenth century to replace the tents used by Methodist parishioners who camped and worshiped here every summer. Observe the no-bicycles rule and quiet time, which begins at dusk and ends at sunrise.

Cycle Around . . . A 10-mile flat bike path shuttles cyclists between Edgartown and Oak Bluffs. The far end of the Edgartown part of the path leads to Katama and South Beach.

FLYING HORSES CAROUSEL (all ages)

Circuit Avenue, Oak Bluffs; (508) 693–9481. Open daily, Easter to Columbus Day. Price: $1.00 per person, $8.00 for a ten-ride pass.

An old wooden building houses the Flying Horses Carousel, a National Historic Landmark that's wonderfully alive with merry-go-round lovers of all ages. It's the oldest operating carousel in the country; the horses were carved in 1876. There's even a brass ring.

HY-LINE CRUISES (all ages)

Information line is (508) 778–2602 or (888) 778–1132; www.hy-linecruises.com. Price: $24 round-trip or $12 one-way for adults, half-price for children 5 to 12; **Free** *for children 4 and under. Bikes are $10.00 round-trip, $5.00 for one-way.*

Hy-Line Cruises has the only interisland ferry service between Oak Bluffs in Martha's Vineyard and Straight Wharf in Nantucket. The two-hour-and-fifteen-minute cruise has a snackbar and plenty of rest rooms on board. Departures are three times a day and reservations are not necessary (the ferry always has space).

I Scream, You Scream Mad Martha's is a Martha's Vineyard institution serving twenty-three great homemade ice cream flavors and seven kinds of nonfat yogurt. My favorite is the red, white, and blue apple pie ice cream. Try one of their unique to-die-for chocolate lovers dream sundaes, such as the Sinful Chocolate sundae or the twelve-scoop Pig sundae (ordered by saying "oink"). There are several locations on the island:

- 12 Circuit Avenue, Oak Bluffs; (508) 693–9151

- 23 Lake Street, Oak Bluffs; (508) 693–8349

- 20 Union Street, Tisbury; (508) 693–5883

- 7 North Water Street, Edgartown; (508) 627–8761

Other Things to See and Do

Take it Easy, Baby, *35 Circuit Avenue, Oak Bluffs; (508) 693–2864.* Specializing in vintage and new clothing for adults and kids.

Where to Eat

Giordano's, *107 Circuit Avenue, Oak Bluffs; (508) 693–0184.* Serves up enormous portions of spaghetti, fried clams, fried chicken, and the like. Open for lunch and dinner, May to mid-September. $–$$$

Jimmy Seas Pan Pasta Restaurant, *32 Kennebec Avenue, Oak Bluffs; (508) 696–8550.* Food served in the pan it was cooked in—brought sizzling to your table. Casual atmosphere, huge portions. $$–$$$$

Where to Stay

Oak Bluffs Inn, *64 Circuit Avenue, Oak Bluffs; (508) 693–7171 or (800) 955–6235.* A cupola-topped, three-story pink building; nine comfortable rooms. Open April to mid-October. Rates are $120 to $215, breakfast included. $$$$

Edgartown

Stately homes line the narrow streets of this seaport village. A great yachting center, Edgartown attracts seafarers today. Walk to Edgartown Lighthouse from North Water Street. In 1828 the lighthouse was built on what was then an island in Edgartown Harbor; after a storm in the early twentieth century, a sandbar emerged from the water and attached the smaller island to the Vineyard. The Chappaquiddick Passenger and Vehicle Ferry (508) 627–9427 operates year-round. Catch it at Dock Street in Edgartown for a short five-minute crossing.

SOUTH BEACH (older children and strong swimmers)

Off Katama Road, south of Edgartown. Rest rooms and changing rooms in season only. **Free.**

Also known as Katama Beach, South Beach is the most popular beach on the island. Lifeguards patrol about three-quarters of the beach. There are no public facilities off-season. South Beach is not appropriate for younger children or weak swimmers, since the undertow can be treacherous. It's accessible by shuttle bus from Edgartown.

JOSEPH SYLVIA STATE BEACH (all ages)
Beach Road, Edgartown to Oak Bluffs. Open year-round. **Free**.

    This 2-mile-long of beach is owned by the state and maintained by the county. The section of Joseph Sylvia State Beach known as Bend-in-the-Road Beach in Edgartown is a nice spot for kids; there are no facilities, although there are lifeguards in-season.

Lighthouse Tours The lighthouses of Edgartown, Aquinnah/ Gay Head (508–645–2211), and East Chop are maintained by the Martha's Vineyard Historical Society (508–627–4441). The society opens the lighthouses on a limited basis from late June to September (for tours and views) usually one hour prior to and one hour after sunset on weekends. The price is $2.00 for adults; **Free** for children twelve and under.

MY TOI AND EAST BEACH (all ages)
Dike Road. Directions: Take Chappaquiddick Road for 2.5 miles to Dike Road.

    The property comprises a Japanese-style garden with ornamental bridges arching over ponds (one of which leads to a serene island). Farther down the road is East Beach.

VINEYARD MUSEUM (all ages)
59 School Street (corner of Cooke Street), Edgartown; (508) 627–4441. Open from July through Labor Day, Tuesday through Saturday 10:00 A.M. to 5:00 P.M.; from Labor Day to July, Wednesday through Friday 10:00 A.M. to 4:00 P.M., Saturday 1:00 to 4:00 P.M.

    For kids, the most interesting item at Edgartown's Vineyard Museum is the original Fresnel lens from the Gay Head Lighthouse, which is lighted for a few hours every night. One room is dedicated to the Native Amercian History on the Island, with tools, artifacts, and arrowheads of the Wampanoag tribe. The children's room is interactive and geared for younger kids.

Where to Eat

Among the Flowers, *North Water Street, Edgartown; (508) 627–3747.* Cafe serving PBJ and other regular fare. Open April through June and September through mid-November for breakfast and lunch; July and August for breakfast, lunch, and dinner. $–$$$

Savoir Faire, *14 Church Street, Edgartown; (508) 627–9864.* Gourmet food served in an elegantly festive atmosphere. For more sophisticated and well-behaved children. $$$–$$$$

Where to Stay

The Shiretown Inn, *44 North Water Street, Edgartown; (508) 627–3353 or (800) 541–0090.* Old whaling captain's home with outlying carriage house and cottage. Lovely gardens; close to the harbor. Rates range from $59 to $359, depending on season. $$–$$$$

The Victorian Inn, *24 South Water Street; Edgartown; (508) 627–4784; www.thevic.com.* Located a block away from the harbor and in the center of the shopping district. Each charming room has its own personality (some with four-posters and harbor views). Rates are $75 to $325, including breakfast. $$$–$$$$

Summer House, *96 South Summer Street, Edgartown; (508) 627–4857.* A comfortable home in a quiet part of Edgartown. It's run by a schoolteacher who's one of the friendliest Vineyarders we've met. Open mid-May to mid-October. Rates are $150 to $180. $$$$

West Tisbury

West Tisbury is a typical New England village, with its prerequisite white church, general store, and fine clapboard homes.

 CEDAR TREE NECK WILDLIFE SANCTUARY (all ages)
Indian Hill Road, West Tisbury.
Three hundred acres with trails through woods, dunes, and beach. Scenic trails and hilltop views. No picnicking or swimming allowed. Owned and managed by Sheriff's Meadow, a Martha's Vineyard Land Trust.

Amazing Vineyard Facts Martha's Vineyard bike paths cover about 22 miles past picturesque villages and scenic views.

MANUEL CORRELLUS STATE FOREST (all ages)

Off Edgartown–West Tisbury Road and Barnes Road; (508) 693–2540. Open year-round dawn to dusk. **Free**.

The 5,140 acres of Manuel Correllus State Forest are crisscrossed with bike, equestrian, and hiking trails. Park near the Barnes Road entrance to the park.

MARTHA'S VINEYARD FAIR (all ages)

35 Panhandle Road, West Tisbury; (508) 693–4343. Held in late August; admission charged.

This old-fashioned fair is a bit more upscale than other state fairs, having dressage and jumper demonstrations, a dog show, and gymnastic events. The midway features rides, games, and fried food.

Swan Lake Our youngest daughter's trip to the Vineyard isn't complete without a stop to feed the swans and ducks in the lovely pond next to the West Tisbury Police Station.

Other Things to See and Do

Long Point Wildlife Refuge, *Edgartown-West Tisbury Road, West Tisbury; (508) 693–3678.*

Menemsha Hills Reservation, *North Road, Chilmark; (508) 693–3678.*

Alley's General Store, *State Road, West Tisbury; (508) 693–0088.* Old-fashioned country store.

Where to Stay

Cove Apartments, *22 Runner Road, West Tisbury; (508) 693–9199.* One-bedroom apartments with kitchens, sleeping up to four people. Pond canoeing and beaches nearby. Rates are from $105 to $125 a night, two-night minimum.

Hosteling International, *West Tisbury Road, West Tisbury; (508) 693–2665, www.tiac.net/users/hienec/index.html.* Five dorms, open April 1 to November 15. Rates are $14.00 to $17.00 a night per person; children are welcome. Credit cards accepted.

Aquinnah (formerly known as Gay Head) and Menemsha

Aquinnah, or Gay Head, is known for its breathtaking cliffs and views of the ocean. It's a more remote, sparsely populated area of Martha's Vineyard. The Aquinnah Cultural Center is opening its first phase, a traditional longhouse, in summer 2000. Eventually a museum, gallery, and visitor center will complete the campus. If you've seen the film *Jaws*, you may recognize Menemsha and Dutcher's Dock, which served as a backdrop in many of the film's harbor shots.

AQUINNAH/GAY HEAD BEACH (all ages)

State Road near Aquinnah Circle, Aquinnah; (508) 645–2300.

Below the colorful clay cliffs, Aquinnah/Gay Head Beach is very popular during the summer. Because parking is limited and the beach extends south for several miles, it's rarely crowded. *Note:* There are no lifeguards here, and the closest rest rooms (50 cent charge—bring change) are on top of the cliffs near the clam shacks. You'll probably see people climbing up the cliffs. Resist the temptation; if caught, you will be fined. The worst of the cliffs' erosion is a direct result of foot traffic. Moreover, the cliffs are the private property of the Wampanoag tribe, who run the town of Aquinnah/Gay Head. *Caution:* Nude bathing on some stretches of beach.

GAY HEAD LIGHTHOUSE (all ages)

Aquinnah/Gay Head; (508) 645–2211. Open mid-June to Labor Day.

The red-brick Gay Head Lighthouse is a spectacular setting. On Friday, Saturday, and Sunday evenings during the summer, you can go up to the lighthouse's observation deck to watch the sun setting over the Sound.

Where to Eat

Home Port, *512 North Road, Menemsha; (508) 645–2679.* Casual seafood restaurant just steps from the water. Reservations required. Open mid-May to mid-October. $$$$

Aquinnah, *on the cliffs, Gay Head; (508) 645–9654.* Fresh seafood, pasta, and Italian specialties; children's menu. Open late May through the summer, seven days a week; Friday and Saturday off-season. $$

Where to Stay

Duck Inn, *off State Road, Gay Head;* *(508) 645–9018.* Comfortable, health-oriented B&B. The kids will enjoy Oralee, the inn mascot, a Vietnamese potbellied pig; parents will love the hot tub and massages. Open year-round. Rates are $105 to $185 in-season (one night Free with a week's stay).

NANTUCKET

Nantucket's stocky Brant Point Lighthouse is one of New England's shortest (it's just 31 feet tall); it's also one of Massachusetts's most photographed spots. Approach it from Easton Street. When you leave the island by ferry, you'll see lots of people throwing pennies overboard as the ship rounds Brant Point. This tradition supposedly ensures that Nantucket visitors will return to the island. For a visitor information packet, contact the Nantucket Island Chamber of Commerce, 48 Main Street, Nantucket (508-228-1700; www.nantucketchmber.org). Also helpful is the Nantucket Visitor Service Center (508-228-0925). For information on hotels, B&Bs, and condos, call (800) 649-5671 or (508) 693-7200. For information on the ferry service to Nantucket from the Cape area, see the Hyannis Ferries sidebar in this chapter. For interisland ferry service, see the Martha's Vineyard section.

CHILDREN'S BEACH (all ages)
Off South Beach Street on Harbor View Way, Nantucket; (508) 228–7213. Free.

Children's Beach is appropriately named because it's perfect for very young children. It offers a bathhouse, lifeguards, an excellent snack bar, a playground, a grassy play area, a horseshoe pit, picnic tables, and organized activities for kids on Friday and weekends. Sunday evening band concerts are held in July and August.

The Black Heritage Trail The African Meeting House is the second oldest structure in the United States built by and for free Africans. It was used as a church, a school, and a meeting place. This historic building is now owned by the Museum of African American History, Boston. For a self-guided tour brochure of important African American sites on Nantucket, call (508) 228-4058.

DIONIS BEACH (all ages)

Dionis Road, Nantucket; (508) 228–7213. **Free.**

Beach swimming is safe for children. Lifeguard on duty in-season; rest rooms.

FIRST CONGREGATIONAL CHURCH AND TOWER (all ages)

62 Centre Street, Nantucket; (508) 228–0950. Open mid-June to mid-October, Monday through Saturday 10:00 A.M. to 4:00 P.M.

The tower offers magnificent views of Nantucket on a clear day (Nantucket is only 14 miles long, and the tower is located near the mid-point of the island).

JETTIES BEACH (all ages)

North Beach Road (off Bathing Beach), Nantucket; (508) 228–7213. **Free.**

Lots of facilities—rest rooms, showers, a snack bar, a playground—plus rental boats, rental chairs, and lifeguards make this Nantucket's best beach for families. This is where the annual Sandcastle and Sculpture Day contest is held in mid-August.

Three memorable Nantucket Lighthouses are:

- **Great Point Lighthouse** (northern tip)
- **Sankaty Head Lighthouse** (eastern tip)
- **Brant Point Lighthouse** (Nantucket Harbor entrance, second oldest lighthouse in the nation)

MADAKET BEACH (all ages)

Madaket Road, Nantucket; (508) 228–7213. **Free.**

Madaket Beach is one of the most beautiful beaches on the islands. Sunsets are to be savored here. The surf can be rolling at times, so it's best to keep a firm grip on children. Rest rooms and lifeguards.

MARIA MITCHELL ASSOCIATION (all ages)

The Maria Mitchell Association (www.mmo.org) properties include the Aquarium, the Hinchman House, the Maria Mitchell Birthplace, the Loines Observatory, and the Science Library. The properties are at various locations just beyond Main Street in Nantucket. The observatories and Science Library are open year-round; other properties are open seasonally Tuesday through Saturday from 10:00 A.M. to 4:00

P.M. A visitor pass including all association properties is $10.00 for adults, $5.00 for children 5 to 14.

Maria Mitchell was the first woman to discover a comet, and she did it on Nantucket, from an observatory that her father constructed on top of his bank building on Main Street in Nantucket (3 Vestal Street, Nantucket; 508–228–9273). The Loines Observatory (59 Milk Street Extension, Nantucket; 508–228–8690) is known for its nighttime tours. Maria Mitchell was the librarian at the Nantucket Athenaeum for twenty years before becoming an astronomy professor at Vassar College. The library of the Maria Mitchell Center (2 Vestal Street; 508–228–9219) has a section for kids, as well as a fascinating collection of Maria's nineteenth-century science books and papers. Next door is Maria's birthplace (1 Vestal Street, Nantucket; 508–228–2896), which has the telescope she was using when she discovered "her" comet. The Mitchell home is topped by the only roof walk on the island that's open to the public. The Aquarium (28 Washington Street; 508–228–5387) gives visitors an insider's look at the marine life of the island through Aquarium-sponsored field trips. The Hinchman House (7 Milk Street, Nantucket; 508–228–0898) is a natural history museum focusing on Nantucket's natural habitats; popular Nantucket ecology trips are offered.

NANTUCKET COMMUNITY SCHOOL'S CHILDREN'S SUMMER THEATRE AND CAMP (ages 8 to 18)

Nantucket High School Auditorium, 10 Surfside Road, Nantucket; (508) 228–7257; www.nantucket.net/children/theater. Children's theater program from mid-July through August.

Children perform in adaptations of popular and widely known plays and musicals. Plays are mounted with professional sets and costuming.

NANTUCKET LIFE SAVING MUSEUM (all ages)

Polpis Road, Nantucket; (508) 228–1885. Open June 15 through September 30, 9:30 A.M. to 4:00 P.M. Admission: $3.00 for adults, $2.00 for children 6 to 12; Free for children under 6.

The museum is a reproduction of an original life-saving station on Nantucket. Memorabilia includes life-saving equipment (a rare surfboat and an authentic beach cart), original photographs, artifacts from sunken ships (the *Andrea Doria,* a luxury cruise ship with registry from Italy, went down in Nantucket waters in the 1950s), and remains from Island lighthouses.

Readers' Choice The Nantucket Athenaeum on Lower India Street (508–228–1110) is one of the oldest libraries in the United States. There's a children's wing, as well as an adjoining park with a play area for kids.

NANTUCKET WHALE WATCH (all ages)
Hy-Line Dock, Straight Wharf, Nantucket; (800) WHALING.
Narrated tour of the feeding grounds of the whales and dolphins from a 100-foot ship.

'SCONSET BEACH (all ages)

Siasconset Road, Nantucket; (508) 228–7213. **Free**.
'Sconset Beach, a long, narrow stretch, can be a bit seaweedy, but your family may overlook the inconvenience if you enjoy having lots of room to yourselves. There's a playground here, too. There are no rest rooms or snack facilities here, but the beach is lifeguarded in season.

Marcia's favorite Nantucket Island biking paths

- **Madaket Bike Path.** The prize at the end of the path (approximately 5 miles) is Madaket Beach, great for sunsets, but dangerous for swimming for kids. The path can have some inclines and sharp curves.

- **Polpis Bike Path.** Nearing completion, this is the longest bike path (8 miles), with some gradual hills and curving corners.

- **'Sconset Beach Bike Path.** Families enjoy biking to 'Sconset Beach via the 7-mile 'Sconset Bike Path, which parallels Milestone Road. There are some mild hills. It's approximately one hour to 'Sconset.

- **The Surfside Bike Path.** A 3-mile-long, flat trail that leads from the town of Nantucket to its best beach. Take Main Street to Pleasant Street; turn right on Atlantic Avenue and proceed to Surfside. The path can be crowded.

Marcia's Top
Annual Events
on Cape Cod, Martha's Vineyard, and Nantucket

- **Daffodil Festival,** April, Nantucket; (508) 228-1700

- **Brewster in Bloom,** early May, Brewster; (508) 896-3500

- **Rhododendron Festival,** mid-May to mid-June, Heritage Plantation, Sandwich; (508) 888-3300

- **Figawi Race Weekend,** Hyannis to Nantucket and back, late May, Hyannis; (508) 778-6100

- **Nantucket Film Festival,** mid-June, Nantucket; (508) 228-1700

- **Maritime Week,** Cape Lighthouses open to the public, mid-June; (508) 362-3828

- **Kid's Day,** Heritage Plantation, mid-June, Sandwich; (508) 888-3300

- **West Tisbury's Farmer's Market,** June through September, West Tisbury, Martha's Vineyard

- **Fourth of July Fireworks,** July 4, Hyannis, Falmouth Heights, Provincetown, and Chatham

- **Mashpee Pow-Wow,** July, Barnstable County Fairgrounds, Mashpee; (508) 477-0208

- **Edgartown Regatta,** mid-July, Edgartown, Martha's Vineyard; (508) 627-4361

- **Barnstable County Fair,** July, Barnstable County Fairgrounds, East Falmouth; (508) 563-3200

- **Falmouth Road Race,** August, Falmouth to Woods Hole; (508) 540-7000

- **Peter Rabbit's Annual Fair,** August, Thornton Burgess Museum, Water Street, Sandwich; (508) 888-6870

- **Carnival Week Parade,** mid-August, Provincetown; (508) 487-2313 or (800) 637-8696

- **Illumination Night,** mid-August, Oak Bluffs, Martha's Vineyard

- **Harwich Cranberry Festival,** mid-September, Harwich; (508) 430-2811

- **Cape Cod Air Show,** Otis Air Force Base, mid-August, Bourne; (508) 968-4003

- **Sandcastle and Sculpture Contest,** mid-August, Nantucket; (508) 228-1700

- **Scallop Festival,** September, Bourne; (508) 759-6000

- **Striped Bass and Bluefish Derby,** mid-September through mid-October, Martha's Vineyard; (508) 693-0085

- **Christmas Stroll,** first Saturday in December, Nantucket; (508)

SURFSIDE BEACH (ages 7 and up)
Surfside Road, Nantucket; (508) 228–7213. **Free.**

Surfside's heavy surf makes it inappropriate for families with younger children, but strong swimmers who love bodysurfing will enjoy it. This beach can be crowded with college kids and surf casters, but Surfside is long enough to accommodate everyone. Facilities include a large parking lot, rest rooms, showers, rental chairs and umbrellas, and a snack bar. Lifeguards.

WHALING MUSEUM (all ages)
Broad Street; (508) 228–1736. Open year-round. Admission: $5.00 for adults, $3.00 for children. An inclusive pass available for an extra fee allows entry to all historical sites operated by the Nantucket Historical Society.

Visit the Whaling Museum to see a vivid explanation of the phrase "Nantucket sleigh ride." That's what happens when your harpoon gets stuck in a whale's back and the whale decides to take you and your companions for a ride through the waves. Start your visit with one of the three daily lectures.

Other Things to See and Do

Brant Point Beach and Lighthouse. Great spot for viewing the ferries rounding the bend into Nantucket Harbor. *Warning:* Strong undertow.

Coskata Coatue Wildlife Refuge, *Wauwinet Road, Nantucket; (508) 228–0006.* Trustees of Reservations property. *Warning:* Dangerous swimming but scenic trails.

Nantucket Babysitters' Service, *5C Windy Way, Nantucket; (508) 228–4970; www.nantucketbabysitters.com.*

Sesachacha Heathlands, *Barnard Road, Nantucket.* Audobon Wildlife Sanctuary on 861 acres; trails open dawn to dusk.

Sky's the Limit, *5 the Courtyard, Nantucket; (508) 228–4633.* Great place to buy a unique kite to fly at a Nantucket beach.

Where to Eat

Atlantic Cafe, *15 South Water Street; Nantucket; (508) 228–0570.* A relaxing, reasonably priced restaurant that serves excellent chowder; children's menu. Open year-round for lunch and dinner. $-$$$

Espresso Cafe, *40 Main Street, Nantucket; (508) 228–6930.* Caffe latte and hot cocoa finished with a rich dessert make for a great family break from a day of touring. $

The Rope Walk, *1 Straight Wharf, Nantucket; (508) 228–8886.* Charming restaurant at the end of Straight Wharf overlooking the sea and the harbor. Food matches the panoramic view. $$-$$$

Sweet Inspirations Chocolates, *26 Centre Street, Nantucket; (888) 225–4843 or (509) 228– 5814.* Chocolate lovers don't need inspiration, just the address. $

Where to Stay

The Beachside, *30 North Beach Street, Nantucket; (508) 228–2241 or (800) 322– 4433; www.thebeachside.com.* Double-decker motel near Jetties Beach; three two-room suites are available. Open mid-April to mid-October. Children under 16 stay **Free** in their parents' room. Rates are $125 to $240 for rooms, $250 to $480 for suites. $$$$

Harbor House, *South Beach Street, Nantucket; (508) 228–1500.* The 216-room

Harbor House prides itself on its Happy Harbor Club Kids Program, offered seven days a week, 9:00 A.M. to 4:00 P.M., **Free** to guests' children ages 2 to 13. An activity staff supervises the kids, and various themed programs are offered. An outdoor swimming pool is open Memorial Day to Labor Day. Breakfast included in-season. Rates are $105 to $380 a night. $$$$

Nesbitt Inn, *21 Broad Street (P.O. Box 1019) Nantucket; (508) 228–0156 or (508) 228–2446.* Pleasant inn that welcomes families who don't mind sharing bathrooms with other guests. There's a swing set in the backyard, a deck overlooking the garden, and games in the living room; families are welcome to use the grill in the backyard. Breakfast is provided. Open March to December. Rates in-season are $75 to $105. $$$–$$$$

Wharf Cottages, *New Whale Street, Nantucket; (508) 228–4620.* Waterfront cottages with decks overlooking the wharf area. Rates are $305 to $650 a night. $$$$

Index